D1590111

Traveler

Traveler

THE MUSICAL ODYSSEY
OF TIM O'BRIEN

★ ★ ★ ★ ★

Bobbie Malone and Bill C. Malone

UNIVERSITY OF OKLAHOMA PRESS : NORMAN

Publication of this book is made possible through the generosity of Edith Kinney Gaylord.

LIBRARY OF CONGRESS CATALOGING-IN-PUBLICATION DATA

Names: Malone, Bobbie, 1944– author. | Malone, Bill C., author.
Title: Traveler : the musical odyssey of Tim O'Brien / Bobbie Malone and
    Bill C. Malone.
Description: [First.] | Norman : University of Oklahoma Press, 2022. | Series:
    American popular music series; vol 8 | Includes bibliographical references and
    index. | Summary: "Tells the story of how West Virginia–born Tim O'Brien first
    made a name for himself as the mandolin- and fiddle-playing lead singer and
    principal songwriter for the 1980s bluegrass band Hot Rize, then pushed beyond
    bluegrass by moving to the US West for a time and building a music ecosystem
    through recording, producing, songwriting, collaborating, and forming new
    bands, a recording label, and a growing audience"—Provided by publisher.
Identifiers: LCCN 2021061685 | ISBN 978-0-8061-9062-4 (hardcover)
Subjects: LCSH: O'Brien, Tim, 1954– | Bluegrass musicians—United States—
    Biography. | Mandolinists—United States—Biography. | Fiddlers—United
    States—Biography. | LCGFT: Biographies.
Classification: LCC ML419.O25 M35 2022 | DDC 782.421642092 [B]—dc23
LC record available at https://lccn.loc.gov/2021061685

Traveler: The Musical Odyssey of Tim O'Brien is Volume 8 in the American Popular Music Series.

The paper in this book meets the guidelines for permanence and durability of the Committee on Production Guidelines for Book Longevity of the Council on Library Resources, Inc. ∞

1 2 3 4 5 6 7 8 9 10

For our sons, Benjamin and Matthew Sontheimer,
but especially for our grandson, Theo Sontheimer,
whose passion for music inspires us all

And for our brother and brother-in-law, Ronnie Scharlack

CONTENTS

★ ★ ★ ★ ★

INTRODUCTION

In 2010, an interviewer asked Tim O'Brien if he had any favorites among his songs recorded by other musicians. His response says a great deal about the musician whose life and work attracted our attention: "If a song is good, it can live many lives, and it won't wear out. I'm always honored and proud when anyone else sings my song, whether it's Garth Brooks or a Facebook fan."[1]

We cannot say for certain when we first heard Tim O'Brien, but we know that we first saw him on July 4, 1986, at a big bluegrass festival in Nacogdoches, Texas. He was there as a musician and lead singer in Hot Rize, one of the most sensational bluegrass bands of that decade. As the years went by, and as he embarked on his own solo career, we followed him, marveling at his singing prowess, at his skill in writing songs, and at his facility with a wide variety of instruments—mandolin, fiddle, guitar, banjo, and bouzouki.

We also began to notice how widely esteemed he was among other musicians. He frequently showed up as a contributor to other people's recordings, providing duet harmonies, playing an instrument, or working as a producer. He even appeared on an album that Rod Moag and Bill did, *Remember Me*, a tribute to the Bailes Brothers, a pioneering country group from West Virginia. For lack of a better description, we began to think of him as the "Renaissance man of country music," and we cannot think of anyone else in the broad realm of roots music who has excelled in such a multiplicity of roles.

Tim hails from West Virginia, a state that many people consider synonymous with Appalachia and what they perceive to be the province of authentic old-time country music. As a teenager, though, Tim couldn't wait to leave that economically depressed state, and he followed his wanderlust to the open skies of Colorado and to his first blossoming as an acoustic musician. Through his sojourn in the Rockies and beyond, however, he found he couldn't shake the dust of West Virginia from his shoes. He discovered there was too much magic in the name *West Virginia*, and music fans quickly identified him and his fondness for roots music with the traditional values of his home state. And over time, West Virginia became nearer and dearer to his heart.

Tim did not grow up as a working-class kid in some factory village or isolated mountain hollow; he was a city boy with a thoroughly middle-class urban upbringing in Wheeling. He was a Catholic, surrounded by an intensely evangelical Protestant culture. From the folk masses in which he participated at the nearby St. Michael's Catholic Church to the varieties of music he listened to at home, Tim easily absorbed America's pop culture. Like Elvis Presley two decades earlier, he was a part of everything he heard. As a teenager discovering Doc Watson on a Pittsburgh television station and attending shows down at the Capitol Theater, home of the venerable *Wheeling Jamboree*, Tim enthusiastically embraced country music. But the performers he saw, and admired, came from all over the nation, and only occasionally from the hills of Appalachia. Neither Appalachian himself nor even predominantly Irish, he nevertheless came to cherish the legend of a great-grandfather who migrated from Ireland to the United States and ultimately wound up in Wheeling after a long trek, by foot, from Cumberland, Maryland. While Appalachia and Ireland eventually became facets of the defining myth surrounding Tim and his music, he is a thoroughly American self-made musician, singer, and songwriter who has digested a broad array of roots styles, reshaping them to his own purposes. Tim's success in navigating the shoals of America's vast reservoir of folk musical expressions, both black and white, took him through the high-powered domain of bluegrass into the realm of what we now know as Americana.

The true measure of Tim O'Brien's genius is his abiding and energetic pursuit of the next musical adventure. He truly has been a traveler, in his wide-ranging and ceaseless explorations of the vast American musical landscape, whether that means the next instrument to play, song to write, songwriter with whom to collaborate, style in which to perform, musician or musicians with whom to play, or setting in which to do so. As the folklorist, radio host, and cowboy poetry impresario Hal Cannon told us, "Tim is not just a pretty voice. Behind that voice is a real . . . human being who knows where he came from . . . from West Virginia to Colorado and back to Nashville."[2] Tim's music is his life, a life built around that singular passion, and a story we wanted very much to tell.

★ ★ ★ ★ ★

Chapter 1

A WHEELING BOYHOOD

By the time Timothy Page O'Brien began his life as the fifth child of Amelia and Frank O'Brien on March 16, 1954, in once-bustling Wheeling, West Virginia, the city had already begun a slow decline. Wedged up against the Ohio River in the Northern Panhandle of West Virginia, Wheeling lay across the river from its western neighbor, Ohio. Travel twenty miles in the opposite direction and you reach the border of Pennsylvania. Once known as the prosperous "Gateway to the West," Wheeling earned the title from its location on the historic National Road. Building the road began in 1811 in Maryland on the Potomac, and seven years later it reached Wheeling. Tim told Derek Halsey in an interview for *Bluegrass Unlimited* that, according to family legend, his great-grandfather Thomas had recently emigrated from Ireland in about 1851, as part of the huge wave of Irish immigrants who left in the wake of the mid-nineteenth-century Irish famine. Thomas took the train to Cumberland, Maryland, where the railroad ended, and then walked the rest of the way to Wheeling on the paved National Road. Because Thomas O'Brien could read and write, he found Wheeling receptive to talented newcomers who could work in its large river trade. Tim said that his great-grandfather "got a job as a clerk soon after he arrived. He was a pretty political guy. He started a Savings and Loan for the Irish immigrants in town and he ended up being the Customs Agent for the Port of Wheeling." The city further burnished its "gateway" luster when, on January 1, 1853, the Baltimore and Ohio (B&O) Railroad reached Wheeling, making it the first rail line to connect the Atlantic seaboard to what was then the beginning of the West, the Ohio River.[1]

Wheeling also served as the site of the convention that, in 1861, wrenched some of the western counties from the parent state of Virginia and created West Virginia as a state, and it served as the capital of the new state on two different occasions in the nineteenth century. The city experienced an exciting and often turbulent history of industrial growth later in that century, profiting from the production of iron, steel, glass, and cut iron nails. Its per capita wealth had emerged as one of the highest in this country. One still finds evidence of that glorious past in the stately mansions gracing the cityscape. The city's population reached its apex of 61,000 in the 1930s, when steel production largely fueled its economy, but by the time of Tim's birth, many of its residents had already begun heading elsewhere. During his boyhood, he remembers, "Wheeling was still a vibrant place. Steel hadn't crashed yet, and the mills were still running." Between the 1950s and his high school graduation in 1973, however, the population declined from over 58,891 to 48,188. Like Tim, who never returned to Wheeling permanently once he graduated from high school, after the steel mills shut down other young men and women increasingly departed from the city and state in search of excitement and better economic opportunity.[2]

Tim grew up in a secure and comfortable environment, completely different from the overworked stereotype of "Southern Appalachian" that any popular notion of West Virginia might connote. Wheeling is far closer to Pittsburgh and Columbus, Ohio, than to its own state capital of Charleston, and its industrial and demographic decline mirrors that of the Rust Belt rather than the Sun Belt. Tim's background—geographically, culturally, educationally, and politically—exemplifies traits definitively more "American" than regional. Even the home and the neighborhood where he grew up, which he termed "Leave It to Beaver" (a popular American television series in the late 1950s and early 1960s) in character, was within walking distance of St. Michael's Catholic Church. There he attended mass regularly with his parents, and he and his siblings spent their first years of formal education at the parish's parochial school. As prominent citizens, Frank and Amelia Gaines O'Brien participated actively in Wheeling's civic, social, and political activities, and in the affairs of St. Michael's Catholic parish. They belonged to a lay organization at church, the Juniper Club, and lived a Catholic-centered life.[3]

Tim's mother, more often referred to by her nickname, Amy, was born on October 14, 1919, in Ansley, Custer County, Nebraska. Her emotionally open and straightforward unpublished memoir that she prepared for her children in the 1990s, "This Will Be All She Wrote," reveals her to be a witty, resourceful, and independent-minded woman. Amy had a sturdy Midwest upbringing. Her people seem to have been mostly small business-men and Republicans and, like most Nebraskans, had originally come from the Upper Midwest (Great Lakes states) or the Northeast. These maternal forebears do not figure prominently, if at all, in Tim's reminisc-ing or in his songs. His middle name, Page, however, came from his mater-nal grandfather, to whom Tim bears a remarkable resemblance, as can be seen in the few available photographs of him.[4]

Tim described his mother as "fun loving" and fond of practical jokes as her own mother was reputed to have been, but with a touch of "her father's hot temper." Tim could also empathize with Amy who would push limits, telling us that she "went her own way very much as I did as the youngest" sibling.[5] Amy grew up in a mainstream Protestant household, and she first asserted her independence as a college student. Although she originally planned to attend the University of Nebraska in Lincoln, at age fourteen she was diagnosed with the autoimmune disorder myesthenia gravis. Her doctor thought it safer for her to remain at home in Omaha to pursue her studies. As an undergraduate at Duchesne College, a Catholic institution in the city, she "received the gift of faith" and converted to Roman Catholi-cism, making her first communion in February 1941. After graduation, she and a close girlfriend moved to Denver to work. They both found employ-ment but soon sought more adventurous paths. Learning that the Marine Corps had created a Women's Reserve, they immediately signed up. These separate but decisively unconventional initiatives on her part brought Amy directly into contact with her future husband. In October 1943, three days after being posted in Charleston, West Virginia, she met a naval officer, Frank A. O'Brien Jr. Soon he was joining her at daily mass and sharing breakfast before they went to their respective offices. After a whirlwind courtship and engagement, they married on December 27, 1943, with both bride and groom wearing the uniforms of their respective military services.[6]

Tim described his father, Frank O'Brien Jr., as "a regular, sorta consis-tent guy who loved his job," had a dry sense of humor, was devoted to his Catholic faith, and lived until the age of ninety-six. He was born in Wheel-ing on June 30, 1913. Although Tim bore the Irish name O'Brien, only his great-grandfather came from Ireland; his other forebears represented other western European ethnicities. Frank's mother, Cincinnati-born Estelle Schlaudecker, for instance, was from a German background. Only

Amy and Frank's wedding day (Tim O'Brien's collection)

his Irish heritage, however, appealed to Tim's romanticism.[7] Frank O'Brien spent his undergraduate years at Mt. St. Mary's in Emmetsburg, Maryland, then followed his father's path, matriculating at the University of Virginia Law School. After serving as an intelligence officer in the Naval Reserve from April 1940 to September 1945, he joined his father's practice in his hometown. In Tim's words, "he loved that relationship." Frank enjoyed his multiple roles as a successful civic-minded attorney who ran for and was elected to the city council once or twice, and a Republican Party advocate, chairing Dwight D. Eisenhower's West Virginia campaign in 1952 as well as that of Republican Arch Moore in his initial campaign for Congress in

1954. But Frank did not follow the party line when he disagreed with its extremist positions; for example, both he and Amy found Joe McCarthy's views alienating. In her memoir, Amy wrote that when McCarthy made his notorious speech in Wheeling about the alleged presence of communists in the State Department, the O'Briens were "unalterably opposed."[8]

Despite her doctor's warning that myasthenia gravis would make childbearing risky, Amy's self-reliant streak and Catholic faith guided her decisions. She and Frank created a family that seemed destined, if not pro-grammed, for a sturdy middle-class professional and Roman Catholic exis-tence. Their children ranged from the eldest, Frank III (Trip) born in 1944, to James (Jim) born in 1946, Brigid born in 1949, Mollie born in 1952, and the youngest, Tim. Amy recalled that Tim "came into this world with a modicum of fuss and caused little disruption during his infancy. He was very agreeable, rarely cried. It was as if he knew he would be taken care of without asking. He must have been thinking deep thoughts even then."[9]

Less than two years after Tim's birth, the first of two tragedies marred the parents' high expectations for their children's futures. Not a month after her sixth birthday, Brigid suddenly became ill on New Year's Eve and died from encephalitis just seventy-two hours later, on January 2, 1956. Brigid's casket lay in the living room of the O'Brien home where the wake was held because Amy couldn't bear to have her go to a funeral home. Mol-lie thought that she and Tim, so young when Brigid died, were probably sent elsewhere during this devastating time. Amy later confessed in her memoir that "losing a child never entered my mind. I had never been exposed to the raw grief of anyone who had suffered such a loss." When Mollie sat on the front steps waiting for Brigid to return from school, Amy wrote that her "heart broke in small pieces," as it did when Tim went look-ing for Brigid in her room the day she died and uttered the first word he'd ever said, "'Big-it,' over and over again." Tim was only two years old, but he undoubtedly recognized that a great void had come into his life, one that he could neither verbalize nor comprehend.[10]

Although Amy was a devoted mother, she was understandably dis-tracted by grief during those trying days. Tim later admitted to Mollie that he'd harbored some resentment toward his mother, probably from mis-perceiving that distraction as neglect. Reading Amy's memoir many years later—which, Tim declared, was "worth its weight in gold to me and my siblings"—he could more fully understand the challenges his mother faced when he was so young. He also could better appreciate her skills as a story-teller, and the unpublished manuscript became a "great reference" for him. He confessed that he continued to find new items of interest in it as he drew "closer and closer to the age she was when she wrote it . . . seeing life from a similar perspective."[11]

As he continued to process this difficult period he could barely remember, he described a vintage Hummel print of a guardian angel protecting a child from a snake that his mother hung on the wall of his childhood bedroom. Tim said, "I got this picture out that had been in a box in the attic for probably thirty years or longer. It was such a touchstone. I mean I looked at it and I couldn't remember when it wasn't around. It really is among some of my earliest memories." He also remembered a statue of a little girl angel, dedicated to Brigid's memory, that sat above the entrance to the auditorium of St. Michael's School. Tim saw that statue daily during the eight years he attended school there. Finally coming to terms with that early loss many years later, he wrote the song, "Guardian Angel," his beautiful tribute to the sister he had come to feel had played that role in his life.[12]

At the time of his sister's death, the O'Briens lived in a spacious three-story house at 10 Lenox Avenue, which intersected the Old National Road (US 40). A block down the street, the children walked to their parish school, St. Michael's. Remembered as a close-knit neighborhood, where children visited freely in each other's homes, the largely self-contained area included a barbershop, drugstore, and a grocery store from which Tim carried home brown-wrapped packages of supplies that his mother had ordered. The family could also walk to a movie theater and Ye Olde Alpha Restaurant and Tavern (opened in 1932, a purveyor of comfort food until 2020). With a paper route like his brothers had once worked, in cold weather Tim would fold papers for his customers in the neighborhood laundromat.[13]

Aside from Brigid's untimely death, the Lenox home held great memories for all the members of the family. Amy described the home's twelve-foot ceilings and its gracious living room with its large fireplace flanked by bookcases. One end of the room opened onto the front porch and the other end onto the front staircase. The dining room, with a table that comfortably seated twelve, also contained a fireplace, and a sun room was located just beyond. The second floor had four bedrooms and a bath, and

Christmas card siblings, from left to right: Jim, Mollie, Brigid (in photos), Tim, and Trip, with their dog, Lady, at their feet (Mollie O'Brien Moore's collection)

the third floor had two dormer rooms and another bath. As Amy wrote, "It was a lot of house, and I ran the steps from top to bottom nearly every day for eighteen years." Mollie commented that, when she was a toddler, television had not yet entered their household but, soon after, she recalled her mother calling Tim the "TV baby" because the TV was then in the den, and he loved sitting there looking at it. When asked by an interviewer if, as a child, he ever wanted to be anything other than a musician, he replied, "I wanted to be a cowboy for sure. One of my earliest memories is running into the kitchen to tell my mom that the cowboys were on TV." As we now know, while being glued to westerns, Tim was also soaking up all the varied forms of music he heard on television.[14]

With Brigid's death, the divisions between the two sets of siblings became more pronounced, not only because of the difference in their ages but also by the decades into which they were born. Trip and Jim could broadly be considered baby boomers, growing up in a decade that, before

Tim as singing cowboy (Jim O'Brien's collection)

the onslaught of the 1960s, seemed so much more settled. By the time Mollie and Tim entered their teens, Amy paraphrasing Bob Dylan, wrote, "The times they were a-changin'." Mom and Dad O'Brien soon found out they had two rebels in their midst. Amy saw 1963 as the turning point, as the two older sons approached adulthood and the parents "watched the world turn topsy-turvy." While Trip and Jim "pretty much escaped all this upheaval, Mollie and Tim were in the throes of the changes." She found that "bracing for the attitudes of Mollie and Tim . . . became a terrific challenge for me." Speaking of his older brothers and the generational transformation they represented, Tim told Derek Halsey, "they were on the other side of the countercultural shift . . . and Mollie and I were really just the red-headed ones of all of them. We were the left-handed ones, and we liked to play music."[15]

Tim and Mollie seemed to have inhaled music almost from the beginnings of their lives, absorbing it first at home. Their parents were not musical themselves, but their tastes leaned toward big band music and the pop offerings of people such as Perry Como. They generously encouraged their children's interests and tolerated their musical choices. Mollie said, "our mother always made sure we heard every kind of music possible," but Tim reassured an interviewer that Amy and Frank were not "stage parents." According to Amy, Mollie "knew the entire score of *My Fair Lady, Sound of Music,* lots of Barbra Streisand songs" by the age of four or five. Amy said that "the artist in Tim was manifested early. He loved to draw, did complicated comic strips, enjoyed art lessons Saturday morning."[16] In addition to drawing, Tim admitted to David A. Mauer, "Growing up, I was kind of artsy. I liked to . . . paint and make up little poems." Amy fondly recalled that she found Mollie "very independent, writing plays, and there was always Timmy to act as her foil." She also described him as Mollie's assistant, and according to Tim, "her actor and singer."[17]

From his brothers Trip and Jim, Tim gained valuable information about popular music and the lore of the outdoors. Mollie, particularly, influenced his love for literature, music, and plays. Tim told Kerry Dexter, an interviewer for *Dirty Linen,* that in addition to performing with his sister, "When I was five or six, my first cousin [Tony Ames] was going off to music college, the Eastman School of Music in Rochester, New York, and he showed me Latin rhythms on the bongos. Then I started getting interested in music." Tim also had a crystal radio. "You use the radiator, the heating radiator, for your antenna. You build one in Boy Scouts, you know."[18] He began listening to Chubby Checkers, Roger Miller, and the Beatles, all available with a simple twist of the radio dial. Bluegrass fans might be surprised to learn that, in his oft-cited recollections of musical explorations, Tim almost never referred to a country or bluegrass musician. Except for Roger Miller, whom he first encountered on television, his earliest influences came from the wide pantheon of pop, rock, and urban folk stylists who dominated American popular culture in the 1960s. He said, "I listened to and learned from every kind of music I could find. So, I guess I just followed my nose on some invisible path between Van Cliburn, Count Basie and Merle Haggard. Still following it." And to a question in a 2014 interview in the *Huffington*

Post about whom he would most love to play with if given the choice, Tim replied, "The Count Basie Band. I would love to be their rhythm guitar player for just a night."[19]

Even as a young boy, he exhibited considerable inner control and emotional strength. Tim underwent serious surgery when he was nine years old to remove a birth mark on his neck, and then to have skin grafted from his buttocks to that area. The procedure kept him out of school for several months. His mother recounted, "He never complained even though changing the dressings made him scream in pain. Going through that had to awaken in him his deep sense of caring for others." That perseverance came in handy when he became a musician and found that he could translate hidden feelings into moving lyrics.[20]

Beyond the little plays in which she enlisted Tim's participation when they were preschoolers, Mollie continued to play a vital role in Tim's musical education as they grew up. Like Tim, his precocious sister responded to any kind of music she heard, from Broadway musicals to rock and roll. She introduced him to the genius of Bob Dylan, incredulous that he had never heard of the Minnesota-born singer-songwriter. As a member of the Beatles' fan club sponsored by local station WKWK, she may have been the first member of the O'Brien family to be dazzled by the British band. But Tim, as a diligent listener to radio and television, also heard the quartet on the Ed Sullivan Show. Learning that the Beatles were scheduled to perform at the Civic Center in Pittsburgh, on September 14, 1964, Mollie and Tim sent off for four tickets (for themselves, their cousin Karen, and their mother) and then persuaded good-natured and ever-solicitous Amy to drive them to the concert. Amy let her children know that they had to help pay the costs by doing extra chores. Both Amy and Mollie later admitted they never understood a single word sung by the Beatles, since the crowd's pandemonium and unbridled enthusiasm obscured the lyrics. Amy described the arena as "a madhouse," when even "getting back to our car was frightening," but they experienced the event as a never-to-be forgotten moment of musical awakening.[21]

The Beatles concert, according to Amy, ignited Tim's decision to become a guitar player. She thought that he received his first guitar for his eleventh birthday, because Trip was still in college at the time and was enthusiastic about Tim's ability. Tim thinks it might have been for his twelfth, but the date is irrelevant. Amy wrote, "What was amazing was his fast learning. Within a few days he was strumming tunes, a year later he was playing along with Chet Atkins records, experimenting with all the other boys his age who were into the same things. . . . When the other boys lost interest, he found new friends who wanted to play. From that early age he worked at his music, played in every kind of band, performed any time he was invited." That first guitar, though significant, was, in Tim's words, "a cheesy [$30] Sunburst Stella harmony." Although left-handed, he learned to play right-handed because all of his friends played that way. He told Steven Stone:

> I was 12 years old and my sister was taking piano lessons, and I had started fooling with the piano, so my parents offered to give me lessons. I learned a few Christmas songs that November and then got a little Harmony guitar and taught myself from a beginner's guitar book, "Go Tell Aunt Rhody" and "Down in the Valley" with the one finger C chord and the one finger G7 chord. My friends had cheap electric guitars, and I'd been learning riffs on one string—like the "Theme from *Peter Gunn*"—from them before I got my own guitar.[22]

During these formative years, like Mollie, Tim sang often and worked on his skills as a beginning instrumentalist. When they were still attending St. Michael's School, they began participating in folk masses at St. Michael's Church, which gave them both the opportunity to perform beyond their household, even if the confines of the Catholic church seem an unlikely training ground for two future roots-based musicians. Most bluegrass and country musicians grew up in evangelical Protestant households. Cajun and Tex-Mex musicians tended to be Roman Catholics, while the folk revival in the Northeast broke the norm with Protestantism by beginning to draw many Jewish musicians such as David Grisman, Peter Wernick, and Andy Statman into bluegrass. Richard Cuccaro, in his interview with Tim, wrote, "While a significant number of songs in Tim's repertoire are bluegrass gospel, generally considered Protestant in origin, the Catholic Church had a great deal to do with his early experience. A big chunk of his practical experience came from playing in the folk mass." The inspiration for Tim's immersion in this religious practice occurred during a historic shift in Roman Catholic liturgy: *Musicam Sacram*, the Holy See's instruction on liturgical music announced in March 1967. The fruit of Vatican II, this innovation wedded "vernacular" musical styles and instrumentation to Catholic liturgy.[23]

To the eventual consternation of religious conservatives, young Catholics around the world began introducing newly written songs in English and borrowing other songs from pop and folk sources. This meant the intrusion of songs like Bob Dylan's "Blowing in the Wind," Pete Seeger's "If I Had a Hammer," and even the Beatles' "Hey Jude" into the liturgical oeuvre. One writer for *Napster* compiled a playlist of folk mass songs and noted that, "To Catholics and lapsed Catholics of a certain age, it might seem like a dream: For a few years starting in the mid-60s, maybe while a formal high mass was being celebrated upstairs, church basements filled with fabric fish cutouts and folding chairs provided a habitat for clean-cut college beatniks—and even young nuns wearing casual clothes!—to strum songs like the Youngbloods' 'Get Together' on acoustic guitars, perhaps with bongo accompaniment. Overnight, a solemn medieval ritual, unchanged for centuries, made way for a hootenanny." This revolutionary change, which inevitably provoked a backlash, initially brought young people back to the church to participate in these "folk masses."[24] As Tim described his experience with the phenomenon at St. Michael's:

> Around the time I was 12 and a half years old, I played at Roman Catholic folk masses. At first there would be about five or more of us sitting in the front pews playing guitars. There was a new young priest, Father Braun, who was musical and directed us. A few years later, the other guitarists dropped out, and it was just me. I started singing and leading from the lectern. I did that through at least the first two years of high school. The same priest was into theater too, and he and one of the moms [Madeline Keys] . . . wrote song lyrics for the mass folk songs, using scripture as the basis. Since I was the best guitarist, they'd have me write music to the lyrics the mom wrote.[25]

In an interview for *M Music and Musicians Magazine*, Tim explained how he started working on the new songs he created that originated in old scripture. He was "into Joni Mitchell" at the time, with his guitar in different tunings:

> I'd play around until it fit the words. It's funny because a couple of them ended up being regular songs in the church. "Look at the

birds of the air . . ."—a famous passage in the New Testament.
This was one that got a lot of play. But that was just my parish in
Wheeling, West Virginia. From the beginning, I seemed to have
an aptitude for music. As an adolescent, I wasn't great at sports. I
liked some sports, but I wasn't a great team player. Music was something of value that I could do on my own. It fed the fire of self-
esteem. I did teach myself to read music. I wanted to diversify to
see what else was out there.[26]

In the building of the Home of the Good Shepherd for the elderly,
Father Braun also started a coffeehouse to attract the younger generation
to the Catholic Youth Organization. Tim loved performing there "just for
the fun of it." While others played games or socialized, he'd play, essentially busking, without the money. Mollie remarked, "Tim's guitar playing
was already outstanding." Because the folk masses and the coffeehouse
playing allowed Mollie and Tim to showcase their talents, they obtained
bookings for a friend's wedding and for talent shows.[27]

Despite Tim's earliest musical exposure to pop, rock, and folk music,
the pivotal moment that eventually spurred his future course as a performer of country music occurred in 1967 when, at the age of thirteen, he
saw Arthel "Doc" Watson in a feature about the Berkeley Folk Festival
shown on a Pittsburgh PBS TV station. In telling the story, Tim exclaimed,
"Wow! That's probably the way you should play the guitar. I'll try to figure
out how to do that. I was playing fingerstyle guitar, but he did the flat-pick
thing, and he was such a good folk music purveyor. He was a major hero
through my life."[28] Always an open-minded artist, O'Brien found that listening intently to Doc Watson encouraged him to follow his own path and
not to fear being unique. This blind North Carolina musician had labored
in obscurity at his home in Deep Gap, North Carolina, until he became
part of the folk music revival in the early 1960s. Doc proved to be a storehouse not only of the rock-and-roll and pop tunes he had been playing for
a living but also of the traditional ballads and gospel songs native to his
home region. Above all, he was a master of the guitar, proficient in many
styles, particularly the flat-picking style of instrumentation—the use of a
flat pick to play tunes with single note precision. His style, demonstrated at
concerts and festivals and on Folkways and other recordings, revolutionized
the playing of young musicians around the world. Although most fond of

Tim and Mollie as high school students (Tim O'Brien's collection)

blues tunes and not at all a bluegrass musician, Doc nevertheless influenced the style of countless bluegrass guitarists. In his earliest days of guitar discovery, Tim had played with finger picks, the technique popularized
by musicians such as Chet Atkins and Merle Travis, but he freely admitted
that "Doc Watson kind of sealed the deal on Bluegrass for me." The exposure to his repertoire and guitar style also opened up Tim's eyes to roots
music of all kinds. As an inveterate student of all that intrigued him, he
began looking into the sources of the pop styles he had embraced as a
child. He soon reached the point in his career that he became comfortable
in describing himself as a "folk musician," akin to his noted mentor.[29]

It didn't take long before Tim formed his first band, The Establishment, while he was still in junior high. Band members included Duffy
Wood on guitar (Tim first learned from Duffy's older brother); Mike Bol-
linger on drums; and Larry Haning as singer. Tim told us that the band
learned about three or four songs that they could play at parties, which he

Tim's band Ice at the Tridelphia Talent show about 1970, from right to left: keyboard player unknown, David Schaefer on bass, Trenny Blum on guitar, Tim on guitar (photo by Cindy Schaefer Sax)

recalled, included "The House of the Rising Sun" from the album *The Best of the Animals*. By the time he turned fourteen, Tim had earned enough money from his paper route to buy an electric guitar. Then he formed his next band, The Evergreen Blues or Shagum, and played all kinds of music, from rock and roll to country. These groups seem to have been primarily rock and roll bands, and, interestingly, Tim did little singing.[30]

Amy wrote that Tim had "a fascination with women and they with him." Being a musician not only fulfilled his passion for music but also fueled his ability to attract girls. In eighth grade, he already had a girl-friend, Susan Ward, whose psychiatrist father collected old instruments, including banjos, mandolins, and guitars. Dr. Ward owned a D-18, the first Martin Tim had ever had the opportunity to play for any length of time. That instrument initiated his love for Martin guitars, one that ultimately led to the manufacturer designing a limited-edition signature Tim O'Brien D-18. Tim commented that the D-18 initially impressed him because his favorite musicians played the instrument, and that Martin offered a lifetime guarantee. He added that the company continued to keep "that integrity. They define the whole thing. There's none finer than a Martin." Dr. Ward also had a patient, Roger Bland, who sometimes showed up for picking sessions at the Ward home. Even though he grew up in a state with a rich heritage of traditional country music, Tim enjoyed no personal organic relationship with country music until, possibly, he met Bland, a guitar and banjo player who had played on a local country music show called the *Wheeling Jamboree* and had at least briefly been a member of Lester Flatt's band.[31]

Bland possessed almost uncontrollable energy. Tim told us that Bland "jumped up in the air when he played." As his nephew wrote about his father and uncle, "They were both Hell raisers [who] travelled many a honky tonk and country music festival together and died too young."[32] Tim, in turn, described Bland as "a hopeless case as far as his personal life, but he was really inspiring as a musician. He showed me what might be possible, just gave me an inkling and awakened that appreciation in me. Playing one-on-one sealed the deal." Tim also found Bland to be a fount of bluegrass knowledge and instrumental mastery. "Everyone in Wheeling kind of learned bluegrass stuff from him." Noticing Tim's finger-style of guitar playing, and his use of finger picks, which he thought would be limiting in country music, Bland urged him to learn to flat pick and taught him the Lester Flatt G-run. As described in *Country Music USA*, this distinctive ascending run "began on the bass E string and ended with a ringing note on the third, or G, string" and became widely copied in bluegrass music. It occurred at the end of a fiddle, mandolin, or banjo sequence or at the end of a vocal phrase, adding "a dramatic note of emphasis or finality to the overall mood of intensity created by the supercharged music." Tim also credited Bland with instilling in him a solid sense of timing and professional excellence.[33]

At about fourteen, Tim also started attending Roger Bland's preferred venue, the *Wheeling Jamboree*. Since January 7, 1933, the powerful radio station WWVA broadcast the Saturday night performances of the *Jamboree* direct from the station's studios in the Hawley Building. The station itself appeared on the air in 1926 and could be heard not only in the Tri-State area it served but as far north as New England and Canada. As one of the longest-running country radio shows in America, during its heyday the *Jamboree* featured the performances of people like Doc and Chickie Williams, Hawkshaw Hawkins, Big Slim McAuliffe, Blaine Smith, Wilma Lee and Stoney Cooper, Grandpa Jones, and other major country performers.[34]

By the time Tim began attending the Saturday night show, the *Jambo-ree*'s glory days were over, and it instead served as a venue for visiting country entertainers making one-night stands at the Capitol Theater. There, Tim witnessed many of country music's leading performers, such as Charley Pride, Jerry Lee Lewis, and Dick Curless. Tim recalled, "I'd go to the *Jam-boree* and buy the cheap seats and my dad would drop me off before I could drive. I'd pay $2.50 for the balcony seats. They had a place where you could take pictures in an aisle on the right side of the theatre as you are walking to the stage with sort of a rope there. You could get in line and walk down there and take a picture, and when you took your picture you had to go. I never had a camera, but I'd get in line so I could get a closer look." Although he was thrilled at getting close to the stage, one moment particularly stood out: the evening sometime in 1970 when he saw Merle Haggard. Long regarded as one of the most gifted interpreters of songs, Haggard was play-ing the fiddle. He was performing songs from a newly recorded tribute to Bob Wills and his version of Western Swing. "That kind of inspired me to play the fiddle," Tim confided. "I thought it was cool, as in 'That's the vio-lin, but that is swinging and it's country. He was a badass.'"[35]

After the O'Brien children completed eight years at St. Michael's, tak-ing advantage of the youth programs as well as faithfully attending church, Tim followed his brothers to Linsly Military Institute, while Mollie went to Mount De Chantal Visitation Academy as a day student where she received classical training in voice. By this time, Mollie was fifteen and Tim thir-teen, and both Trip and Jim had already left home for college. Continuing to follow in his father's footsteps, Trip also matriculated at Mt. St. Mary's, intending to attend law school afterward and join his father's firm. Jim emphasized that his parents always encouraged their children to follow their hearts, and he had his set on getting an appointment to the US Naval Academy, which he gratefully achieved. Then Jim received his commission as a helicopter pilot, flying from ships in Vietnam. Upon returning to the United States, he became a career naval officer. The house on Lenox Ave-nue now seemed too large for the family still in Wheeling. Amy also indi-cated that the neighborhood had begun to be noisy and crowded when a new convent and parking lot were built on their block.[36]

In 1967 the O'Briens sold the house and bought one at 430 Oglebay Drive, a smaller house on a half-acre lot where they moved in the late summer. The larger lot afforded the family more privacy. Mollie and Tim,

Tim as Linsly cadet (Tim O'Brien's collection)

now aged fifteen and thirteen, profited from the new house's proximity to Oglebay Park, a self-supporting municipal park named for Earl W. Oglebay, who in 1926 had deeded his estate with its magnificent grounds to the city of Wheeling for the express purpose of public recreation. The two-thousand-acre multipurpose park contains golf courses, tennis courts, a zoo, gardens, walking paths, a nature center, a museum, and other public buildings including a theater offering performances of all kinds. In the winter, part of the golf course becomes a ski slope, complete with facilities for making snow. Amy felt that "within a few years we were very satisfied having a small house," but she confessed in her memoirs that "the Lenox house will always be the one I look back on with the greatest love and affection."[37]

Not many months after their move to the new home, tragedy struck the O'Brien family a second time. Spurred perhaps by the patriotism of his parents and their own military service, Trip interrupted his career path by joining the US Marine Corps Officer Training program in 1966 while still an undergraduate, now planning to serve his country before going to law school. When he announced that decision to his parents, Amy wrote, "I choked up with all kinds of emotion, pride, fear, excitement, wonderment, apprehension." Sadly, her fear and apprehension were well placed, and the O'Brien family suffered an irreparable loss when they learned that their beloved son and brother had been killed in Vietnam a decade after Brigid's death. Trip, by then a commissioned officer, died during the TET Offensive on March 24, 1968, the victim of a land mine. He never even saw his parents' new home. Although he'd seen photographs of the Oglebay Drive house before he left the country in the summer of 1967, he did not want to see photos of the interior until he walked into it himself. As Amy said, "He wanted to think of us in Lenox."[38]

Amy believed that she had a premonition while at Mass on the day Trip died, when she felt "a great black cloud" settling over her that she had trouble shaking off. Trip's loss not only cut short his promising career but also deprived Tim of a brother and mentor. Like his older brothers, Tim was an active boy scout—and he even became an Eagle Scout, which neither of them had accomplished—and Trip had taken him camping. Trip enjoyed the outdoors and shared that passion with his youngest brother, who idolized and emulated him. Then, before he left for Vietnam, Trip took him and several friends on a fifty-mile hike, which Tim thought was "pretty cool." He told interviewer Derek Halsey, "I had just turned 14 when my brother died. I wasn't there when the soldiers walked up to the door, but I was in eighth grade and my neighbor, who lived down the street from us, came and picked us up from school. She said, 'we're going to take you home.' We didn't know why. And then, we got the word. A soldier that was in his unit came by later and told us about what had happened." Trip's death also called into question the cause for which he died. The family took pride in his sacrifice and commitment to military service, but like many Americans, they had doubts about the larger decisions made by his country. Tim himself felt "that the country was abandoning the men in Vietnam." As Tim slowly entered the adult world, the events surrounding his brother's death left him torn. "The 1960s were a touchy time. With politics, there was a counter culture move towards a moratorium on the Vietnam War and all that stuff. Meanwhile, I had a brother that had just died over there. I was into the music and I was thinking, 'Gee, I'd like to go to this protest, but I was too young, probably about 16. But, I always sort of synthesized both sides because my oldest brother was my hero." Tim made peace with his inner conflict by believing that Trip had honored the commitment he made, and in keeping his honor, his death was not in vain.[39]

Just a toddler with little understanding of what was going on when Brigid died, Tim experienced Trip's death with acute immediacy. This beloved brother had liked virtually every style of music, including doo-wop, which he sang with his buddies. He generously supported Tim's efforts as a budding instrumentalist, supplying him with pop records and encouraging his early guitar attempts. Trip and Jim also introduced their siblings to music from the folk revival, soul singers like Sam Cooke and Ray Charles, and jazz musicians like Miles Davis. While Trip was serving in Vietnam, he and the family exchanged tapes. Tim recorded some of his guitar playing for Trip, who responded by suggesting that Tim listen to the playing of the great guitarists Andres Segovia and Manitas de Plata. Tim told us, "with Trip's death, it was once again a major factor as I was trying to be an adult at fourteen. I was trying to honor Trip with my music, and live up to his ideals or what I invented as his ideals or something. He was another saint in the family. It wasn't until I got much older that I finally realized that his life and Brigid's were cut so short, there's no way to tell who they might have become, good or bad. Still hard to get free from this stuff." When Trip died in Vietnam, he left money to his siblings. With Mollie's portion, she bought a piano; with his portion, Tim bought his first Martin D-28 guitar, "brand new off the rack from Gerrero's Music in Wheeling."[40]

As for many musicians in all genres, music stores played a significant role in Tim's life from his Wheeling days forward. Not only did he look for and find instruments or recordings that he coveted, but such venues offered musicians and wanna-be-musicians a place to encounter like-minded individuals. Music stores, therefore, served as informal community centers where musicians often could find potential band hookups or just develop relationships with people with whom they could pick and sing informally, learning from each other. As Tim said, even though record stores had more fans, "music stores are the places you meet other musicians, especially when you're fourteen or fifteen years old." A Croatian musician who played tambouriza music with an ethnic group over local radio, Walter Shalayka had a small music store where Frank O'Brien had his banjo mandolin repaired and where he also purchased Tim's first guitar. Tim recalls the bouzoukis in the window there, probably the first time he ever saw one and, not surprisingly, it was an instrument he ultimately mastered. Tim later bought his electric guitar and a fiddle from Shalayka's, but he also liked to see what the action was at C. A. House and Nick's, two music stores located closer to the Capitol Theater, like Gerrero's.[41]

Musicians and music stores, though fueling a major part of Tim's quest for creative outlets, were not his only source of inspiration. A few favorite teachers that he encountered at Linsly Military Institute fostered his passion for both music and literature. Founded in 1814 and the oldest preparatory school west of the Alleghenies, Linsly served as a compulsory military academy but also had an excellent music department and a strong liberal arts component. Tim actively participated in the school's annual minstrel shows, a variety show directed by the band teacher and director of the men's chorus, Major Douglas Haigwood. In its earlier history, the minstrel show had featured performers wearing blackface, but by the time Tim attended, these characters had been transformed into hoboes with dusty unshaven faces. Once at Linsly, he also became close friends with Willie Neumann, who had similar interests. Willie told us, "Tim was kind of a loner in a way. He didn't have a lot of friends because his interests were elsewhere." Neither of them engaged in sports, but they both enjoyed being in the glee club, doing show tunes like "Seventy-Six Trombones" as well as performing together in the minstrel shows. Willie had started taking piano lessons when he was only five, so he helped Tim with reading music. Sometimes students like Mollie at Linsly's sister school, Mount de Chantal, performed in the minstrels along with the Linsly students. With the schools' reciprocity in musical productions, Mollie was thrilled when one of her best friends hired the siblings to perform at what her friend called the "'Wheeling Woodstock,' which took place on the lawn at the Mount in 1969—capitalizing on the real Woodstock that same year."[42]

Like Tim, Willie spoke highly of their shared academic successes: both made it into the top twenty students nationally in national math contests, even though Willie believed Tim to be a more consistent achiever. Speaking of his own experience at Linsly, Tim said, "I got my love for literature there." He remembered especially the books *How Green Was My Valley* and *For Whom the Bell Tolls*, capturing his attention, and one particularly good teacher, Captain Max W. LaBorde, who cried when he read passages from the former work. "I really wanted to do well in his class," Tim recalled. Linsly eventually established the Laborde Award, given to superior English students. Willie served as the editor of the school paper, *The Cadet*, with Tim as one of the two assistant editors; all three were best friends. Remembering Tim as very "focused," Willie sees their friendship as "part of their shared music, creative, and self-challenging interests." Off campus, they'd go to each other's houses, or bring some of the boarding students home for the weekend since Frank and Amy always welcomed their children's friends. More often, Tim and Willie would listen to records for hours in Tim's downstairs bedroom.[43]

Tim did not study music professionally until many years later when he took some lessons in Denver from a jazz guitarist, Dale Bruning, who encouraged a discipline for learning the guitar fingerboard. But as a teenager Tim absorbed more than a rudimentary understanding of technique from a few music courses in grade school and high school. He said, "Singing in church or at camp, I was always able to find harmony parts," and through his choral experiences at Linsly, he learned more "challenging harmony." Always a self-confident risk taker, he commented, "After I learned a few scales and chords, I could make up simple lines to go with stuff. I guess as a result, I wasn't afraid of making mistakes." And even though he took about "a dozen guitar lessons from a couple people at the time," Tim spent more time "watching others and learning stuff from records, slowing the 33rpms on the turntable." He appreciated the 1960s as a decade where people just enjoyed playing informally, with no pressure. "I reached into any situation I could as a guitarist, though, not just because it was fun, but because it was something I could do . . . music helped my self-esteem. It was safe and rewarding." And Willie recalled that when Tim was "into Bob Dylan," he played piano, guitar, and harmonica, and both boys admired Randy Newman and Doc Watson. Willie also told us about musical adventures he and Tim shared. Sometimes they drove to some "godfor-saken" farm in places like Elkins, West Virginia, where they jammed. Willie would also drive Tim to little clubs where he played; once they drove to see the recently formed New Grass Revival when the band played at West Liberty College outside of Wheeling. Sam Bush and his band eventually became some of Tim's closest musical friends.[44]

Mollie and Tim were in their teens when they moved to their Oglebay Drive home, and Oglebay Park played a huge role in their year-round extracurricular activities: athletic, vocational, and cultural. As Mollie informed us, the park has "the most wonderful amphitheater" where she performed growing up, mostly in musical theater. "In the summers, they produced outdoor concerts where I ushered and then was able to stay and hear the show. I heard Buddy Rich, Ray Charles, Sergio Mendez and Brasil 66, Ferrante and Teicher and so many other touring acts." Tim and Mollie both entertained there when they got older. Amy thought that the park took advantage of the cheap labor that neighborhood teenagers willingly offered, but both Mollie and Tim appreciated being able to work there and each held several different jobs, during the summer and the winter months.[45] Tim began by picking up trash, then "graduated to more respon-sibility," including driving tourists around on a little train. He and Mollie learned to ski and "got hooked" after they moved to their new home, just walking distance from the ski lift where they obtained season passes. Mollie told us that the "lift went up and down the hill on the golf course." While she worked renting skis, Tim achieved such proficiency at skiing that he soon became an instructor to other youngsters. Amy mentioned that "watching him downhill ski was a joy to behold, especially because he learned on our simple little old slope at Oglebay."[46]

Tim and Mollie also drove up to Blue Knob, Pennsylvania, which Mol-lie described as "a rustic place in the Alleghenies." Tim played music in any receptive setting and with any interested musician in any style—folk, rock and roll, country—but Mollie remained his favorite music partner. At ages sixteen and fourteen, they managed to get a few gigs at a bar at Blue Knob by lying about their ages, which suited their dual purposes in being there. As Tim said, "You got paid *and* you got to go skiing."[47]

Tim's interest in many forms of music probably betrayed a restlessness that inevitably broke the bonds of West Virginia. While organized athletics never appealed to him, he excelled at individual outdoor activities such as skiing, swimming, and hiking. His immersion in the Boy Scouts, in fact, led to his initial sojourn in the West and initiated his ongoing fascination with the region. At fourteen in the summer of 1968, he attended the premier national Boy Scout camp, Philmont Scout Ranch, near the village of Cimarron, New Mexico. Founded by a bequest from Waite Phillips of the Phillips Oil Company and described as "a high adventure" camp, Philmont sat on 140,000 acres of wilderness in the Sangre de Cristo mountains. Campers typically took part in strenuous backpacking "treks" that might last as long as two weeks.[48]

After Philmont Scout Ranch, Tim spent providential summers at camps run by Jay and Cynthia Devereaux. In the summer of 1969 he began as a camper at their rustic outdoor adventure Rawhide Ranch Camp in Dubois, Wyoming. Then, in 1971, when the owners of a more established camp near Kelly, Wyoming, retired, the Devereauxs moved their operation to the new site. The new camp became known as the Teton Valley Ranch Camp where Tim served first as a junior counselor. He became friends with Matt Montagne at Teton Valley where they worked as counselors for children aged eleven through fifteen during the summers of 1972 and 1973. Tim described the new location as "a gorgeous property with warm springs and pasture land along the Gross Ventre River, looking directly at the Teton range." These Wyoming summers introduced him not only to the grandeur of the Rocky Mountain West but also to the life of cowboys. The new campus operated as a working cattle ranch, and some of the ranch hands impressed Tim with their knowledge of the backcountry. Jack Davis, the oldest cowboy, regaled Tim with the exploits of his earlier adventures driving cattle from Texas to Wyoming and rekindled Tim's fascination with the television cowboys he had admired as a youngster. These cowboys ran the pack trips, packing the mules and tending to the corrals at the trailhead during excursions that lasted between one and six days—quite demanding for campers and counselors alike. Tim enjoyed the exhilaration and challenge that Teton Valley offered. During the day, activities kept campers busy, and every night they gathered around a campfire where the programs included skits, stories, and songs. Although the leadership of the campfires rotated, Tim often entertained.[49]

In the summer of 1970, when Tim was sixteen, he borrowed his mom's VW bug and set out with his friend Pete Bachman for Elizabeth, West Virginia, to attend a fiddlers' convention. There, he heard Franklin George play a hammered dulcimer and Ira Mullins play the old-time fiddle. Merle Haggard may have stimulated Tim's interest in the fiddle, but this event inspired his lifelong fascination with traditional fiddling and his involvement both as a listener and, not so many years later, as a winning contest participant. Tim's Aunt Katrine Rempe had played violin in the Wheeling Symphony, but after marrying she never picked the instrument up again. He told Halsey that when he graduated from Linsly in 1972, she said, "'Well, maybe you can use this. Maybe you should try and play the violin.' I took it from her, but I couldn't make any sense of it." He did think enough of the instrument, however, to ask his parents for a new bow as his graduation gift. But Tim only fully realized the value the fiddle held for him after he had sampled college.[50]

★ ★ ★ ★ ★

Chapter 2

THE CALL OF THE WEST

Even before Tim graduated from Linsly Military Institute, his father clearly sensed his youngest son's restlessness. Tim always liked quoting his father, whom he likely heard say more than once, "You just want to go as far away as you can, don't you?" Wheeling was beginning to bore Tim, but his summer camp experiences in New Mexico and Wyoming awakened his romance with the Mountain West. As he mentioned to us, "Wyoming figures pretty big in my adolescence." First, though, Tim had to deal with the matter of going to college, a stepping stone to adulthood highly valued in the O'Brien family. Tim chose Colby College for its sterling liberal arts academic reputation and, equally important, for its proximity to ski country, a location he had already enjoyed. He set off on his journey into academia in 1972 and managed to remain an undergraduate until a few weeks into his sophomore year. The peripatetic years between 1972 and 1978—when he coorganized the famous Hot Rize Band—garnered him all the information that an autodidact and lifelong learner needed to prepare himself for the musical career that he then relentlessly pursued. Ironically, not long after he left the state, he began to realize that being a native son of West Virginia lent him a certain "authenticity"—enough so, that it served as a cultural credit card from which he could continually draw.[1]

Founded in 1813, Colby College is a private liberal arts school located on Mayflower Hill in Waterville, Maine, overlooking both the Kennebec River valley and downtown Waterville. With its picture postcard–perfect campus, Colby presented an archetypical version of everything one might seek in a classic New England academic setting. With former students like Margaret Chase Smith, Elijah Lovejoy, Doris Kearns Goodwin, and Benjamin Butler, the school prides itself on its contributions to national public service. When asked about the instruction he received at Colby, Tim responded wryly, "I don't remember many Colby professors' names! Not surprising really. I was mostly learning how much pot I could smoke, and how Doc Watson played 'Muskrat' between classes. I took an intro/ overview Classics course from a guy named Peter Westervelt. He was a tiny guy with a kind of twisted body, not sure what from, but he was very articulate, very much in love with his subject—Ancient Greece and its artifacts and literature."[2]

Intending to major in some form of literature, or perhaps the classics, Tim found the curriculum compatible with these aspirations, and he especially appreciated an innovative program known as the Jan Plan, which fostered "independent study by the whole student body, on a diversity of subjects." Tim explained:

> I think the guy who taught Irish history and politics as part of a co-ordinated study program (I think the other element was literature), was named Paul Sacks. He raised my awareness of the Irish strife with England, its literary revival, the Troubles. The whole month of January 1973 was dedicated to independent study of Joyce's *Ulysses*. There must have been a faculty member involved but it was mostly me with a study guide, getting through it, and writing a paper. I have read parts of it again in recent years, and partly because I've been to Ireland and read about it a lot since '73, I understand it more easily. At the time, it was foreign and nearly impenetrable. My dad commented on my upcoming study over the Christmas holidays, saying it seemed like an awful tough subject—I was trying to read it over the break.

This rigorous exercise in literary understanding helped to whet his interest in Irish culture, a fitting predecessor for his later fascination with the music of Ireland.[3]

Although Tim became settled into coursework, music never loosened its grip, and musicians have a way of finding each other. He and Jeff "Smokey" McKeen, who lived down the hall, were immediately simpatico; they became friends and frequent jam partners. Together, they discovered a "vibrant coffeehouse scene" at the college, as well as a coterie of people who enjoyed playing bluegrass and old-time music. Smokey, a product of Worcester, Massachusetts, grew up in a family well-connected to Maine and Colby. He insisted that he enrolled at Colby in order to "go to Maine." His parents had already introduced him to the music of Pete Seeger and

Brownie McGhee. From there, like Tim and many young aspiring musicians, he gravitated toward Doc Watson and bluegrass. When Tim enrolled at Colby, of course, he brought his guitar along, and his playing impressed Smokey, who told us, "his musical proficiency was pretty amazing. He was playing great finger style things, and just beginning flat-picking, very influenced by Doc Watson at the time." Even though Smokey's skills did not measure up to Tim's, they discovered that their music sounded particularly sharp and resonant while playing in the stairwell of their dorm, Dana Hall. When the two of them played at a coffeehouse on campus, someone shouted, "Which one is Doc, and which one is Merle?" (Merle was Doc's super-talented son.) They were thrilled to see the premier musicians Joe Val and Don Stover when they came to campus to play at the coffeehouse. Tim remembers asking Stover to play "Sitting on Top of the World." During the spring semester, the two friends hitchhiked to Boston to see Doc and Merle play, then spent the night in Smokey's parents' rec room. When Tim spied a ukulele mandolin hanging on the wall, he "reached for it, tuned it up, and started playing it. The instrument had a great sound. We took it back to Colby, and Tim got to playing it there."[4]

Smokey had a *Sing Out!* magazine collection. His parents had taken him to the Newport Folk Festival in 1967 during his high school years, where he saw, among others, Jack Elliott, John Hartford, and Pete Seeger. Smokey's father belonged to a record club, and Smokey sent away for three folk music records: Sandy Bull, Ian and Sylvia, and Doc and Merle Watson. "I brought that record [Doc and Merle's] with me to Colby, and Tim and I must have listened about one hundred times." To add to the music that inspired Tim and Smokey, Mollie sent her brother the Nitty Gritty Dirt band's influential album *Will the Circle Be Unbroken?* Always ready to hear live music, when Mollie visited Tim at Colby, the three attended a Beach Boys concert.[5]

Tim, Smokey, and their bluegrass cohorts also found a loyal benefactor in Shirley Littlefield, a longtime dining hall employee at Dana Hall, who warmed to the music she heard the bluegrassers playing there. She and her large family had a farm outside of town, and she frequently invited the young musicians to the farm for dinner and a session of music out on the front porch. Tim and Smokey became regulars. These informal gatherings ultimately inspired a fiddlers' contest and music festival, the East Benton Fiddle Festival, begun in 1974 and hosted by the Littlefields on their farm every year since.[6]

In 2000, Tim told an interviewer from *Colby Magazine,* "Jeff McKeen had a mandolin. He went away for Spring Break, and I stayed. I borrowed that mandolin and started playing it. That was the start." Tim had also borrowed a copy of *Sing Out!* magazine from Smokey's extensive collection and found there the mandolin tablature for two songs, "Fisher's Hornpipe" and "Rickett's Hornpipe." As he shared with us, "I learned them on the mandolin, and then I went home to where my fiddle was and I started working it out. I figured out how the fingering worked just from those two tunes, because the mandolin's the same."[7]

After his freshman year, Tim returned to Wyoming in the summer of 1973 to resume his job as a camp counselor at Teton Valley Ranch Camp, where he rejoined his friend and fellow counselor, Matt Montagne. Matt remembers that Tim was just beginning to work on his bowing techniques on his fiddle. He practiced during any break during the day and then performed for the campers around the campfire. Jack Davis, the old ranch hand whom Tim had gotten to know during his previous summers, noticed Tim carrying his fiddle along on one of the extended excursions in the mountains. Tim told us, "I brought my fiddle to take on a trip and he said, 'The trail's no place for a banjo.' I told him it was a fiddle, but he still said, 'Banjo don't belong on the trail.' The others liked it ok." Matt observed that, even while at camp, Tim gained proficiency as an outstanding fiddler, which, in turn, inspired Matt to learn the mandolin. "It seemed that he was doing what he was doing effortlessly, even though it took a great deal of practice to achieve that ease." According to Matt, Tim also wrote a couple of "tear-jerking camp songs that kids really loved and identified with." The two friends remained in touch in between and after those Wyoming summers. During their "off-season communication" while at Dartmouth, Matt began to realize the extent of Tim's dedication to his music, which became more evident at Colby. Although they enjoyed comparing their collegiate experiences, Matt could see that playing music dominated Tim's focus and that he appeared ready to "choreograph his life to follow that path."[8]

Indeed, fiddling had captured Tim's full attention, and the mountains he loved in the West beckoned. Only two weeks after returning to Colby in the fall of 1973 to begin his sophomore year, Tim decided that collegiate life interfered with his working toward his real goal: music making. According to John Lawless, this realization seemed to come during a course on Beowulf. Tim told him that "I was just playing the guitar and fiddle, mostly the guitar, all day." He also learned that the campus bluegrass group with whom he had played the previous year had replaced him with another guitar player. That led him to declare, "The wind went out of my sails, and I thought 'I don't want to be here. I just want to play music.'" He told an interviewer for *Colby Magazine* in 2000, "I felt like my life was over," when he discovered that his outlet for performing at the college had evaporated. That realization, in turn, propelled him to move on, even though he did not yet know just how to proceed to get himself out west again.[9]

As Derek Halsey wrote, Tim "grew up in a family of professionals, and a life plan that mentioned the word 'musician' was not exactly on the forefront of his parents' imagination." Tim told him, "I suppose my parents had other career paths in mind, but I was the youngest, and I think my older siblings wore them down, really." His sister, Mollie, had preceded him in dashing their parents' aspirations to see all of their children graduate from college. As Amy wrote in her memoir, "Coping with the changing times, tolerating the ideas tossed at us, bracing for the attitudes of Mollie and Tim . . . became a terrific challenge to me." Mollie had matriculated at the University of West Virginia her freshman year, transferred to Bethany College, then dropped out. She, too, wanted to pursue her musical dreams: making it into Broadway musicals in New York. After she dropped out of college and moved to New York City to try to get into auditions, she had to support herself, first as a clerical worker and then as a buyer in a men's wear department. She found the city in the 1970s "in bad shape . . . tough . . . and expensive." Mollie sang in a municipal choir for about a year, auditioned but didn't get anywhere, and finally moved back to Wheeling to figure out her next moves. As Tim told us, Mollie had already given up college, and now he was following suit. He felt that his folks "were angrier with or more protective of her" than with him, though perhaps she had taken the brunt of their disappointment since she had already flouted their expectations.[10]

After that brief return to Colby, Tim explained, "I told my parents I was withdrawing and I would stay in Maine for a bit to decide what to do next. They got in their car the next day, and drove to Maine to bring me right home." Tim's withdrawal occurred early enough in the semester that Colby fortunately reimbursed his tuition. He hung around Wheeling for a few months, honing his skills on guitar, fiddle, and mandolin, and playing music locally. Most often Tim played with a group led by his friend, Pete

Bachmann—West Virginia Grass—that consisted of Pete on mandolin, Ed Mahonen on banjo, Laura Cramblet on guitar and vocal, Mac MacFadden on guitar, and either Bill Gorby or Vick Marshall on bass. Tim told us that he believed "Mac quit the band soon after Pete invited me to join. He had been lead guitar, but I was crowding him out. It was a little uncomfortable—I learned after that about band politics and the etiquette of such things. We were all so young!"[11]

Tim even made a banjo from a kit provided by Stuart McDonald in Athens, Ohio. Just like Mollie, he had to figure out how to support himself while pursuing his career as a musician. He worked at Teeter's Tree Nursery for six weeks and, unsurprisingly, discovered "some hard, physical labor there and didn't hold up too well. After unloading a truckload of flagstone one day, my back told me to work harder on my guitar playing." He told Kavanagh he did work at the nursery long enough, though, to buy a 1965 Volvo, and then he set out on his "walkabout." Armed with a new car and a young man's confidence, Tim prepared to pursue his heart's desires: skiing and making music. In November 1973, shortly before Thanksgiving, he told his mother, "I'm heading west. I know 200 songs now, and I figure if I keep learning more I should be all right." He was soon on the road to Jackson Hole.[12]

John Sidle, attracted like many fellow musicians to the proposition of skiing and music making, moved in 1969 from the Boston area to Jackson Hole. Although he had played in a funk music club in Cambridge in the 1960s, once out west, he became immersed in cowboy and country music, which he continues to pursue at area dude ranches and cowboy poetry gatherings. He recalled that in the early 1970s he was asked to put together a four-piece bluegrass group to play at the Million Dollar Cowboy Bar. He recalled that while he was playing there, a young Tim O'Brien walked in with his guitar on a night off from being counselor at Teton Valley Ranch Camp. Tim asked to play with John's band, which he did that night and on several subsequent evenings. They saw each other infrequently after that summer, but whenever their careers intersected, John remembers being impressed with Tim's dedication and discipline. Tim remembers their encounter quite differently. He told us that, "while a camp counselor, I doubt I'd have gone in the Cowboy Bar in Jackson because I was underage. But when I moved there, I got a gig playing in a bluegrassy band called Bluegrass After the Shoot-Out, which referred to the daily mock shoot-out

on the square there. Basically, a happy hour gig. 6–8pm or so." Tim also
said that he didn't recall John's being a part of that band, adding that he
would not have walked into the Million Dollar Bar with a guitar until late
November of 1973, after he'd moved to Jackson.[13]

Tim told us that he chose to spend the winter in Jackson, because he
knew Matt Montagne and other friends from summer camp, he loved the
mountains and skiing, and he was sure he could make some money singing
in bars to cover ski expenses. Once he arrived in Wyoming, Tim found at
least part of what he'd hoped for. While frequent skiing in and around
Jackson Hole cost more money than he expected, he secured a job at the
Calico Restaurant, popularly known as Calico Pizza, housed in a building
that was once a Mormon meetinghouse. He told Halsey, "I could play and
sing, and I had enough guts to say, 'I can entertain your crowd in your
pizza joint.'" Later he elaborated in an email:

> An Australian guy named Kim hired me to play après ski in Calico
> Pizza on the Wilson Road. He fed me burned pizzas and provided
> a room in a house behind where he lived. Onstage, I played a mix
> of Norman Blake and John Prine songs on my guitar, adding a
> fiddle tune now and then to break things up, but my fiddling was
> shaky. The wages were such that I couldn't afford many lift tickets,
> but I could cross-country ski for free by the Snake River behind
> the house, and that house behind the Calico became my musical
> woodshed. On long quiet afternoons, I'd roll a joint and put a
> clothespin on the bridge to muffle the sound, then just go at it. I'd
> arrived in November, and when I left the following spring, I was
> able to play in time and in tune with other musicians.[14]

Sitting in with John Sidle's band provided part of Tim's learning experience that winter in Jackson Hole. And Tim's memories of John are vivid.
Not only did he play solo après-ski gigs at The Alpenhof in Teton Village,
John also was "part of the Stagecoach band that played every Sunday night
at the Stagecoach Bar in nearby Wilson. I went there often to sit in and
learn. The Stagecoach was wild and the band was a motley crew, led by
long neck banjo player Bill Briggs, who's also a skiing pioneer, the first person to ski down the Grand Teton. The repertoire of the Stagecoach band
included selections from 'Fraulein' and 'Up Against the Wall You Redneck
Mother' to Swiss yodeling songs." Elsewhere Tim reminisced, "You practice

until you can play in tune and play in time and get a pleasing tone. I wanted to play other instruments so I would be valuable to somebody in a band."[15]

After spending the winter in Jackson Hole perfecting his fiddle playing and becoming more confident as a multi-instrumentalist, Tim moved on, still partially on his "walkabout," before relocating in 1974 to Boulder, Colorado, in response to an open invitation from a musician friend, Ritchie Mintz, who had told him about the bluegrass scene there. Hailing from Brooklyn, Ritchie had first heard Scruggs-style banjo picking, which he called "a psychedelic experience," when he was ten years old and attending camp in the Berkshire Mountains. As a banjo player, he had chosen to attend Bethany College in West Virginia to get closer to the music he loved, but he was disappointed not to find it on campus. Ritchie remembered sending his bluegrass buddy Ned Alterman a letter from West Virginia to tell him about meeting "a fifteen-year old who could play guitar like Doc Watson and was learning the fiddle." Although he was likely already at Colby when the two met, Tim's youthful looks probably made him look not a day older than fifteen! Tim thought he was probably already twenty at the time they first saw one another when he was back in Wheeling one summer after camp and visiting bassist Bill Gorby in nearby Bethany. "If I'm not mistaken, Ritchie and I played some music in Bill's parents' living room in Bethany. If Ritchie saw me play on that visit to WV, it would have been with the West Virginia Grass, at the Hilltop Club, which is between where my parents lived and Bethany."[16]

Although their accounts of meeting differ, the event itself furthered Tim's thoughts about becoming a musician. Talking with Ritchie, he had asked if one could make a living playing music. Ritchie then asked Tim to come west to work in the music store in Boulder where he was employed and play in a band that he and some friends had organized. Although Tim did not immediately act on this enticing information, he filed it away for future use, and he and Ritchie intermittently kept in touch.[17]

After graduating from Bethany College, Ritchie returned to New York but soon became involved in a project with one of his former banjo students, Ned Alterman, who moved to Boulder in 1971. There, Ned and his wife, Laurel, established a music store, Folk Arts Music, and convinced Ritchie to join and work for them, teaching morning and afternoon lessons. Once in Boulder, Ritchie met Chris Battis and Sam Replin, who taught him not only how to fix instruments but how instruments work, the science of instrument building, splicing wood in, and other skills. Ritchie took his newly minted talents to Folk Arts Music. He told us, "The great fun of having a music store is you never know who is going to walk through the door." He and Ned also made music in a series of groups including the Wheeling Steel Band, Dixie Wind, and the Town and Country Review, playing in rowdy bars throughout the region. Three years later, Tim finally accepted Ritchie's offer.[18]

According to Ned, "ten minutes after Tim entered Folk Arts Music, he was working in the store" and playing whenever he could with Town and Country, even if it seemed "a bit too modern for his taste." The most important place to be on a Saturday night, Ned reported, was the Millside Inn in Ward in the mountains above Boulder: the locus of the local bluegrass scene where folks could play and jam. Ritchie, Ned, and Tim often played together informally around Boulder back then, and Ritchie admitted, "Those days were the most musician I ever was." Both Ritchie and Ned took pride in the musician that Tim became, and they understandably vied with each other about the roles each played in his life. Ned, for example, told a story about riding to the festival grounds at Telluride with Tim and some other people. Tim told the folks in the car how much Ned had influenced him. Ned said, "What about Ritchie? After all, Ritchie introduced you to me. 'Yes,' said Tim, 'but YOU gave me the job.'"[19]

Ritchie had sufficiently convinced Tim to come to Boulder, but Tim probably did not fully comprehend that his arrival coincided with the burgeoning interest in bluegrass there and on Colorado's Front Range. With the advice and assistance of Bill Monroe ("The Father of Bluegrass Music"), the Colorado Bluegrass Music Society had been founded only a few years earlier, and in 1971, the society organized the first annual Rocky Mountain Bluegrass Festival. An estimated sixty-five hundred people attended the first gathering. The Rocky Mountain Bluegrass Festival, which met at the Adams County Fairgrounds in Henderson, marked the real beginning of bluegrass on the Front Range. The Telluride Bluegrass Festival, founded just three years later in the tiny and picturesque old mining community of Telluride, became synonymous with the idea of a quasi-mystical Colorado bluegrass scene.[20]

Tim was only one of a large contingent of people, musicians and otherwise, who poured into Colorado during the late 1960s and early 1970s. Exulting in the freedom and expansiveness of the Rocky Mountain West, they succumbed to its mystique. Each member of the historic band Hot Rize—Tim, Pete Wernick, Nick Forster, and Charles Sawtelle—arrived in the region during those years. John Denver, who hailed from Fort Worth, Texas, sang often of the beauty and freedom of the region, in songs like "Rocky Mountain High." Some poets and songwriters, in fact, believed that the spirit and splendor of the Rockies shaped much of the region's music, reflecting the vast openness of its terrain. Professional skier and band leader Mark Morris, for example, of the Colorado-based Rapidgrass, linked his band to the state's blend of topography. The band's website states that Rapidgrass "embodies the notion that nature, and particularly mountains, can bring out the best in our art, and we have dedicated much of our creative energy into bringing that art back to the people of the mountains. . . . We focus our energy to outdoor mountain lifestyle/culture events." Tim gave his own version of the alluring Colorado scene to Brian Turk:

> Colorado being such a beautiful spot with great weather, it kind of draws a certain type of people. The immigrants to Colorado over the years, and I was one of them when I moved there in 1974, go there for the mountains and the weather and the recreation, and it turns out that people like that tend to enjoy music. . . . The audiences in Colorado have always been strong. New groups will break in Colorado early on before they break anywhere else. It's a real great environment for music.[21]

In the *Aspen Times* on March 16, 2006, the reviewer Stewart Oksenhorn commented that Tim had seen the West Virginia scene as "overly respectful of tradition, and lacking in innovation. Around Boulder he saw a vibrant acoustic music scene with a healthy dose of irreverence." After the release of a Hot Rize reunion recording in 2014, Tim spoke of the perceived freedom of the mountains in an interview for *Mandolin Café*. Referring to the title of Hot Rize's new CD, he said, "*When I'm Free* is a reference to the western vibe and the Colorado bluegrass scene and the freedom of the mountains and the fresh air that gave birth to the band. Pete, Nick, and I all moved west from darker, grayer climates, so it's sort of a story about us." Ironically, even as Tim continued embracing the Rocky Mountain mystique (and prospering from its popularity), he simultaneously became aware of the power exerted by the name "West Virginia," the home state he had worked so hard to leave behind. He learned that he won legitimacy among country and bluegrass aficionados when they discovered he came from the Appalachian state, a region famous for its traditional musicians. Although not "Appalachian" himself, Tim freely embraced this identification and in fact soon began trying to learn as much about it as he could. Over the years that followed, Tim became a marvelous interpreter of old-time styles and songs, and a passionate advocate of his home state's musical traditions.[22]

Before, during, and after his move to Boulder, Tim put a lot of miles on his Volvo, satisfying his cravings to make music anywhere that an opportunity presented itself. This meant playing bluegrass music wherever he could as he traveled back and forth to visit his parents, just like he did when meeting Ritchie Mintz the first time. After he dropped out of Colby, Tim's ramblings also included forays into Chicago. In the fall of 1974 while back in Wheeling for a visit, Tim decided to survey the folk scene in Chicago. After his friend Jay Odice secured an audition for him at the folk club Somebody Else's Troubles (named for a Steve Goodman song), Tim drove to Chicago and managed to book a one-night gig there. Like most young people who aspired to a career in folk music, Tim was in awe of Goodman. The following summer, he booked a week-long gig at another Chicago club, The Earl of Old Town, alternating with folk singer Marty Pfeiffer. They played altogether about ten sets that lasted until five o'clock the following morning. Steve Goodman played frequently at the club, and Tim met him there during a Saturday matinee performance. Already a widely esteemed singer, guitarist, and the composer of exceptional songs such as "City of New Orleans," Goodman tragically died from leukemia at the age of thirty-six, less than a decade later. He treated Tim to a Mexican dinner, invited him to his apartment, played music with him, and then gave him some advice about playing his guitar (putting out "a good steady groove") and dealing with an audience. "They were good lessons," Tim said, "and I took them in like a student of a guru should." He understood the importance of this encounter: "Here was a guy who was successful who told me I was good. It gave me the confidence to pursue music and, for the first time, I accepted 'this is what I do.'"[23]

Steve Goodman served as only one of many "teachers" from whom Tim learned in his evolution as a professional musician. His acknowledged mentor, the Ohio musician JD Hutchison, also entered Tim's life about the same time he met Goodman, similarly, on one of Tim's many trips back home. Tim had actually seen JD in Nick's Music Store on Market Street in Wheeling, when Tim was eighteen or nineteen, but the two did not actually meet then. As Tim told us, "I just wandered into the store to see if there were any good instruments to look at. He was behind the counter holding a guitar, and I imagine I just nodded to him and him to me. I looked around and he played 'Nine Pound Hammer' fingerstyle ala Merle Travis. I didn't ask his name and he didn't ask mine." JD grew up in Belmont County, in southeast Ohio, just across the river from Wheeling. His father had the reputation of a renowned old-time fiddle and guitar player in the Barnesville area. The Hutchisons were not backwoods people, but JD enjoyed creating that illusion and playing it full tilt. JD eventually made his home in Athens, Ohio, and he and his brother Zeke played all around that area. Tim loved his sense of humor. JD and Zeke sang and played music together since their childhood, and before Tim met him JD had played with Roger Bland on the *Wheeling Jamboree*, a shared connection.[24]

Tim and JD met a few years later in the summer of 1975. As usual, when in Wheeling, Tim contacted his bluegrass friend Pete Bachmann to check on current musical events and gigs. Pete invited him to a new club, Tin Pan Alley, to hear a bluegrass band—the Hutchison Brothers—with whom Pete was playing. The Hutchison Brothers played in the tradition of the groups Tim and Pete particularly admired: the Lilly Brothers (Everett and Bea), the Delmores (Alton and Rabon), and the Monroe Brothers (Bill and Charlie), bands with the "spirit and enthusiasm" that JD found particularly appealing. But JD described his own band as "a cross between the Stanleys [Carter and Ralph] and the Whites [Clarence and Roland]." The meeting proved providential for Tim on many levels because it introduced him to a network of other relationships that were to prove fruitful for decades to come. In addition to Pete's playing mandolin that evening, Tim got acquainted with JD and Zeke (Robert, "Sour Bob"), and bassist Tim Sparkman ("Rocky"), and he joined the band on one number, as he recalled, probably playing "Sailor's Hornpipe."[25]

Soon after the Tin Pan Alley gig, Tim visited JD and Zeke at their parents' home in Barnesville where they talked about music and instruments. Not many weeks later, Tim attended a bluegrass party on the banks of Big Wheeling Creek and saw JD once again. Tim thought that might be the first time they really played much together. As JD recalled in typically earthy language: "We went back in the house, and after we had been there for a little while, we were pissing around with some instruments, and man, he was playing his guitar, and we were all gathering around and getting in tune." Tim started playing "Peach Pickin' Time in Georgia" on his guitar and "fittin' right in" while they fooled around for about an hour, and Tim really impressed JD, who wanted to know all about his future plans. When Tim hemmed and hawed, JD told him that he shouldn't do anything *but* make music.[26]

Every time JD and his band did anything around Wheeling at that time, Tim would bring his instrument to join in: doubling on the fiddle or playing his guitar. His sitting in pleased JD, who informed us, "It was always a great delight to me when Tim would show up." JD proudly witnessed Tim's having picked up "a lot of mannerisms and stage presentation" from the older musician, who also said, "I have never known him to make a false move. He's always been completely forthright. He's been most generous with everybody he knows. I always thought that he was one of those people who just wants to know how everything works. I think most people in the music business are in it for the wrong reasons—to impress people—but Tim was in it for the love of the music." Early on Tim realized that Hutchison had "a great overview of American music, the roots and branches that I was diving into at the time." While Tim marveled at JD's humor, musicianship, and downhome warmth, JD in turn was amazed at the versatility shown by "the little red-haired boy" from Wheeling. In the years that followed the two musicians remained close, continuing to inspire each other. As JD put it, "Ever since I've known Tim, it's been right next to being a blood brother."[27]

While JD was "plottin' and prayin'" about how he could fit Tim in to his band, Tim told him that he intended to stay in Boulder. JD mentioned that his friend Mike Kemnitzer had recently moved there, and that Tim should look him up when he returned out west. Though JD talked about the musical and personal kinship he felt with Tim, Mike was part of JD's greater family. From Central Ohio and a graduate of Ohio University in Athens, Mike "Nugget" Kemnitzer remained there to work at Blue Eagle Music, repairing instruments and carving banjo necks. While working there, he met the Hutchison Brothers, became a friend and ardent fan of their music, and ultimately married the sister of Zeke's wife. On one of his road trips with the Hutchisons in Ohio, JD joked about a pair of orange corduroy pants that Mike was wearing. The pants' flamboyant color earned him the name "Nugget." More than a nickname, Mike used it as a brand name gracing the headstock of his instruments. While working at Blue Eagle, Mike studied building mandolins and served as an apprentice luthier under the direction of master craftsman Bob White. When the Hutchisons made a short foray to Berkeley, California, in the summer of 1974, Mike and his wife soon joined them, remaining there for about seven months. During this short period, Mike finished the construction of his first mandolin, and an impressed JD told him that he should make more of those instruments. Coincidentally, Tim's friend Ritchie Mintz had heard the Hutchisons in West Virginia and became an instant and ardent fan, telling us they were "the most amazing musicians—a step beyond what you had hoped to hear." Ritchie visited Berkeley when the Hutchisons were there and often joined those listening to them when they played music on the sidewalk on Telegraph Avenue adjacent to the University of California. After a crowd materialized, a guitar case would fill with bills. In that context, when Ritchie saw the mandolin that Mike had built, he passed word on to Tim about its beauty and tone.[28] Up until this time, Tim had been using borrowed mandolins or the banjo-mandolin given to him by his father.

The Hutchisons' talents gained them limited recognition, but their personalities and predilections probably inhibited their becoming better known. As Mike told us, "They'd rather starve than play a gig that didn't suit them—and very few jobs suited them."[29] When the brothers returned to Ohio, Mike instead moved to Boulder where he had been offered a job with OME Banjos. In addition to his other duties, he worked in the basement continuing to fashion a mandolin on which he had long been experimenting. Back in Boulder, Tim followed JD's advice and contacted Mike who told us that, within minutes of their first encounter in the fall of 1975, Tim asked about the mandolin Ritchie Mintz had seen in California. Mike immediately agreed to make one for Tim. Bearing the Nugget label, and purchased in 1976, this mandolin became Tim's principal instrument, a prized possession that he carried on stage throughout his tenure as a member of Hot Rize. This black-topped A-5 Model Nugget, one of the earliest that Mike crafted, was the first of three different models that Nugget made for Tim. In the process, the two became good friends. Mike told us that, around Christmas that year, Tim rode back to Ohio with him and his wife,

Loyal friends always: Mike Kemnitzer, Tim, and JD Hutchison (Mike Kemnitzer's collection)

and they visited JD at his parents' house in Barnesville. The following day JD and Mike drove Tim to his parents' in Wheeling. When JD bragged to Tim's father about his son's music, Mike said, "his dad acknowledged [the compliment], but stated the importance of a 'real' occupation. Tim's dad was more than serious." Although Tim is quiet, with a wonderfully dry sense of humor, he develops deep friendships easily, and he values and sustains them over time. Nugget's fame rose as Tim's did, sufficiently so that by 1981, Mike's career and name had become so well established that he and his wife felt secure enough to move back east, to Central Lake, Michigan. There, they could live among their extended families, and Mike could continue his profession as luthier, fashioning beautiful mandolins for players all over the nation.[30]

Making his way through the musical culture of Colorado, Tim had two complementary assets: his brilliant musicianship and his extraordinary ability to make friends and useful contacts. He made music constantly, on the streets, in fiddle contests, in clubs, and with a wide variety of musicians. One of his most fortuitous connections came in the context of his "discovery" of the Denver Folklore Center, only about forty minutes away from Boulder. The two communities constituted the nerve center of Colorado music. Later, when Tim returned for the fiftieth anniversary of the Folklore Center, he remarked, "It's over 30 years ago that I moved there, so I guess I am part of that legacy in a way. Harry Tuft starting the Denver Folklore Center is a big thing. I might not have moved there if it weren't for the Denver Folklore Center. . . . Harry Tuft should get a lot of credit for the Colorado music scene. When you look at what he's done, it's just so remarkable, and it was done humbly. The Folklore Center became a meeting place, and every town needs that to get a music scene going."[31]

Born in Philadelphia in 1935, Harry Tuft became another northeasterner who fell in love with the Front Range. While he was studying architecture at the University of Pennsylvania, the folk music revival swept him away, propelling him instead to become both a musician and a student of folk music. He considered Roger Abrahams, another Philadelphia resident, singer, and guitar player (and later a distinguished folklorist), his mentor. Members of the same Jewish high school fraternity, Harry learned dozens of songs from Roger, who helped him buy his first guitar. In 1960 Harry visited Israel "Izzy" Young's Folklore Center in Greenwich Village. Young had founded the center three years earlier at 110 MacDougal Street, and it became "the beating heart of the folk revival" where aspiring folkies gathered to meet like-minded others. The Greenwich Village Folklore Center sold records, books, instruments, sheet music, and music-related periodicals—some mimeographed—and it also had a small performance space where, in 1961, Bob Dylan performed for the first time in the city. That ambience enticed Harry. When he and a musician friend left on a ski trip to Colorado in the winter of 1960, they stopped at the Old Town School of Music in Chicago where courses in folk performance also impressed him.[32]

Once Harry was in Denver, a friend told him someone could make a living part-time by establishing a folklore center in the city. Harry sought Izzy Young's advice about how to set up such an operation. He found a good location with cheap rent at Seventeenth Avenue and Pearl Street, in an area just east of downtown known as Swallow Hill and, on March 13, 1962, opened the Denver Folklore Center (DFC). Like Izzy Young's Greenwich Village Center, Harry's store supplied its customers with all the materials of folk music: the recordings and the books, and what are now called "vintage" instruments. From his initial location, he expanded several times, adding spaces for classes, a repair shop, then a coffee shop and a concert hall, where Harry established a hootenanny on Sunday afternoons. The DFC never made Harry rich, but it nonetheless fulfilled his dreams.[33]

The DFC thus became an all-purpose music emporium, hosting such major entertainers as Joan Baez, Pete Seeger, and Arlo Guthrie but also

Tim rehearsing at Weiser Fiddle contest, 1975 (Tim O'Brien's collection)

operating as a merchandise and repair center for musical instruments and other material. Above all, it became the employer of many of Colorado's most important bluegrass musicians—including the original nucleus of Hot Rize. Tim remembered, "I used to play at the DFC Tuesday or Wednesday nights. It was a weekly gig for a band that included Peter Wernick, Charles Sawtelle, and Warren Kennison, and various bass players and fiddle players. I was one of the fiddle players. . . . We were all just kind of there. It was a good catalyst for a lot of good music."[34]

Jamming at the DFC and at other venues throughout the Front Range, Tim became acquainted with several musicians who proved crucial to his career. He played music briefly with one of them, David Kelly McNish, in a country band called the Bluebirds. McNish charmed Tim with his "silvery hair and southern charm and enigmatic, superficially simple but stylishly sophisticated presentation," as well as his finger-picking style of guitar playing and expert blues and country singing. At about the same time, Tim began a fruitful association with Dan Sadowsky at the Folk Arts Center in Boulder, where Dan was repairing instruments. Their friendship continued to grow through innumerable gigs and festivals in Colorado and Wyoming. Both had a fondness for fiddle contests, with Tim soon proficient enough to be a frequent winner. A musician named Duck Baker (an American who moved to England) recalled hearing and playing with Dan and Tim in the formative period when the Ophelia Swing Band (OSB) was taking shape. In the summer of 1975, while living in Boulder, these young musicians often played on the streets of Denver "to survive." On one trip made with Dan, Duane Webster, and Tim, Duck Baker recalled:

> We had heard that we could do well playing on the streets of Aspen, so we piled into my car, with Tim and Duane in the back seat with Duane's stand-up bass across their laps and the headstock sticking out the window. We then drove the 200 miles up to Aspen with barely enough cash to pay for gas and no idea where we would sleep that night. We set up and started playing but before long a cop came along and told us almost apologetically that we could play for tips but had to be very low-key about it, because of a recently passed ordinance against busking. We could leave the guitar case open for tips but couldn't pass the hat, which cut into our earning capacity considerably.[35]

Touring brought its highs and lows as well as a host of colorful anecdotes. Although Tim said he had always tried to take good care of his cherished instruments while on the road, he admitted, "I've certainly had my share of mishaps. It's not a long list, but it's an interesting one." Even though duly proud of his Nugget mandolin, at first he lacked a proper case for it and instead carried it around in an old cardboard suitcase stuffed with foam, which was not nearly secure enough protection. Tim had traded his old Volvo for a Ford wagon but managed to total it one night on Togwotee Pass on the way to an OSB gig at the Mangy Moose Saloon in Jackson, Wyoming. Ophelia's bassist Duane Webster had to hitch a ride to borrow his brother's International Harvester pickup with a topper over the truck bed. The only problem was that the topper lacked a proper door, so they "put a tall board against the tailgate that mostly closed off the gear." Finally, they were back on their way when, as Tim told us:

> We were flagged down by a trucker on I-80 west of Rawlings. He told us something had bounced out of the pickup bed, and another

trucker had stopped to retrieve it. We turned around and came back from the exit behind to where an eighteen-wheeler was pulled over. We parked on the berm behind and walked to the front of the truck. The trucker was holding my mandolin in the headlights. It had survived the bounce. The foam case and the trucker's benevolence had saved it, but after that trip I carried it inside the cab.[36]

Born in St. Paul, Minnesota, Dan Sadowsky grew up in Rochester, New York, where he attended Rochester Institute of Technology. He arrived in Boulder in 1970 as part of a children's theatrical production that featured marionettes, and he settled down there in 1972 when he was offered a job with a local marionette production of *The Hobbit*. After the show dissolved, he got a job as instrument repairman with Folk Arts and soon met Tim O'Brien. Puppetry had paid his bills, but Dan's real love had always been music, particularly the swing rhythms favored by his mother—the pre-bebop sounds of the 1930s and 1940s played by Louis Jordan, Fats Waller, Roy Eldridge, and others. But he claimed, "It had never crossed my mind to play swing music til I got to Boulder" where he found some "colorful characters" willing to play it with him. Dan said that "forming the Ophelia band was a very organic business," which evolved out of street jams and other informal gatherings. In 1974, it coalesced as the Ophelia Swing Band, with Dan (guitar), Duane Webster (bass), Linda Joseph (fiddle), Washboard Chaz Leary (percussion), Mike Scap (guitar), and Tim O'Brien (mandolin, fiddle, and guitar). Ophelia earned a reputation as a freewheel-ing band that won audiences as much through its personality and madcap humor as through its musicianship. According to Dan, the band delivered an eclectic blend, "part jug band, part bluegrass band, part swing band. It was a horse of a different color but fortunately, Boulder was a very accept-ing place." Tim similarly described the band as "a cross between Dan Hicks and the Hot Licks, the Jim Kweskin Jug Band, and the Hot Club of France. We paid a lot of attention to the arrangements, attempting to compress big band call and response riffs into a small band." They played regularly at the Colorado Coal Company on North Broadway in Boulder, to "mostly a listening rather than a dance crowd."[37] Dan told us, "Every band in town played that venue, and they kinda took a shine to us." According to journal-ist Steven Oksenhorn, Ophelia had the good luck of forming during the city's thriving music scene. Tim further commented wryly that "in the course of three years, we alternately confounded, delighted, and confused audiences, leaving broken fiddles, wrecked vehicles, and even a horse's head in our wake."[38]

Through Harry Tuft's influence, and after a well-received show at the DFC, the Ophelia Swing Band managed to secure a recording contract from a local label called Biscuit City that specialized in folk music. They recorded two albums, with Tim appearing prominently only on the first. *Swing Tunes of the 30s and 40s* (BC 1313), recorded in 1977, exemplifies their idiosyncratic repertory and infectious style of performance. It consisted of various swing tunes, including "A Chicken Ain't Nothing But a Bird," "I Got Rhythm," and "Man from Harlem." Tim played both fiddle and mandolin, and his brief stints at singing already revealed his distinctive and ear-catching vocalizing, most affecting on an old Bob Wills tune, "Mean Woman with the Green Eyes," written by Sheb Wooley (who later wrote "Flying Purple People Eater"). Mike Kemnitzer commented that when the Hutchison brothers heard the album, they were surprised, since they had no idea Tim could sing as well as demonstrate his mastery on string instruments. Tim also appeared on the second OSB album, *Spreadin' Rhythm Around*, from August 1978, but only as a guest on "Old Rocking Chair's Got Me."[39]

In the mid-1970s, the OSB actively performed on the Front Range: on the street, in the clubs (including an extended gig at the Colorado Coal Company from March 18 through October 30, 1974), and at the Telluride Bluegrass Festival. Dan turned out to be such a crowd favorite at Telluride that, after the demise of the OSB, he moved to the community and hosted the *Pastor Mustard* show on the radio there and emceed the Telluride Bluegrass Festival for many years. Ophelia's farewell show occurred August 16, 1977, at the Blue Note on Pearl Street in Boulder. Although not given top billing, Tim gained invaluable experience with this band and later said that he had developed "his chops" playing alongside the powerful rhythm section of Duane Webster and Washboard Chaz.[40]

Tim had been playing in gigs with Peter Wernick at the DFC and elsewhere, and in 1977 he joined in Pete's banjo project. Pete already had a strong track record as a banjo player and now wanted to put out a "progressive" album that, among other things, would showcase his receptivity to innovation. To achieve this goal, he invited some of the most progressive

Ophelia Swing Band promo, from left to right: Linda Joseph, Duane Webster,
Tim O'Brien, Dan Sadowsky (Mike Kemnitzer's collection)

bluegrass musicians in the nation, including Andy Statman and Tony Trishka, to participate in the recording. One or two cuts even included a flute and a synthesizer. Released on the Flying Fish label that year, *Dr. Banjo Steps Out* featured Tim playing fiddle and mandolin on a diverse array of songs such as "Whiskey Before Breakfast," "Shady Grove," "Sally Ann," "Cross-Eyed Fiddler," and "Blueberry Ripple." Tim sang on a few of the songs: "Beatin' My Time," earlier recorded by Eddy Arnold, the Delmores' "Life's Too Short," and "Wichita Lineman," a huge pop country hit from the recorded repertory of Glen Campbell. In fact, Pete specifically wanted Tim on the album because Pete loved "Wichita Lineman," with its difficult tenor reach, and he felt that Tim could more than do it justice. That performance proved to be providential for Tim's career.[41]

At this point, Tim's confidence in his own music making had grown strong enough that he felt ready to do some recording of his own. The same year as the release of *Dr. Banjo Steps Out*, Tim gathered some of his musician friends to back him up on an LP for the Biscuit City label named *Guess Who's Coming to Town* (BC1317). The recording's notes accurately described its contents as "eclectic." The "little red-haired boy" who had been struggling to master the fiddle when he came to Jackson Hole in 1974 now played with self-assurance in any style required to suit the occasion and its audience.[42]

Four of his Ophelia bandmates—Dan Sadowsky, Duane Webster, Linda Joseph, and Washboard Chaz—joined him on several songs on the album, as did lap steel guitar player Lemuel Whitney Eisenwinter, and two musicians with whom he had traded licks at the DFC, Pete Wernick and Charles Sawtelle. Tim sang on only four cuts, including "Ninety Nine Years (And One Dark Day)," later a staple of the Hot Rize repertory. Instead, he played fiddle or mandolin on a remarkably diverse mixture of hornpipes, country breakdowns, western swing pieces, blues tunes, and 1930s pop songs. When JD Hutchinson received his copy of the LP and heard Tim playing the old western swing tune "Beaumont Rag," he was bowled over by the progress made by his little buddy. Tim even included a newer song, "Kit's Waltz," written in tribute to his sweetheart, Kit Swaggert, who was soon to become his wife. Although the album cover bore Tim's name, in the liner notes he drolly noted that the Buffocle County Boys and Howdy Skies performed the recordings, the latter being the nickname Tim donned while playing with the Ophelia Swing Band.

Even as Tim's musical stock rose rapidly in Colorado, he never missed an opportunity to perfect his skills. This quest took him to one of the Front Range's master musicians, Dale Bruning. Born in Carbondale, Pennsylvania, Dale built a reputation as a jazz guitarist in that state and in New Jersey and New York before spending four years with the US Navy jazz band in the mid-1950s. He left a lucrative position on Philadelphia television, leading the house band for the Del Shields Show, before relocating with his family to Denver in 1964. Tim went to see Dale when he was playing in a quartet with the tenor saxophonist Spike Robinson, in Sunday night gigs at the Walrus in Boulder in the mid-1970s, and Tim told Dale he wanted to study with him. As Dale told us, when Tim heard him in the jazz quartet, Tim tried to fully comprehend "the way the guitar will sometimes substitute for the piano," since a large part of Dale's role was playing accompaniment to the saxophonist. This arrangement whetted Tim's quest to accomplish something similar in his own music. In addition to playing locally, Dale was teaching such personalities as guitarist Bill Frisell when Tim became his student. "He wanted to know the chords that worked as a rhythm guitar accompaniment. He was curious about the jazz guitar and repertoire," Dale continued. "He came to study with me with a lot of questions, and I would give him assignments. . . . We did talk about jazz phrasing and articulation, but harmony was his main interest." According to Tim, "In those first lessons, he taught me enough theory and technique to get around the neck of the guitar." Tim applied those lessons first to the mandolin, then to the fiddle. As he began to master harmony and jazz progressions, Tim felt that he was "learning the language of what you already hear and know." The admiration was mutual. Dale mentioned that, years later, when he, Bill Frisell, and Tim recorded *Life Lessons* on Wendell World Records, with *eTown*, "We talked about the guitar in its many guises, and that was very satisfying. I respect their talents ('my nephews'), and I am grateful to have played a small part of their development."[43]

While studying with Dale as he pursued and began to fulfill some of his musical goals, Tim also found fulfillment in his personal life. He met Kit Swaggert in the spring of 1975 when she was twenty, and he had just turned twenty-one. Born and raised in Minneapolis, Kit was living in Boulder when she and Tim saw each other for the first time. On the evening of May 9, 1975, Kit and her roommates went to a "Beer and Steer" party up in the mountains north of Boulder, a celebration held by Charlie Papazian, a Montessori school teacher and home brewing advocate. Papazian held one of these affairs each spring, asking guests to pay a three-dollar fee and bring a dish, and inviting a band to play. He eventually became the founder of the Homebrewers' Association and a galvanizing force in microbrewing throughout the United States. On this particular night the Ophelia Swing Band played, and Kit and Tim met and talked during an intermission. After the show, Tim told Dan Sadowsky that he had met the person "who's going to be my girl for the rest of my life."[44]

Their brief courting days forecast what Kit's life with Tim would hold in store. They went to shows at the Colorado Coal Company, the Telluride Festival, and other Ophelia Swing Band gigs. They moved in together a couple of months later, in July 1975, but Kit had artistic ambitions of her own and returned to Minneapolis in August 1976 to enroll at the Minneapolis College of Art and Design.[45]

That same summer, Tim and Mollie went to Cornwall in the United Kingdom to visit their brother Jim who was stationed there. After their week-long stay, Tim and Mollie parted, because they had differing travel agendas. During this first trip abroad, Tim spent an additional two and a half weeks in Ireland. When The Dayhills, musician friends from the Twin Cities, performed in Denver, they introduced Tim to Pat Flanagan, who played tunes weekly, and Tim learned from him. At the time, migration waves back and forth across the Atlantic fascinated Tim, who learned that new immigrants moving to the city and integrating into the existing community continually refreshed the traditional Irish music played locally. An Irish woman musician friend in Minneapolis had told him about a huge music festival in Ireland. His interest thus piqued, Tim took his fiddle to Ireland, since the festival coincided with his travels. Given Tim's enormous networking skills, he met many musicians there and found Ireland simultaneously "so familiar and so mysterious," an impression that matched his developing involvement with the music.[46]

Tim ended up in Dublin at a bluegrass jam and felt immediately comfortable as he made crucial contacts with Irish musicians, important for his eventual odyssey to Irish music. When Hot Rize played in Ireland a few years later, he encountered some of the same folks he had met on that initial trip when he was just feeling his way around Irish musical culture. Touring Ireland with Mollie in the 1990s, he noticed how well listeners responded to the duet's music, once again reassured that he had learned "the etiquette of things" in the music scene of the Emerald Isle.[47]

Just months after this interlude, Tim joined Kit in Minneapolis. In her memoir, Tim's mother had written about his decision to leave Boulder: "Early in 1977, he'd come home from Boulder for a short visit and was quite despondent about a girl named Kit. He had fallen in love with her but, for whatever reason, she decided to leave him and return to Minneapolis. He confided in me that he could not live without her and my advice was 'go to her and tell her this.'" Tim, of course, followed his mother's counsel. Love temporarily trumped other career ambitions, and Tim left the Ophelia Swing Band before moving to the Twin Cities, then returned to Colorado that summer when the state's arts and humanities division booked the band for a five-week Chautauqua tour. Traveling in a state-owned station wagon, they were part of a variety entertainment package, staying four days with local families at each stop in small towns such as Brush, Paonia, Monte Vista, and Rangley. Returning to Minneapolis and Kim, he played music whenever he could, but he secured only a few paying jobs. He taught lessons at the West Bank School of Music in Dinky Town near the University of Minnesota and booked gigs occasionally at coffeehouses and folk clubs and freelanced with bluegrass groups. He also made some important contacts with a number of musicians including Peter Ostroushka and others connected with the then-fledgling radio show in St. Paul, *Prairie Home Companion*, even managing to appear on the show at least once at that time.[48]

Sometime in the fall of 1977, Tim received a fateful telephone call from Pete Wernick, asking him to return to Colorado to join a bluegrass band he was organizing. By this time Kit had dropped out of art school, and she and Tim welcomed the chance to move back to Boulder. The couple decided that they should get married before they left Kit's hometown. As she explained:

> I grew up in Minnesota, part of a large family, and three of my siblings had gotten married the summer of 1977. I couldn't see putting my parents through another big wedding, so we made a plan to "elope" in our Minneapolis living room. We had a friend, Bill Teske, who was an Episcopal priest and he agreed to marry us at our home. We got married on October 23rd, 1977, and our witnesses were our friends Bill Hinkley and Judy Larson . . . two of

the founders of the Minneapolis folk scene. We had invited about a dozen friends, mostly artists, to brunch after the ceremony, not telling them what the occasion was. As people arrived, we answered the door with the pronouncement that we had just gotten married! I made some soufflés (thinking back, I have no idea how I did that) and we had a case of champagne and a very fun, small celebration. After our guests left, we took a bottle of champagne to my parents' house, walked in, and told them we just got married. My mother looked at me and said, "Thank you!" They were delighted.[49]

Although learning about the marriage after the fact disappointed Tim's family, his parents, sister Mollie, and brother Jim got their chance to extend congratulations at a much larger celebration. As Kit described it, "They threw us a huge party with a live band, food, an open bar, and about three hundred people. They got to have their celebration too, and everyone had a wonderful time. Tim's brother and his family came to Wheeling for the party and we all spent Christmas together." The next month, Tim and Kit moved back to Boulder, where a new chapter awaited them.[50]

Chapter 3

THE REMARKABLE RISE
OF HOT RIZE

Within a relatively short span of years, Tim O'Brien had become one of the most highly regarded musicians on the Front Range. His ascent to national fame, though, came after 1978 as a member of the bluegrass band Pete Wernick was organizing. Pete already had chosen a name for the proposed band, Hot Rize, inspired by the legendary leavening agent found in Martha White Flour, a longtime sponsor of bluegrass music on the Grand Ole Opry. Martha White agreed to allow the band to use the title "Hot Rize," but with "the stipulation that we had to keep the show clean." Everyone in bluegrass music knew the jingle that Flatt and Scruggs and the Foggy Mountain Boys sang and played to advertise the product:

> For the finest biscuits, cakes and pies.
> Get Martha White self-rising flour
> The one all-purpose flour,
> Martha White self-rising flour
> It's got Hot Rize.

The audiences' responses to the young band's music soon echoed the jingle's famous tag line, "Goodness Gracious, It's Good!"[1]

At age twenty-three in the summer of 1969, Pete had finished his oral exams for the PhD at Columbia University and decided to drive to Boulder to visit his musician friend Fred Weisz. Happily, once there, he met and subsequently married Joan "Nondi" Leonard, a Colorado native. Several years later, he abandoned academia, and he and Joan moved back to the Boulder area. Seeking a rural retreat from the congestion and hectic pace of his urban roots, in 1976 they settled down in the little community of Niwot, about ten miles northeast of Boulder. Pete soon became an active participant in the local bluegrass scene. He joined the contingent of musicians who worked at the Denver Folklore Center (DFC) and began playing with them on the street, or in any available venue. He performed most frequently in a band variously known as either the Drifting Ramblers or the Rambling Drifters, which included Warren Kennison and Charles Sawtelle. At the DFC, he also got to know Tim O'Brien who taught there once a week and whom he heard performing with the Ophelia Swing Band. Sometimes Tim also sat in with the Rambling Drifters.[2]

Pete brought impressive bluegrass credentials to his adopted state. He was born in the Bronx, New York, on February 25, 1946, and as an undergraduate at Columbia University he was already hosting a bluegrass show ("the only one of its kind in New York") on WKCR. He told an interviewer years later, "At 17 or 18 I became important, if you can call it that, as the guy who played bluegrass on the radio." Even as a boy wonder undergraduate (he'd entered the university at sixteen), he could boast of having interviewed Bill Monroe and many of the first-generation bluegrass performers for his radio show and for the bluegrass songbook he authored. Pete also played banjo at every opportunity, jammed in the folk music scene at Washington Square, and from 1965 through 1969 attended the first bluegrass festival, launched by Carlton Haney in Virginia. This propensity to be present almost everywhere when historic events were taking place lent luster and credibility both to him and to the new band he was now creating.[3]

After attaining the PhD as a sociologist, Pete had begun a research position at the International Population Program at Cornell University in Ithaca, New York. But his love for bluegrass music and the five-string banjo won out over the stable, if staid, life of academia. By the time Pete moved permanently to Colorado, his diverse talents and academic credentials had already earned him the sobriquet of Dr. Banjo. While still at Cornell, he had written a popular (and still in-print) instruction book, *Bluegrass Banjo*, which offered readers a step-by-step guide to the famous Earl Scruggs–style of banjo picking, and had organized a progressive band, Country Cooking, with Joan as the lead vocalist. On the strength of the royalties earned from his books and recordings, he decided he would rather rely on the music he loved than his equally promising academic career.[4]

As Pete later indicated, "The idea with Hot Rize was that I really wanted to be in a band with Tim. Tim had never been a lead singer and, in the band he was in, he only rarely sang harmony. I knew he was way too good a singer to not be the lead singer of a bluegrass band, so I proposed we put that together, and he agreed." Tim's "fantastic rhythm mandolin style, which is so easy to play banjo over," also attracted Pete, since he knew that "most bluegrass mandolin players do not play that kind of rhythm."[5] But Tim's clear tenor and bell-like vocal tone had most impressed Pete. As noted earlier, Tim's vocal performances on *Dr. Banjo Steps Out* included the superb rendition of "Wichita Lineman" that Pete relished. He, in turn, had played banjo on Tim's first solo LP, *Guess Who's in Town*. Although Pete's long-range goal for Hot Rize is now uncertain, at the time he argued that the band could serve the immediate purpose of advertising the LPs that he and Tim had recorded. Nick Forster, who joined the band in May 1978, later insisted that he envisioned little activity beyond the summer of that year. He did not reckon with Pete's drive and ambition, however. Pete soon booked gigs for the group all over the Front Range and beyond. He believed that Hot Rize got a boost from its Colorado location, because the music fans there maintained a "wide-open" attitude to all kinds of roots music, and those fans—"our people"—quickly became the "musical community [that] nourished us from the start."[6]

The first incarnation of Hot Rize included Pete on five-string banjo, Tim on mandolin and fiddle and as the lead singer, Charles Sawtelle on bass, and Mike Scap on guitar. Scap (his real surname is Scoppetuolo), a brilliant guitarist from New Jersey, had played with the Ophelia Swing Band. His instrumental breaks invariably elicited gasps of wonderment and enthusiasm from listeners. Unfortunately, his eccentricities, which included a reluctance to ride in an automobile, made him an unreliable member of a band that hoped to tour widely. He also felt uncomfortable being in the same band with Charles Sawtelle, whom he perceived as very different and not supportive of him. In fact, Mike Scap had never lasted more than three months in any band and he didn't last any longer in Hot Rize.[7]

Born in Austin, Texas, on September 20, 1946, Charles Sawtelle's wide array of talents contributed immeasurably to Hot Rize's popularity and endurance. His musical skills, combined with his unsmiling countenance and solemn demeanor, contributed to his self-cultivated reputation as "the bluegrass mystery." His fusion of gravity and musical mastery contributed wonderfully to Hot Rize's magnetic stage presence. As the son of a petroleum engineer whose job took him all over the West and into Canada,

Charles had seen and lived in much of North America, from Winnipeg to Wyoming. He started college at Northern Colorado but transferred to Colorado State "where he fell in love with pottery."[8]

Charles played in a variety of bands before joining Hot Rize: the Monroe Doctrine, the Drifting Ramblers, the XX String Bluegrass Band (so-called because twenty equaled the sum of strings of their five-piece band, which included Mary Stribling on her one-string bass). Although she would become an outstanding performing and recording multi-genre bassist, Mary was still in high school at the time, having met and played with "Old Weird Charles," as he was known in the band, and other future XX String Bluegrass Band members at the "hoots" or hootenannies at the DFC. About the same time, Mary's friend and high school buddy Sumi Yamashita also enjoyed hanging out at the DFC, where she met Charles and later became his wife. Mary told us that the money she saved from earning a typical twenty-five dollars per gig eventually allowed her to purchase an acoustic upright bass. Her new instrument gave the band more than twenty strings, so the band then adopted a new name, City Limits. One telling anecdote she shared about Charles involved gigs the band played at the Red Ram, a bar in the mountain community of Georgetown. Charles would pick her up, and after the gig he would put the jeep in neutral as he coasted back downhill to Denver. He told her if he ever wrote a book about guitar playing, it would be called *How to Play Like Me*, an apt example of his "whacky" sense of humor.[9]

During his tenure with City Limits, Charles demonstrated his prowess as a fiery flat-picking guitarist, provoking fellow band member Jerry Mills to recall that "he goes through so many flat picks in one night that the stage ends up looking like it's tiled." Like Mary, Jerry stayed active as a musician, and he was a well-respected DJ, specializing in broadcasting bluegrass music across the mountain west.[10] All who knew Charles spoke of his profound knowledge of American roots music. His fellow Hot Rize band members profited from the road tapes he made of the songs of the Stanley Brothers, Flatt and Scruggs, other bluegrass luminaries, and bluesmen like Blind Willie Johnson. Nick Forster described Charles as a "remarkable human," indeed a marvel of virtuosity, who carried a business card containing only one word: "Expert." While the term suggested his wry sense of humor, it also came close to encapsulating his wide-ranging skills as a college-trained potter, student and collector of musical instruments, connoisseur of vintage motorcycles and automobiles, and master of musical sound production—a quality sorely needed by bluegrass and other acoustic musicians. Sumi described the way he loved all the "trappings" of the band—the image that he, above all, helped Hot Rize embody: the Cadillac, the suits and the ties—just as he loved his Lucchese cowboy boots and cowboy hat. As Jerry Mills noted, Charles's theory of musicianship could be summed up, "'You look sharp, you are sharp.' He wanted the music to be taken seriously, much like Bill Monroe." Commitment to style and musicality did not exhaust Charles's multifaceted personality. Bluegrass fiddler and singer Laurie Lewis noted that "Charles was outgoing and friendly, but when he decided you were important to him and you were going to be his friend, then it was unconditional affection."[11]

Hot Rize made its professional debut in January 1978 with a set of performances at the Hungry Farmer Restaurant in Boulder. Less than a month later, the band opened for Doc Watson at a concert at Colorado Women's College in Denver. Tim described the event as the group's first formal show, which he likely found fulfilling because he considered Doc Watson such a hero. With Scap's departure at the end of April, Charles moved from electric bass to his preferred instrument, acoustic guitar, and they recruited Nick Forster to take over his previous role, giving the group a new look and ambience.

Nick was born in Beirut, Lebanon, in 1955, the son of a State Department employee, originally from New York. In fact, Nick's middle name is Stuyvesant, after the thirteen generations of New Yorkers he followed. Returning to New York two years later to work in Governor Nelson Rockefeller's cabinet, his father brought his family home to the ancestral farm in the Hudson River valley. Nick loved growing up in the vicinity of the music of Pete Seeger, John Cohen (a former member of the New Lost City Ramblers), and fiddler Jay Ungar. He honed his musical skills and repertory playing mandolin, guitar, and banjo for square dances (as well as calling sets). When he graduated from high school, he knew he had no interest in going to college but instead decided he wanted to make mountain dulcimers. His first gig was opening for Jean Ritchie, the famous Kentucky dulcimer player, songwriter, and folk singer, who had relocated to New York City in 1946. By the end of 1974, Nick had made his way to Colorado, where he found himself in the company of a host of other musicians who had similarly been drawn there from various parts of the country and were open to any musical style. The first band in which he played included "a bunch of Texans," including Jimmie Dale Gilmore, David Halley, and Tommy Hancock. They were all following the spiritual guidance and learning to meditate under the tutelage of a young guru named Maharaj Ji, who had established the Divine Light Mission in Denver. Nick met Tim on New Year's Eve 1975, when he tried to attend a concert that the Aspen-based band Liberty played at the Oxford Hotel. Although they were twenty and twenty-one, respectively, neither Nick nor Tim could get in because they looked too young. As a consequence, they had their first conversation that evening on the outskirts of the event taking place.[12]

Lacking the proper tools to repair his mandolin, Nick went into the DFC soon after his arrival to see about getting the work done. Because he had the skills necessary to do the job himself, he immediately gained employment as an instrument repairman there. Charles Sawtelle already worked there, and Tim and Pete joined them soon after. Adept at playing several instruments, Nick nevertheless had usually concentrated on the electric guitar. Charles had already become the acoustic guitar player for Hot Rize when Pete asked Nick to join the band. When interviewed, Nick said, "Pete asked me to play bass in Hot Rize, even though I hadn't played bass, and I didn't even own one." Neither Pete nor Nick seemed bothered, and Nick quickly learned what he needed to know. Now the band attained the configuration that eventually took the bluegrass world by storm.[13]

Given his extraordinary musicianship, singing, and songwriting, Tim became the cog around which all the others revolved. As John Lehndorff reported, Nick became, in his words, "emcee by default, [since] he was the one guy who didn't have to tune much." In the same interview, Tim added that Nick's success as a "great emcee" was also due to his being "photogenic with a smile that hypnotizes people and brings them in." This defining version of Hot Rize began inauspiciously with a gig on May 1, 1978, at the Ramada Snow King in Jackson Hole, playing for five nights in the courtyard for a TOPS (Taking Off Pounds Sensibly) weight loss convention. Any assumption that the band would last only through that summer, as Nick initially believed, was soon dispelled. He had told Lehndorff, "We didn't think Hot Rize would last very long. We got together for the summer in 1978, because Pete and Tim had already put out solo records and thought they'd just follow up with a band to play festivals, promoting their records. But the band members clicked, put on some good shows." Nick continued,

"It was a band that started with a lot of commitment. We were really in all the way, even though we were young and brand new." He recalls that, in their first year, making one hundred dollars a week each seemed a feasible goal. "We did that, and I never went back to my day job."[14] The rest is bluegrass history.

Each musician in Hot Rize had specific strengths that shaped the group's style and assured its popularity. Nick described Hot Rize as "a bluegrass band with four really distinct personalities . . . who bring different skills and sounds to the party."[15] From the beginning, Tim's prowess as a singer and gifted multi-instrumentalist set the band apart. Pete had not only mastered the Scruggs sound and dissected it in publication, he had begun experimenting with a phase shifter, a device that, when plugged into his banjo and an amplifier, enabled him to extend the notes into a kind of organ-like warble. He had used this effect to accent particular passages on *Dr. Banjo Steps Out.* Nick found Charles "a completely original guitar player who, remarkably, stayed inside the tradition while really pushing the boundaries." Nick himself broke with bluegrass tradition by replacing the time-honored standup bass with an electric instrument, but he enjoyed "especially dancing around the low notes with Charles—that became a part of our sound [and] that was both inside the tradition and new."[16]

Not only did the aspiring members of the band bring their individual gifts as musicians to Hot Rize, they contributed useful practical assets, which added mightily to the internal cohesion of their emerging organization. Given Charles's sensitivity to and expertise on sound, he insisted that the band use its own sound system—a crucial decision—and with top-of-the-line components, which Charles personally owned, oversaw, maintained, and soon sold to the band. Employing its own sound system and sound manager, Hot Rize became one of the few bands in bluegrass music to do so, key assets that contributed to the band's early success. Charles remained the sound system guru and started training his protégé, Frank Edmondson, whom the band hired in 1981 as roadie and driver.[17] In time, Frank took over the job of full-time sound engineer for the band. Actually, even before Hot Rize, the band members all knew Frank well. He and Nick had begun working in the repair shop at the DFC on the same day in 1975. Frank became so indispensable to the band that he became a fifth Hot Rize member with full voting rights in their decisions and received a fifth of their earnings.[18]

Drawing on his wide range of contacts in bluegrass music and his enthusiasm for the band's potential, Pete became the band's indefatigable and unpaid booking agent until a few successful years later. Once the band initially formed, Pete made call after call to book gigs throughout Colorado and in dozens of other states nationwide. He happily relinquished booking tasks in 1981, when Hot Rize hired Keith Case, a highly regarded agent in bluegrass circles, who agreed to work under Pete's oversight. As a jack-of-all-trades, Nick Forster could repair instruments and automobiles and do much of the driving for their gigs. Pete correctly referred to Tim as the "musical front man," but he could also be called the band's muse: writing some of their most enduring songs and demanding the best of himself and his fellow musicians.[19]

Not only concerned with how the band sounded, Charles also wanted to give the band a distinctive look. He knew that many of the young bands in bluegrass—such as New Grass Revival, Country Gazette, and the New Deal String Band—were bending the stylistic rules of bluegrass and decking out in hippie attire. Instinctively, Charles recognized that image and appearance meant as much to a band's success as its music. He scoured the racks at Goodwill and other secondhand stores to find inexpensive suits and ties that he and his comrades could wear. Nick commented that they "made a conscious effort to separate ourselves from the pack" so that both older and more traditional bluegrass audiences could say, "'Oh, my, look at those nice young men and aren't they good and don't they look good in their suits.' But if people looked closer they would see that we were wearing thrift store suits. . . . We were wearing vintage ties as an homage to the people who came before us. So, there was a certain amount of tongue-in-cheek from the get-go." Tim commented that, as much as Charles liked combing through thrift stores for apparel, both he and Pete preferred proper suits. "Charles already had a western cut suit he got at Sheplers in Denver, and I think Pete got one there once as well. Nick had a good thrift shop suit and I wore a couple in the early years that weren't very good at all. Somewhere in there I got a proper suit from a shop in Boulder." As Pete put it, "We realized we were trying to look like Flatt and Scruggs. And that made us look different from all the other bands. Then we all started wearing boots. Southern audiences liked us, in spite of our looking (hair and glasses) like 'collegiate leftovers.'"[20]

Charles also found a smooth-riding 1969 Cadillac Deville, black with a white vinyl top, and with big leather seats. Nick and Tim painted a U-Haul trailer to match, for the band's gear. Charles and Nick did all the repairs on the Cadillac. Nick did 80 percent of the driving; Charles did the navigating; Tim and Pete shared the back seat, smoking pot. As Hot Rize pulled into bluegrass festival grounds, other musicians and fans immediately recognized the custom designed-to-match rig, perhaps also a not-so-subtle promise of a similarly well-crafted performance. The Cadillac carried Hot Rize all over the Mountain West and much of the United States until its 120,000 miles of service—and success—encouraged them, in 1980, to replace it with a used Greyhound bus.[21]

The band played in virtually every imaginable venue. Hot Rize frequented Peggy's Hi-Lo Club, a low-level honky-tonk in Boulder. Some patrons recalled the club as a "dive," but others remember it with great affection. Somewhat classier, the Blue Note, also in Boulder, featured some of the best-known rock and blues performers in the nation, even though it occasionally held topless contests as well. Since band members never mentioned these contests, evidently, they occurred when Hot Rize played elsewhere. Charlie Brennan remarked that "the area seemed to have been a hippie place, with wild stuff in the clubs." According to Nick, who had played with musicians from Texas, he learned that the music scene in the Lone Star state depended on songs for dancing. In the hippie scene in 1970s Colorado, Hot Rize played all the bars, so they, like Willie Nelson in Austin, "united the ropers and the dopers," although very little dancing occurred.[22]

Pete claimed that the "low end" of their early career came with a series of gigs, every Wednesday for six months, at the Colorado Coal Company, a bar that gave them a quarter of the night's bar receipts. On the other hand, an infrequent house party or private soiree might earn them something like eight hundred dollars for an evening's work. Occasional radio shows on local KGNU brought no money but did provide needed publicity. Hot Rize first appeared on the station on a morning show, not long after KGNU first went on the air on May 22, 1978. Typically, the bars required musicians to play four sets, a grueling schedule that could exhaust a young band's repertory rather quickly. Pete admitted that he was

> all over the place stylistically, and Charles could play some really good bluegrass, so that's how we did bluegrass. . . . We mostly played clubs around Boulder, which Charles really hated—especially

when the crowd got loud later in the night. Everybody liked Hot Rize, but the audience was more into pot-smoking than into drinking. The cash register didn't do well enough. People were just listening, not dancing. In Fort Collins and in Durango, people did dance. But we couldn't keep the clubs hiring us in Denver or Boulder.

As Nick related, "In the 1970s, you played in the bars from 9:00 to 1:00, and they [folks in Colorado] likened traditional country to bluegrass in a way that didn't happen elsewhere." Pete added, "Tim didn't want to play four sets of bluegrass the whole night." That became one of the reasons the band began doing some old-time country songs borrowed from folks like Jimmie Rodgers and Hank Williams. Tim had suggested introducing the dobro, but Pete got a lap steel and began learning how to play it. Hot Rize's alter-ego band, Red Knuckles and the Trailblazers, slowly emerged from these interludes and proved to be almost as popular as their parent band.[23]

At the suggestion of Pete's wife, Joan, the band eventually found a stable and respectable venue at the Left Hand Grange in Niwot—located in Left Hand (or Boulder) Valley, about halfway between Boulder and Longmont. This gave Hot Rize a steady winter gig with paid customers and no drinking. The Left Hand Grange #9 was a carryover from the late nineteenth century when a national farmers' organization, the National Grange of the Order of the Patrons of Husbandry, had fought for economic security, political power, and social camaraderie for farmers. The Left Hand Grange, one of over fifteen hundred such lodges in the United States, no longer asserted the political power it once possessed, but it remained a meeting place for various social and religious groups. For Hot Rize, the venue presented a real lifesaver, with its comfortable environment, friendly audience, and the ability to charge admission, two dollars at first, which by 1983 rose to three dollars, with a dollar added each year thereafter.[24]

Despite the grueling one-night stands, Hot Rize also had some striking good luck, even as the band took its first tentative steps. During his brief residence in Minnesota, Tim had made some crucial contacts with musicians there that opened up performance possibilities. Tim's musical acquaintance from his Jackson Hole days, John Sidle, recalled that when playing in Wilson, Wyoming, on Sunday nights (from 1970 to 1985), Tim and some of his other band members would occasionally sit in and play with John's Stagecoach Band. John also hosted a bluegrass radio show and recalled interviewing Pete on it when Hot Rize played in the area.[25]

Not much more than two weeks after Nick joined Hot Rize, they secured some important gigs in Minnesota, scoring a place at the first annual Minnesota Bluegrass Festival from May 19 to 21, and an invitation to be on Garrison Keillor's *Prairie Home Companion* in St. Paul. At that time the long-running radio show existed strictly as a one-state enterprise, carried by only five radio stations, but it already exerted great influence in the Upper Midwest. This initial appearance at the World Theater, just weeks after *Prairie Home Companion* moved there, proved to be the first of many made by the band down through the years.[26]

Hot Rize, of course, did not emerge immediately as a smooth and polished band. Professional poise came only after repeated performances and experimentation. Evidence of a few of their early shows still exists and eventually appeared on the Internet. These performances reveal a group of young musicians who seemed remarkably self-confident and whose initial shows improved markedly over that first summer. With sometimes clumsy stage patter, too often marked with the tired clichés often heard in country shows, the band's music, nevertheless, felt both fresh and memorable, even though they weren't yet writing their own songs. They easily transmitted the pleasure they obviously enjoyed parlaying with one another during performances. Listeners appreciatively imbibed this infectious joy. Hot Rize members possessed the quintessential qualities that facilitated their appeal: youth, good looks, and impressive talent. They transported this winning combination of virtues into the national arena of bluegrass.[27]

When Hot Rize formed in the summer of 1978, Ronni Lundy, a bluegrass and food writer and Kentucky native, lived out west and saw the band at a small, off-beat, "goofy" bluegrass festival held at the Isleta Pueblo, about fifteen miles south of Albuquerque, New Mexico. She had seen Tim previously at Telluride when he played with the Ophelia Swing Band, where he had "seemed like a kid with a young band," even while his performance on the fiddle and his vocals had really impressed her. At Isleta, Hot Rize performed on a stage outside under the trees. Ronni loved what she identified as the "Rocky Mountain bluegrass sound" when she first heard Pete use the phase shifter on his banjo on *Dr. Banjo Steps Out* and was otherwise "blown away" by the Hot Rize performance that day. She felt that she had witnessed something "subversive." Although Ronni described the band's sound as "traditional" in many ways, she felt that she ascertained a certain "edginess" with Pete's experimentation with the banjo and Tim's bringing in a "jazzy, swinging thing" to bluegrass instead of the straight-ahead Monroe drive. She likened the experience to watching a live radio show. That evening, Ronni ran into Pete and Nick in the picnic area, and they all started talking under the shade of a cottonwood tree. While working on a piece about New Grass for *Bluegrass Unlimited*, she decided to write about Hot Rize too. During the conversation, Tim, hidden in the branches above, "sent down sardonic comments" from time to time before eventually climbing down, and she actually got to meet him.[28]

Along with their retro outfits, which reassured traditional fans of their sincerity and commitment, Hot Rize also paid their debts to old-time bluegrass by resurrecting the use of one vocal microphone, the practice used by all bluegrass bands back in the 1950s but mostly popularized by Lester Flatt and Earl Scruggs and the Foggy Mountain Boys in their wide-ranging tours. By the time Hot Rize emerged, most bluegrass bands had embraced using individual microphones, generally standing behind them without much body movement. Hot Rize instead used individual mics for their instruments but gathered around one microphone when they sang. Their seemingly effortless darting back and forth around the one mic, in an almost choreographed fashion, added excitement to their performances. But while they kept one foot in the traditional camp, they nevertheless remained a thoroughly modern unit. An innovative but straight-ahead Scruggs-style banjo player, Pete freely made use of the phase shifter, particularly on instrumental tunes. Frowned on by Bill Monroe and rarely heard in the old-time bands, the electric bass became more acceptable to bluegrass musicians when Nick demonstrated that his subdued style could be employed without overpowering the acoustic instruments. Attached to a long cord, the bass never impeded his movements across the stage, and fans particularly enjoyed seeing him lean into the mic for vocal harmony. Like a lengthy retinue of bluegrass guitar players, Charles Sawtelle gave testimony to the revolution wrought earlier by Doc Watson who, in the 1960s, had freed the acoustic country guitar from a purely rhythmic function. Doc demonstrated that the guitar could more than hold its own in sharing lead passages with other instruments. While not as flashy as Tony Rice and a few other bluegrass guitarists, and playing fewer notes, Charles believed that the low tones of the guitar provided a resonant counterpoint to the higher sounds of the other instruments. Feeling that less is more, Charles displayed a superb sense of timing, playing with great subtlety, alternating between the bass and treble strings to achieve a dramatic tone and syncopated shower of notes. According to one observer, Charles's "bass runs were surprising and sure, sparse and tasteful, and full of soul."[29] Tim once poetically described Charles's unique style:

> As he starts his solos . . . I hear us bracing for another wild ride, holding tight like you do the steering wheel on a twisty mountain road with a steep drop off on the right. He imitates the dobro and the fiddle, cannon and machine gun fire, and impressionist paintings. His whole persona exists within the sound of that 1937 Martin D-28. It contains his musical influences, his loves and sorrows, vintage clothes, even what he ate for dinner. He comes and goes in the sound, sometimes bold, sometimes subtle, but even when inaudible, he's always felt.[30]

Tim switched easily from mandolin to fiddle in each Hot Rize set. He typically kicked off their concerts with a powerful mandolin break filled with drive and precision, issuing a string of single notes, interspersed with a strong tremolo. All bluegrass mandolin players have usually been judged by the precedent set earlier by Bill Monroe. Though partly beholden to Monroe, Tim nevertheless features less of his percussive sound and often opts to let the strings ring out instead of being dampened.

Tim's vocals and rhythm mandolin energized the inimitable Hot Rize sound. His musical partners readily agreed with this assessment. Pete, for example, said, "with Tim singing lead, we could immediately get anybody's attention, even when he was 24 years old." Tim sang with power and clarity and could later say that "after becoming the front man, I started paying more attention to precision and direction. You watched for the right chemistry and then you used it in your favor." Tim sang lead on virtually all of Hot Rize's vocal numbers and shifted to tenor harmony on the choruses of their songs.[31]

In keeping with their distinctive cross-audience-appealing look, Hot Rize's repertory in the early years also seemed carefully crafted to appeal to both traditionalists and modernists. The band made sure to include the Martha White theme, while keeping their program as "clean" as the flour company had stipulated. They chose a few songs from the canon introduced years earlier by Monroe, Flatt and Scruggs, the Stanley Brothers, and other bluegrass pioneers. And Charles Sawtelle regularly sang at least one song on a set, such as "Think of What You've Done" from the Stanley Brothers or "Ain't I Been Good to You," from JD Hutchison. Tim said, "Charles heard them [the Hutchison Brothers] before he and I played together, maybe before we met, having provided the sound system for the Walnut Valley festival in Winfield when the Hutchison Brothers played there."[32]

Hot Rize exhibited their considerable talents as instrumentalists with a few vintage fiddle tunes such as "Durham's Reel," "Sally Ann," or self-penned tunes like Pete's "Pow Wow" (complete with phase shifter). Similarly, in a clear nod to the traditionalists, they did two or three gospel numbers, but with little sectarian flavor, such as "Prayer Bells of Heaven" or "Standing in the Need of Prayer." They were performing for audiences beyond the evangelical South where gospel was a staple, but as an atheist raised by Jewish parents, Pete felt uncomfortable with songs that spoke of Jesus or Christ. Tim had always loved traditional songs, and he reprised a few like "Ninety Nine Years (and One Dark Day)" (borrowed from the West Coast blues singer Jesse Fuller), "High on a Mountain" (from the pen of Ola Belle Reed), and "Blue Night" (learned from Bill Monroe, but written by the veteran Grand Ole Opry musician Kirk McGee). "Blue Night" soon became Hot Rize's opening song, and performed down through the years it signaled that the band, poised to soar, was inviting its listeners into its orbit.

Like "Blue Night," other songs performed in the early shows remained in their live performances for much of the band's career. This list alone, though, would never have nourished Hot Rize members' creativity nor their desire to distinguish themselves from other bluegrass outfits. They soon realized they needed a fresh catalogue of songs to build and sustain an audience and also augment their income. From the beginning, Pete exhorted band members to write new songs. He contributed one of their most popularly received songs, "Just Like You," which he revived from his days with Country Cooking. His band mates at that time had passed on doing this compassionate song about the need to empathize with the problems of others. Tim, too, felt initially hesitant about it, but by experimenting with different keys and vocal arrangements, they finally came up with a version that satisfied them. "Just Like You" ultimately became one of their best loved songs and in 1987 appeared on their fifth album, *Untold Stories.*

While each member of Hot Rize contributed to the band's repertory, Tim became not only their most successful lyricist but also one of the most respected writers in bluegrass music. Journalist Randy Barrett asked him how he went from learning "200-plus songs"—those he'd told his mother he already knew when he originally left for Wyoming—to songwriting. Tim responded that "Hot Rize was a catalyst":

> I'd already been dabbling in it and never thought much about it. And then when Hot Rize started, everybody said it's a good value if you write your own songs. So, that was the idea, and Pete Wernick had done it, and I figured maybe I could, too. So, Nick and I and Pete all put our pens to paper separately and as collaborators. We wrote songs and then I found that people liked them so we recorded them. It's a carrot at the end of the stick. It encourages you to keep doing it.[33]

Tim's songs, like his picking and singing, proved indispensable to Hot Rize's long-range success.

Before their first recording session, Tim came up with a "western" song, "Nellie Kane," inspired by memories of his favorite cowboy movie, *Shane*. Shane (played by Alan Ladd) adopted the young boy whose family he had protected, and Tim remembered that his friend Mike Kemnitzer had also adopted his wife's son. In Tim's well-crafted ballad, the rambling fellow, who "as a young man riding out on the western plain" fell in love with a young single mother "living in a lonely cabin with a son by another man." She had waited for the boy's father "as long as a woman can." So, our protagonist steps in, stops his rambling, and settles down as both a husband and a father to her young son. According to Pete, the melody for the song came from "Bowling Green," which bluegrass fiddler and singer Laurie Lewis performed at the time, while "the strange harmony came from Bill Monroe." "Nellie Kane" immediately surged as their most popular number and soon made its rounds as a staple at bluegrass jam sessions and amateur performances. It also took on a new life after February 1993—as well as a happy source of additional income for Tim—when the rock band Phish added it to their repertory and frequently included it in their concerts. In fact, Nick Stock interviewed Tim about the band covering his songs:

STOCK: I'm sure you've been asked before, but what was your initial reaction when you learned that Phish was covering "Nellie Kane"?

TIM: Did you ever hear what Bill Monroe said to Elvis Presley when he sang "Blue Moon of Kentucky" on the Opry when he was first coming up? Elvis was worried Monroe wouldn't like the way he'd changed it up, but Bill told him that if it would help him, he should do it. . . . Phish ain't Elvis, but they're nothing shabby, and I had the same reaction as Mr. Monroe.[34]

Beyond writing original songs, Hot Rize added another exciting ingredient to their recipe for crafting enticing performances. From the beginnings of their career, they learned that humor could be both a relief from boredom and a way of capturing an audience's attention and allegiance. The creation of their alter ego band, Red Knuckles and the Trailblazers, achieved these dual objectives. This beloved bogus group evolved over the years, and no one in the band could later pinpoint the precise moment when Red Knuckles members, decked out in their western garb, got spliced into Hot Rize performances. Pete, Tim, Nick, and Charles had always approached their music with an intriguing mixture of seriousness and fun. They, in fact, had given themselves comic names as early as the Minnesota Bluegrass Festival in May 1978, only five months after Hot Rize formed. The band members had always loved country and western songs and early on had eagerly included them to add variety to their shows and to delight their late-night, hard-to-please Colorado audiences. The change certainly appealed to those who frequented clubs not so much to listen to straightforward bluegrass music as to drink, dance, and converse with their friends.[35]

Diversion, then, not comedy, originally underlay the move toward Red Knuckles and the Trailblazers. Pete explained, "Red Knuckles, in essence, was Tim's idea, because he didn't want to be a band that played only bluegrass." They performed under the new guise at least once on KGNU, probably in 1980, minus most of the elements the band would bring to their comical subversive act. But, little by little, a change of instruments and the adoption of nicknames heralded the emergence of this new group. Later, the addition of a change of clothing sealed the deal. When Hot Rize members brought their alternative band on stage, they found that the assumption of faux personas necessitated appropriate attire. Charles, as always coming equipped with sartorial ideas, suggested cowboy hats and shirts, bandanas, and dark glasses. The country music world, of course, provided plenty of inspiration, with easily available visual evidence of the gaudy, colorful, sequined garb—"Nudie suits," originally made by their West Coast creator, Nudie Cohen—that such singers as Jimmy Dickens, Hank Snow, and Porter Wagoner had sported back in the 1950s. On March 27, 1982, Hot Rize and Ernest Tubb and the Texas Troubadours appeared on the same *Prairie Home Companion* show. As Tim, years later, told Chris Thile on *Live from Here*: "Nick struck up a friendship with the [Troubadours'] bus driver and ended up making the connection where we bought the clothes they were wearing that night. . . . They say 'TT,' sort of western Ranger style with the bib," and Nick piped in, "Triple knit polyester."[36]

Pete said he gave Nick the nickname Wendell Mercantile, earnestly deserved because of his dreaming up ideas for merchandise, then promoting and selling those items at concerts and festivals—T-shirts, records, and quirky items like big red fly swatters with a cartoonish rendering of Red Knuckles emblazoned on the business end. Thus, Nick became the first Trailblazer to appear on stage with a comic name. Minus the Trailblazers' persona, Nick, the most gregarious member of Hot Rize, also happily manned the merchandise table at festivals and other venues. Pete told us, "Once the Red Knuckles thing started blossoming, Nick's stepfather designed the Red Knuckles logo on the shirts. The 'merch' really helped the bottom line."[37] Tim, who had sometimes been called Howdy Skies during his tenure with the Ophelia Swing Band, adopted the moniker of Red Knuckles. In this guise, he did most of the lead vocalizing and played the rhythm guitar. Waldo Otto, a name Pete conjured up, performed on the electric steel guitar as a Trailblazer, while Charles Sawtelle, true to his reputation as "the bluegrass mystery," came up with the most intriguing persona. Shifting to the electric bass, he became Slade, a character that echoed the bad men of grade B western movies. Dressed in black and wearing a black hat and dark glasses, Slade glared at the audience and remained silent throughout the Trailblazer portion of the show.

Not simply content with the alternative repertoire, stage attire, alternative personalities and instruments, Pete developed the backstory of the Trailblazers. As a prelude to the Red Knuckles portion of the show, Pete talked about traveling through the fictitious little town of Wyoming, Montana, on the way to other western venues. Stopping at the Eat Café, they encountered a group of local cowboys who fed nickel after nickel into an antiquated jukebox filled with pre-1954 hillbilly records by the likes of Faron Young, Webb Pierce, and their contemporaries. The jukebox had not been replenished since that time. Discovering that these retro-loving cowboys were also passable musicians who played along with their jukebox heroes, Hot Rize decided they needed to get beyond the Eat Café and out of Wyoming, Montana. The band invited these fellows to join their tour, riding in the back of the bus, keeping it clean, and occasionally filling in on stage when Hot Rize needed to take a break. This newborn group, Red Knuckles and the Trailblazers, quickly became a crowd pleaser and an integral part of Hot Rize's success.

Typically setting up the act after a lengthy first set, Pete would remain on stage, telling the backstory while the others went backstage. Soon, the others would return in their flamboyant garb, sporting new identities and playing a different configuration of instruments. With his rhythm guitar Red Knuckles fronted the Trailblazers, mostly singing vintage country and western songs from the repertories of people like Lefty Frizzell, Hank Williams, and Johnny Horton, all heard on that jukebox in the Eat Café. The Trailblazers conveyed humor visually, with Pete returning to the stage as a goofy-but-competent steel guitar player, who sometimes dropped his steel bar on the strings or let it roll the entire length of the fret board without missing a note. At other times, he would saunter away from his steel guitar and come back just in time to play his instrumental part of the song. On occasion, as the band endured and its members aged, Pete even employed the steel guitar as a walker as he tottered on to the stage. Slade maintained his menacing presence but sometimes demonstrated a "walking bass," leaving the stage in the middle of a song and taking advantage of an extra-long cord on his electric bass. Electric guitar–picking Wendell Mercantile postured as a flashily dressed pretty boy constantly seeking the limelight and unabashedly playing up to the audience. He and Red Knuckles sometimes moved their guitars in unison and did coordinated dance steps as they played a song. As the emcee, Red Knuckles uttered numerous "mighty fines" and other hackneyed phrases taken from the lexicon of country and western performers. Above all, he sang beautifully on all of his songs and, like the other members of the Trailblazers, demonstrated his deep understanding of and feel for the honky-tonk and western swing genres.[38]

Before Hot Rize initiated Red Knuckles and the Trailblazers, they knew of precedents for an alter ego band with comic personas that had existed in bluegrass and country music. In molding his Slade character, for example, Charles was most likely familiar with Raymond D. Smith who, performing as Son, made up one half of the Geezinslaw Brothers. This popular comic act served as a mainstay of CBS's Arthur Godfrey radio show for several years and were frequent guests on Ralph Emery's *Nashville Now* television show. Son, a fine singer and guitar player, never spoke, smiled, or lost his staid composure during the wild antics and hilarious monologues of his partner, Sammy Allred. Bluegrass and mainstream country entertainers, of course, had their own burlesque acts. If Hot Rize did not know about Chicken and Pansy Hot Rod and the Banty-Roosters, a slapstick skit replete with drag and other ridiculous costumes, featured by Don Reno and Red Smiley in their stage shows, they certainly would have been aware of a popular routine used by the mainstream country act the Statler Brothers. In 1974, the Statlers produced an album *Alive at the Johnny Mack Brown High School*, featuring Lester "Roadhog" Moran and the Cadillac Cowboys, an LP spoofing small-town country radio. Backed by some of Nashville's finest studio musicians, the Statlers succeeded in butchering every song on the record, while Roadhog (Harold Reid) uttered an unending and guttural stream of "all rights" and "mighty fines." The mythical evening at the school gymnasium ended with a wild melee in the alcohol-fueled audience.

Unlike the Statler Brothers, Hot Rize, while having great fun with their characters and their audiences, never made fun of the music they played. Red Knuckles and the Trailblazers made magnificent music. Leon McAuliffe, the legendary steel guitar player for Bob Wills's Texas Playboys, famous for his 1936 recording of "Steel Guitar Rag," admired the Trailblazers and the music they were reviving. Tim told us:

Hot Rize met Leon McAuliffe in Stillwater, OK, I think, where he was teaching some and we were playing an outdoor show that he was also playing. Later he would come to Winfield and other places close to his area, and he would sit in. Our friend in Boulder named Clover held an annual Lap Steel Day where he and fellow steel players would get together and compare notes. He asked if we thought Leon would consider coming if he paid for a flight and a small fee. So, we asked Leon and suggested he could play with Red

Knuckles and the Trailblazers at Peggy's Hi-Lo the night before. He agreed and it was epic. Such an honor and such ridiculous luck that we got to experience that.[39]

The act as a whole appealed irresistibly to other bluegrass musicians who, when they were playing at the same festival or program, welcomed the opportunity to take on the personality of Waldo's fiddle-playing brother, Elmo. Each Elmo—played by Sam Bush, Darol Anger, or Eddie Stubbs—differed from the others, but they all wore an oversized orange coat that Pete had bought in some Goodwill store. According to Tim: "John Cowan sat in either as drummer (Green Krupa was one of his names) or dressed in drag as Red's ex-wife Bunny Knuckles." All performers had a terrific time playing with Red Knuckles, and their exhilarating enthusiasm was picked up immediately by the audience.[40]

The group's renditions of western swing and honky-tonk also won the praise of the critics, their act always a highly anticipated feature of every Hot Rize concert. When Red Knuckles and the Trailblazers appeared at the Kentucky Fried Chicken Festival in Louisville in about 1980, Ronni Lundy had moved back to her home state and was there to see them. She became the first journalist to interview the Trailblazers, an honor she recalled fondly. For the occasion, Zoe Evermont became Ronni's alter ego, and she said that all of them wore sunglasses. Sometime later, Tim told Ronni that this interview actually "crystallized" their personas as Red Knuckles and the Trailblazers. During the interview, Slade, true to his mysterious identity, would only answer questions with "yes" or "no."[41]

In truth, many people enjoyed Red Knuckles and the Trailblazers even more than their parent band. The country music critic Geoffrey Himes spoke for such fans in a review of the band's 1983 concert at the Birchmere Restaurant in Alexandria, Virginia. Opening for Jerry Jeff Walker, Hot Rize received a dismissive critique from the reviewer who called them a "Colorado quartet . . . locked into the timeworn formulas" of bluegrass. But, he said, in their guise as Red Knuckles and the Trailblazers, "the four-some played with a looseness and spirit that made their honky-tonk and western swing numbers more enjoyable than their bluegrass picking." Another reviewer, Karen Boren Swedin, concurred, "I think Hot Rize had better worry a little about this band that makes honky-tonk country-western music a delight to see as well as hear."[42]

By 1981, with Red Knuckles and the Trailblazers laying out in the back of the big bus and ever ready to take the stage, Hot Rize prepared for a major launch into the world at large. When Hot Rize came into existence, bluegrass as a distinct commercial sound had only existed about thirty years. Named for Bill Monroe's influential band, the Blue Grass Boys, the music had taken shape as a popular entity in the late 1940s when young musicians began imitating the sounds heard on Monroe's records, Grand Ole Opry radio shows, and his many personal appearances throughout the country. To many musicians, fans, and publicists the syncopated three-finger style of banjo played by Earl Scruggs, the smooth bluesy sound popularized by fiddler Chubby Wise, and the hard-driving jazz-inflected phrases heard in Bill Monroe's mandolin playing provided a core sound that should be preserved and never altered. By the time Hot Rize appeared in 1978, however, musicians had taken the style in many different directions. Bill Monroe remained duly revered as the founding father of the exciting genre, but bluegrass had assumed a shape far distant from the sounds heard in the 1950s. "Traditional" bluegrass musicians still clung to versions of the "original" sound, while "progressives" experimented with styles and songs borrowed from rock, pop, and jazz music and even dabbled with electric instruments and drums. To the chagrin of many traditionalists, some of the progressives dressed so casually that old-time fans saw such attire as almost sacrilegious. The emergence in 1971 of the greatest hippie band, Sam Bush's New Grass Revival, whose stylistic experimentations knew no bounds, wrought revolutionary consequences for the music's overall sound and acceptance. "New Grass" became the generic term applied to those bands that carried bluegrass way beyond its traditional limits.[43]

Along with stylistic innovations came dramatic changes: southern and blue-collar bluegrass audiences no longer predominated as when the genre first took shape, nor did white males make the music their exclusive domain. Women now played decisive roles in the music's development. While never losing its original audience, bluegrass was well on its way to building a worldwide following that encompassed virtually all classes, genders, and ages. Its demographic expansion began in the late 1950s and early 1960s when bluegrass became part of the urban folk music revival. College students throughout America became aware of its rhythms and dynamism when groups like the Osborne Brothers and the Stanley

Brothers began appearing on campuses and in folk clubs and at festivals. The famous folklorist Alan Lomax captured the music's essence in a 1959 *Esquire* article—while communicating its mystique to literate middlebrow readers—when he described it as "folk music with overdrive." Soon thereafter, mass media discovered and utilized the sound of the five-string banjo and other bluegrass instruments in movies such as *Deliverance* and *Bonnie and Clyde* and on television with the theme tune of the popular *Beverly Hillbillies*.[44]

The ascent of bluegrass to international prominence did not come without occasional hazards and pitfalls. Mainstream country music too often treated its offspring like a stepchild, and during the first ascendancy of rock and roll, bluegrass musicians struggled to gain radio airplay and jukebox exposure. The bluegrass community responded by building its own infrastructure and culture. By the time Hot Rize appeared on the scene, bluegrass had developed its own network of publicity, marketing, and merchandizing and could now boast of magazines such as *Bluegrass Unlimited*, along with record labels, radio shows, and trade associations that fostered and promoted its interests. Above all, music festivals, which became the chief sites for bluegrass bands in America, now convened all over the nation, especially during the summer months. These welcoming venues provided musical exposure, social camaraderie, and networking opportunities for fans and musicians alike.

Hot Rize, then, entered a thriving bluegrass scene. As a Colorado band they conveyed the mystique of the open and expansive Rocky Mountain West, even though they may have initially aroused the suspicion of some traditionalists who identified bluegrass exclusively with the Mountain South. Recognizing this predilection, Hot Rize strived in various ways to demonstrate their respect for the traditions bequeathed by bluegrass music's pioneers. Combining youth, spontaneity, and musical expertise, they were capable of playing New Grass—but chose not to. Their own songs and song choices, their compelling energy, good looks, and youthfulness combined with their solid musicality, definitive stylings, and outstanding singing set them apart from their contemporaries. The members' sense of style and humor also helped to create a fan base among both traditionalists and progressives. In fact, their entire gestalt delivered a complete Hot Rize package or brand that made them unique in bluegrass music and contributed mightily to their commercial and popular success.

Hot Rize's appearance on *Prairie Home Companion* just a couple of months after they initially organized had already sparked a few inklings of that future ascent to glory. Soon after, playing at the still young Telluride Bluegrass Festival accentuated the aura that surrounded Hot Rize in its forays from there into the eastern sections of the United States. Nestled deep in the San Miguel Mountains, in southwestern Colorado, and surrounded by thirteen-thousand-foot mountain peaks, the little community of Telluride struck most people who visited it as one of the most beautiful places they had ever seen. Once a rugged mining town in the late nineteenth century, Telluride had suffered serious population decline. But the town revived dramatically in the 1960s when promoters saw how the combination of picturesque scenery and plentiful snow would provide a great draw for developers and ski enthusiasts. Their gamble paid off: Telluride became one of the best-loved ski resorts in the nation.

The town had already become a popular destination when nature worshipers and hippies convened in 1974 for the first Telluride Bluegrass Festival. After Fred Shellman and his band Fall Creek made a trip to the well-known Walnut Valley National Guitar Flat-Picking Championships Festival in Winfield, Kansas, he returned to Telluride and became the principal organizer of what he hoped would be a similar festival. The relaxed attitudes toward drug use that prevailed in the community increased Telluride's magnetism for musicians and others who sought the seemingly unbridled freedom they now associated with the Rocky Mountain West. Progressive musicians such as Steve Goodman, John Hartford, Peter Rowan, Bryan Bowers, and Sam Bush became regular participants every year. Tim O'Brien noted that "the festival was kind of Fred's yearly party, a chemical experiment." John Cowan, the bass player and lead singer for New Grass Revival, even more explicitly recalled, "We'd all take acid and people would walk around naked and people would just do the craziest shit imaginable. It was just guys and girls feeling their oats." Already a veteran when he traveled to the event in 1978 with Hot Rize, Tim had appeared at Telluride on a couple of occasions with the Ophelia Swing Band. Recalling his time there, he commented, "This is ritual, really. It's a family reunion, the gathering of the clans in ancient time, a celebration of the summer solstice: we're celebrating the longest day of the year, we're going to take advantage of the bounty of the earth. We're going to dance and sing and maybe mix up some alcohol in it. The people who come for the first time

Hot Rize at Telluride, 1979, from left to right: Pete Wernick, Nick Forster, Tim, Charles Sawtelle (Rick Gardner photo)

are almost in a state of shock with the air and the sun and the mountains." But alcohol and pot did not dominate every moment, as he conveyed about a particularly heartfelt occasion: "Honestly, nothing beats seeing my one-year old son in the arms of Bill Monroe when he's singing 'I Saw the Light' with a bunch of hippies dancing around him. That must have been in 1983. We were backstage, and my son, this little newborn baby, was just kinda passed around to people. At one point someone's holding him, and Bill says 'bring that baby onstage' and all of a sudden, there's my son."[45]

After their first appearance at Telluride, Hot Rize made annual trips to the festival and, along with New Grass Revival, became virtually the house band of the event. Although remaining basically traditional in repertory and style, simply from its association with Telluride, Hot Rize acquired the reputation of a progressive band. The members did not discourage the common perception that the Mountain West, with its open skies and welcome acceptance of new arrivals, fostered experimentation and innovation in music. While they continued to play in small venues throughout the Front Range, Hot Rize quickly branched out into the larger bluegrass world. During their first year as an organization, they began landing prestigious gigs as far off as the East Coast. A few shows were arranged through fortuitous personal associations. Through the help of some old friends, Nick booked a gig at the Towne Crier Café in Beekman, New York, and Tim secured a show at his childhood stomping grounds, the *Wheeling Jamboree*—with an additional bonus when his parents graciously offered to put up the band. Pete landed them on the bill at O'Lunney's Pub in New York City, a gig attended by some of his old bluegrass buddies. Most of the other gigs probably came through Pete's connections in the bluegrass community or through his diligent work. They drove for three days to play a show in Myrtle Beach, South Carolina, staying at Motel 6's along the way. They were paid eleven hundred dollars for the show, the most money they had ever yet received for a performance. Their trip in June 1978 to the Indian Springs Bluegrass Festival, near Hagerstown, Maryland, proved to be not so lucrative but more advantageous in other ways. Sponsored by *Bluegrass Unlimited Magazine*, this festival provided an excellent showcase for young bands and a convenient place for networking with other musicians. In this case, Hot Rize met Dick Kimmel, a musician and respected bluegrass writer, who invited them to stop by his place in West Virginia on the way home. Less than one year later, that chance association produced an outstanding outcome. Only fourteen months after they began, in March 1979, they appeared on the cover of *Bluegrass Unlimited* and were featured in a prominent article that Dick wrote, "Hot Rize: Pete Wernick's Secret Ingredient." The article's title suggests the stature that Pete already enjoyed in the bluegrass world and the important role his name played in gaining widespread recognition for the band.[46]

Later in 1979, Hot Rize recorded its first LP, modestly but aptly entitled *Hot Rize*, produced by the Flying Fish label in Chicago. The six-year-old label established by Bruce Kaplan, a professionally trained folklorist, was already building a roster of outstanding roots musicians such as Pete Seeger and John Hartford. Graced by a front-cover illustration of a savory biscuit and also sporting a photo of the band members wearing aprons and bakers' caps, the album contained fourteen songs that replicated their stage shows. One could hear a few fiery instrumentals, a couple of gospel songs, and other items that showcased Tim's supple lead singing. "Nellie Kane" appeared for the first time (with Tim doing both the lead vocal and the tenor harmony on the chorus) along with other songs like "Blue Night," "High on a Mountain," and "Ninety Nine Years (and One Dark Day)," which remained frequently featured in their live performances. The band could now take great pride in being "recording artists," as well as profiting from the increased exposure. As Pete mentioned, "We went up a notch when we had our first album out. . . . The reviews were very good and I made sure people saw them." Album and T-shirt sales also helped pay bills, "which got bigger once we got the bus, around the same time."[47]

This valued publicity soon bore fruit when Victor Woronov, owner of a record store in Paris, heard the album and liked it enough to arrange a three-week tour for Hot Rize to France, Holland, Denmark, Belgium, and Sweden in the summer of 1980. Nick Forster later remembered the venture as simultaneously grueling and exciting. Woronov booked the shows, but he seemed indifferent in the quest to find them adequate housing. One late night in Stockholm, after they had completed a show, they asked about sleeping accommodations and found that Woronov had done nothing to find rooms for them. Some of the boys were already sleeping under a table in the bar, while Woronov negotiated with a young woman there for a couple of beds where they could sleep for the night. Nick remembered, "We did something like eighteen shows in twenty-two days. Victor didn't get us hotel rooms the last night of the tour, and we waited for the first ferry to Denmark, sleeping in the car. Audience reactions were all over the place. The best audiences were in France, where no one was in a hurry, although the most knowledgeable audience was in Stockholm." Pete pronounced it "a really special thing for us to have a chance to go travel abroad and be able to come back to Colorado as people who had been asked to play in Europe, you know. That made us special among Colorado musicians."[48]

This trip to western Europe became only the first of many international ventures during their career, which took Hot Rize to places like Finland, Australia, Holland, Ireland, and Japan. Japan had become a haven of bluegrass interest since at least 1968 when Flatt and Scruggs played to responsive audiences there. Hot Rize played three gigs in Japan—Osaka, Kyoto, and Tokyo—in February 1985, supported by a travel allowance of about four thousand dollars. The trip on Korean Air took them about thirty-six hours to complete. Despite the tiring journey, the band came away from the experience impressed with both their hosts' gracious courtesies and the audiences' quiet but attentive behavior during their performances. Hot Rize made no concessions to listeners who, for the most part, may not have understood what they were saying or singing. But bluegrass with its virtuosic instrumentation and high lonesome harmonies had already become a universal language. The band presented their usual show, complete with corny stage banter and introductions. Red Knuckles and the Trailblazers also performed their usual hijinks. While Japanese fans tended to remain silent during a performance, once it was over, they exploded with enthusiasm. After one such occasion, their Japanese sponsors introduced them to different kinds of local cuisine, complete with copious servings of saki.[49]

Hot Rize had now emerged as one of the premier bluegrass bands of the 1980s. Along with bands like the Johnson Mountain Boys, the Nashville Bluegrass Band, and Doyle Lawson and Quicksilver, Hot Rize formed a central part of a youth movement in bluegrass music that effectively combined a feel for tradition with progressive and dynamic performance. The band achieved this recognition through hard work and constant travel, now in a converted 1957 Greyhound bus. Nick and Charles rebuilt the interior of the bus to accommodate their needs, and Nick designed fold-out bunk beds that permitted both sleeping and places to practice music along the road. They added one extra bunk to the bus, and sometimes band members invited people like Jody Stecher or Mike "Nugget" Kemnitzer to ride with them. Tim often stocked the bus with drinks and maybe a few snacks, mainly juice, water, and club soda. Nugget fondly remembered the fellowship enjoyed by all.[50]

Not always exciting, life on the road could also be exhausting and monotonous. The unglamorous routines included driving all night to get to a gig in time for the sound check, setting up their own sound system if the venue's rig seemed inadequate, doing two sets a show, hanging around the merchandise table until the last item was sold and the last autograph signed, taking down the sound system, loading the instruments and equipment, and then hitting the road to repeat the same routine at the next venue. Unfortunately, tires sometimes blew out, engines overheated, accelerator cables froze, and accidents were always a possibility. Luckily, both Nick and Charles had outstanding mechanical skills. Still, they could not avoid some totally unexpected road hazards that later became legendary stories. Late one night, Nick was at the wheel. He pulled into a gas station to fill the tank but failed to see Pete leave the bus to go into the station. As Pete told us, Nick assumed that everyone was asleep in their bunks and "headed on out. I was just heading back for the bus when I see it pulling away. Nothing to do at first but run after it, but he never saw me and no way he'd hear me yell, so I stood there and watched the bus pull out onto I-70. This was way before cell phones, of course. So, I went back in and got on a phone and called state patrol." As Tim recalled, "about 25 minutes later, this flashing light pulls behind us and the cop pulls us over. The policeman comes up to the bus window and says, 'You got a Pete Wernick on board?' When I tell him yes, the cop said 'Guess again.'"[51]

These extended road tours definitely did not include band members' families. If Hot Rize played somewhere like Telluride or a day trip away from Boulder, then the band relaxed its Males Only rule, and wives or a few guests could travel along on the bus. But otherwise, in Pete's words, "being in the 'traveling locker room' for a series of road dates was understood to be not workable." And undoubtedly, members' wives would have found the routines of the road of little interest—even when the travel occurred abroad. On the other hand, band members were concerned that they not stay away from their families any longer than necessary. As Pete explained, Hot Rize had policies to which they adhered, such as "'no road trip longer than 3 weeks' (the only one that long, ever, was our 1st Europe trip in 1980), and 'at least 2 weeks of home time between 2-week road trips.'"[52]

And how did those left-behind wives fare while their husbands were gaining popularity and adulation in all of those live venues? Joan and Pete and Sumi and Charles were older and already married; Kit and Tim were newlyweds; Robin and Nick already had daughters. The women were all working either full- or part-time, and except for Sumi and Charles, were having and raising children. Robin spoke frankly and not surprisingly about the tough life of being married to a musician and talked about how challenging the rise of Hot Rize was and how it affected all of them, especially in the early days when the band earned little money. "The effort it takes to make a band known takes a big toll on the family," Joan asserted. "If you're married to someone who needs a lot of attention, forget it. Pete was constantly on the phone. When they've achieved their goal, and they're in their groove, that's when marriages sometimes break up."[53]

When Kit and Tim moved back to Colorado, they first lived in Aurora, about thirty minutes east of Denver. Then Kit went to Colorado State University in Fort Collins, where they lived in married student housing. The following year, when she transferred to the University of Colorado in Boulder, they rented half a house on Grove Street. Tim's sister, Mollie, moved to Boulder in 1980 and lived with them, becoming part of the tight sisterhood that the band wives formed, all great friends at the time who continue to keep up with each other over the years. Robin mentioned, "We would often celebrate each other's anniversaries when the husbands were out of town." Mollie met her future husband, musician Rich Moore, and moved in with him around the same time that Tim and Kit's older son, Jackson, was born. Sharing houses with other folks like themselves worked well until Jackson arrived, but then the three of them needed to live on their own. Tim's older brother, Jim, cosigned a loan ("He was a little nervous about it, [and] I don't blame him," Tim said) that allowed Tim and Kit to buy a basement condo on Valmont. Tim recalled that Kit "was alone on a lot of weekends with Jackson from his birth to when Joel was born eight years later. I remember a lot of times in the condo . . . watching Jackson while she was at school, calling folks on the phone for gigs before Hot Rize had an agent, or carrying him in a backpack while I put up posters on the Boulder mall. She started making a real income after she graduated from CU, working in a biochemistry research lab. At that point Hot Rize was making real money as well."[54]

In addition to her own household and work responsibilities, Sumi did much of the band's bookkeeping. She told us that she and Kit cleaned the bus after an extended tour. According to Joan, at the self-promoted Hot Rize shows at the Niwot Grange, she ordered cookies from a bakery or the wives would bake brownies to sell with the CDs at the merch table there. Tim added, "We made coffee in the Grange's big urn and sold that in Styrofoam cups." Kit joked that luckily both of the O'Brien sons, eight years apart, were born on Tuesday mornings when Tim could be home to welcome them. Jackson was born the day after Tim returned home from Telluride, while Joel arrived during the spring of 1990 during the Hot Rize extended farewell tour when Tim had taken a week off around Kit's due date. She explained that she had worked out a routine, allowing Tim to dispense with most family responsibilities in the day or two before he left for a tour and then made the same kind of allowances for him to transition a day or two after he returned home. Transitions were a two-way street for both Tim and Kit, as he explained, "When Hot Rize started mostly flying to a destination on a Thursday or a Friday and coming home on a Sunday or Monday, I would still be helping with the children, the cooking and grocery shopping on those weekdays at home." Those emotional shifts were difficult for both partners in a musical marriage, and as Joan reminded us, "A lot of the band's success and the individuals' success depended on the support they got at home. That includes all the wives and kids. I don't think that one was more herculean than the others."[55]

Getting left at a gas station could be embarrassing and mildly inconvenient, but falling to the *ceiling* of an airplane, while clutching your six-year-old son to your chest, and then finding yourself in the middle of an Iowa cornfield was a decidedly more nerve-shattering and heart-wrenching experience. But on July 19, 1989, this is exactly what happened to Pete. He, Joan, and their son Will set out from Denver on United Air Lines flight 232 headed toward O'Hare Airport in Chicago, the first leg of a journey that would ultimately take them to New York for a visit with Pete's parents near Albany. Afterward, they planned to rendezvous with the rest of the band for the Winterhawk Bluegrass Festival held nearby. About an hour into the flight, engine issues resulted in an explosion. During the emergency landing at the airport in Sioux City, Iowa, the aircraft broke apart and flipped over. Miraculously, Pete and his family were virtually unhurt, although all the families' baggage was destroyed, and his steel guitar and banjo were badly damaged (though restorable). The Wernicks were among the 184 survivors of a crash that killed 112. They finally arrived at his folks' house the next day for some needed "rest and recovery" before going on to the festival about an hour away. One can scarcely imagine the relief and jubilation that his fellow band members and the audience felt, well aware of the ordeal. Tim, while known for playing his cards close to his vest, upon seeing Pete at Winterhawk, gave him a big bear hug, holding onto him for a long time. Although Tim did not verbalize how much he appreciated and valued Pete, "the hug said it all." Captured by a fan who filmed the band's performance that day, one feels the palpable relief and love that the other Hot Rize musicians expressed.[56]

Although Pete had performed invaluable service as booking agent, Hot Rize won even greater exposure and commercial reward after 1981 when Keith Case became their agent. During a successful stint as a restaurant owner and chef at Café York in Denver, Keith became consumed with music through his association with the musicians who played in his establishment. He moved to Nashville and became the agent for many of America's leading old-time music and bluegrass performers such as John Hartford, Norman and Nancy Blake, Seldom Scene, Tony Rice, and Alison Krauss. His first encounter with the full Hot Rize band came in an unexpected way. Driving to Telluride for their annual show in 1980 the Hot Rize bus broke down, and Case, who just happened to be following the same route, stopped to give them a hand. They hired him almost on the spot, pleased with his aggressive promotion style and, above all, with his insistence on getting "top dollars" for his clientele. According to Pete, "when Keith Case agreed to take over the booking, in late 1981, we had our feet in a lot of doors, and he helped raise our price, something he was good at. At the first meeting I asked what's the minimum he would book us for. When he said $500 we were amazed and almost giddy. He said he would never book a band for no guarantee. So, our pricing was going higher and he of course took 15% off the top, but the take-home pay went steadily up."[57]

The band's hooking up with Steve Goodman at the 1980 Telluride festival special also heightened the quality of that summer. It marked Steve's initial appearance at Telluride and likely the first time Tim had seen him since the Chicago days they had shared some years earlier. Tim had contacted him earlier that year, though, with the release of Hot Rize's first record. Knowing that Steve was undergoing treatment for a relapse of the leukemia that eventually killed him four years later, Tim got the address of the hospital and sent him a cassette of the album's mixes with a little note. Tim told us that when Hot Rize was playing at Telluride later that year:

> Steve came over to our old bus and thanked me for sending the cassette, saying it was helpful to have music in his room at the hospital. He asked if we'd sit in on the last song of his set, which was "City of New Orleans," and then we'd play an encore, if there was one, of "Mama Don't Allow." I said sure without asking the other guys and was flattered. From then on, whenever we were in the same place, he'd generally ask us to sit in—always the same songs— and we found a new way to mess up the chords of "City" each time. I figured out later that he always asked whoever was opening the show to do the same, but it was special to me and to us. He brought Jethro Burns to Somebody Else's Troubles one night when Hot Rize was playing, and we got them up to play. Man, what a thrill. And several times, either at Troubles or at McCabes in Santa Monica (he'd moved there), he would come and ask if he could sing a song unannounced before we started our second set. He would try something new in front of an audience, then he'd stay around and we'd do "City" and "Mama" again at the end.

I was much impressed with Steve as a writer, instrumentalist and performer. His energy was astounding and he seemed to grow a few feet onstage. His early endorsement was gold. It was after that first meeting that I learned he'd battled leukemia before and that afterwards he'd sorta made a deal with himself to do his best with the time he had. He was generous to me and so many others. He was sorta shy offstage, but in a group after hours he could be hysterically funny. I still try to honor him as I go along.[58]

Tim's recounting of that event and amplifying it with his own meditation on Steve's tragic death at the age of thirty-six gives the reader some insight into Tim's personality: his kindness, his sense of humor, and his deep sense of connectedness to those he loved, respected, and after their deaths, mourned deeply.

The members of Hot Rize never expected to get rich playing their music—or otherwise, they would not have chosen bluegrass as their profession. Dedication to a musical form, ardent love for performance, and the acclaim won from other fans and other musicians kept them on the road. Combining record and merchandise sales with concert fees, they nevertheless attained comfortable incomes. The six albums they made up to 1990 were generally well-received and brought a welcome source of compensation. *Radio Boogie*, their second album in 1981, was another Flying Fish production. The title cut, originally recorded in 1953 by its creator Ralph Mayo, during a country boogie craze, proved to be one of their most popular numbers.

For their third album, *Traditional Ties*, Hot Rize shifted to the Sugar Hill label, owned and directed by Barry Poss. Like the owner of Flying Fish, Poss was also a professionally trained folklorist with an ardent affection for bluegrass and other styles of roots music. Under his direction, Sugar Hill became the premier label for tradition-oriented bluegrass artists such as Ricky Skaggs and Tony Rice. Hot Rize's first Sugar Hill album proved crucial for both the band's future and, separately, Tim O'Brien's. As the album's title suggested, it featured a wide variety of old-time songs, such as "John Henry" and three gospel songs of African American origin, "Working on a Building," "Keep Your Lamp Trimmed and Burning," and "Hear Jerusalem Moan." Tim and Nick contributed a song with old-time feeling, a modern murder ballad called "Footsteps So Near" and were delighted when one of the patriarchs of bluegrass music, Ralph Stanley, recorded it. Nick said later, "That was as high a compliment as we could dream of." Tim also provided two songs, "Hard Pressed" and "Walk the Way the Wind Blows," that became among Hot Rize's most successful numbers. Country star Kathy Mattea so successfully covered "Walk the Way the Wind Blows" that the royalties allowed Kit and Tim to buy a dining room table and, most significantly, turned Tim's head toward Nashville.[59]

The 1980s also witnessed the band's profiting from a few prestigious and high-profile engagements. Hot Rize made appearances on the coveted *Grand Ole Opry, Mountain Stage,* and *Austin City Limits.* Setting foot on the *Opry* stage for the first time was a dream come true, as it was for most young country entertainers. On Saturday evening, September 12, 1982, Hot Rize appeared on an early show sponsored, fittingly, by the Martha White Company. Among their hit songs, they made sure to include the Martha White theme. Like all who attend the Ryman Auditorium during an *Opry* show, band members were intrigued and delighted by the almost chaotic mix of fans and performers that they found backstage and even on the stage itself. During their stay in Nashville they made the first of what would be several appearances on *Nashville Now,* a popular television program hosted by the longtime media personality Ralph Emery. By 1986, they had been on the show at least five times.[60]

Hot Rize's performance on *Mountain Stage,* in Charleston, West Virginia, satisfyingly reinforced Tim's identity with and allegiance to his home state. Tim's mother, Amy, secured the engagement after sending a postcard to the show's founder and emcee, Larry Groce, suggesting that her son and his band would be perfect fits for the program. *Mountain Stage,* now a venerable public radio institution, was only in its second year in May 1984 and was heard only once a month in West Virginia at the time Hot Rize first performed on the show. Someone connected with the Piccolo Spoleto Festival in Charleston, South Carolina (a seventeen-day extravaganza of the performing arts), heard that show and suggested that *Mountain Stage* broadcast from there the following year. National Public Radio (NPR) carried that show live, which gave Hot Rize a huge radio audience and *Mountain Stage* the boost it needed. In 1986, the radio program achieved its goal of becoming affiliated with NPR, more recently carried on about 250 stations. Always champions of Mollie's and Tim's music, Amy and Frank O'Brien also became vigorous supporters of the radio show. Tim has been a fixture ever since, appearing there year after year either with Hot Rize, with Mollie, or by himself. Larry Groce, the show's founder, described Tim as "humble" with a "staggering" talent, and he praised Tim's willingness to play with all kinds of people on any show on which he has appeared, thereby elevating every performance in which he's been involved.[61]

With roots music forms becoming an important part of the cultural scene in the capital city of Texas, *Austin City Limits* began its broadcast in 1974 on the public television station KLRU to showcase this diverse assortment of local musical offerings. Its pilot program featured Willie Nelson, and the show soon emerged as a staple of PBS Saturday night programming. Watched by millions, *Austin City Limits* provided invaluable exposure for musical acts of varying descriptions and eventually won the reputation of being "the longest running musical showcase in the history of television." When Hot Rize appeared on the show on February 10, 1987 (season 12, episode 5), they shared billing with the cowboy revivalist act Riders in the Sky. A group that delightfully spoofed the Hollywood cowboy songs of yesteryear with loving care and artistic mastery, Riders in the Sky made a perfect match for Hot Rize and their alter egos, Red Knuckles and the Trailblazers. For this show Hot Rize pulled out their greatest hits, including "Blue Night, "Nellie Kane," and "Radio Boogie," while Red and the boys did a little skit called "Red Remembers the 60s" and other time-tested favorites. By this time, Red Knuckles had gained stature with albums featuring the Wyoming, Montana, musicians. They first appeared as early as 1982 (it was the third Hot Rize recording): *Hot Rize Presents Red Knuckles & the Trailblazers*, and then, *Hot Rize Added Attraction Red Knuckles & The Trailblazers in Concert* (1984), both on Flying Fish.[62]

Although large individual concerts in auditoriums or theaters provided important vehicles for winning new converts, it was the bluegrass festivals that served as the band's real bread-and-butter venues. Festivals had become indispensable ingredients of bluegrass music's infrastructure in the mid-1960s when bluegrass felt the economic pinch of country music's neglect. Finding it difficult to obtain airplay on country radio, bluegrass musicians welcomed the outdoor festivals where they not only gained significant commercial exposure but also relished the casual camaraderie of both fans and fellow musicians. Veteran musician Bill Clifton had organized a one-day all-bluegrass affair in Luray, Virginia, in 1961. But the first multiday exclusively bluegrass gathering convened at Cantrell's Horse

Red Knuckles & The Trailblazers at *Austin City Limits*, from left to right: Waldo Otto, Red Knuckles, Slade, and Wendell Mercantile (Pete Wernick's collection, photo by Scott Newton)

Farm, near Fincastle, Virginia, on Labor Day weekend in 1965, promoted principally by Carlton Haney, who hoped not only to give the music a new means of exposure but also to reunite Bill Monroe with his earlier musicians. Festivals soon spread to virtually every state in the Union. Almost like religious gatherings—comparisons to the nineteenth-century evangelical camp meetings were often made—the festivals brought the faithful together and provided unending music both on the stage and out in the campgrounds where earnest amateurs could meet and play with the professionals.

It would be a decided understatement to say that the festivals differed widely in character and style. Most of these events tended to emphasize their family-friendly nature and their status as a pastoral retreat from the pressures of urban life. Pete Kuykendall, founder of the Bluegrass Unlimited Festival in Hagerstown, Maryland (commonly referred to as Indian Springs), announced in ads for the affair, "NO dogs; NO drugs; NO alcoholic beverages." Kuykendall reacted against those bluegrass events like the Old Time Music and Bluegrass Festival at Union Grove, North Carolina, that had drunk freely from the elixir of unlicensed freedom unleashed by the giant rock festival in Woodstock, New York. He touted his own "the friendliest festival of all" in 1978 when Hot Rize appeared there. The band stumbled into one of the not-so-family-friendly festivals in the early 1980s after a harrowing trip that saw their bus disabled and left at a shop in Pennsylvania, while they slowly made their way separately to their destination: the Great Northern Bluegrass Festival in Mole Lake, Wisconsin, the site of an Ojibwe reservation. Mole Lake became famous for the great bluegrass bands that played there—and notorious for the largely uninhibited behavior that surrounded the music. Tim remembers arriving several hours before their scheduled music set and strolling through the "unusual concessions" area, seeing a "Shot and Beer" booth and a "Show Us Your Tits" teepee. The Hot Rize musical set that followed was a real challenge. Walking up on stage, they heard a roar coming from the crowd, and Tim thought, "Wow, this crowd is excited about bluegrass." Then he continued, "but after we went on stage, the roar stayed exactly the same throughout the set. They were just drunk and who knows what else. My lingering memory is of a sunburned guy in the crowd wearing nothing but a pair of cutoff jeans and a watermelon rind for a hat, both fists in the air, yelling something, who knows what, through most of the show."[63]

While Hot Rize considered Mole Lake an outlier in outrageousness, the band continued to headline the more family-friendly festivals all across America. They journeyed south to the Bill Grant Bluegrass Festival in Hugo, Oklahoma, which claimed to be the oldest festival west of the Mississippi River. There they were billed in 1979 as "Pete Wernick and Hot Rize." In the Northeast, they were regulars at the Grey Fox Festival (formerly Winterhawk) in Ancramdale, New York. Further down the East Coast, the band performed at the Delaware Valley Bluegrass Festival in New Jersey, one of the earliest festivals in the East; at the Doyle Lawson & Quicksilver Bluegrass Festival in Denton, North Carolina; and elsewhere in the state at Doc Watson's Merlefest in Wilkesboro. In the Lone Star State, they performed at Rod Kennedy's Folk Festival at Quiet Valley Ranch near Kerrville, Texas, an extravaganza that welcomed all varieties of roots music and was famous for having given a jump start to the careers of musicians such as Lyle Lovett, Tish Hinojosa, and Guy Clark. Other Texas festivals that welcomed them over the years included ones held in Nacogdoches and at the Old Settlers Festival at Round Rock. The World of Bluegrass Music Festival held each year by the International Bluegrass Music Association (IBMA) arguably provided the capstone of their festival season. Described as "the largest urban indoor bluegrass festival in America," and now held in Raleigh, North Carolina, IBMA includes virtually every major American bluegrass band as well as groups from around the world.

As Hot Rize approached its tenth anniversary, band members could reflect on a career almost unparalleled in bluegrass music. It is rare for any group to endure that long without a change in personnel, but Pete, Tim, Nick, and Charles consistently presented the predictable format that Hot Rize fans anticipated and relished. The band frequently introduced new songs to their repertory, but their style of performance remained rock solid, smooth, and filled with humor. It all seemed like it could last forever. In 1988 the band celebrated its anniversary with a gig at the Left-Hand Grange. Pete told us that a *Rolling Stone* journalist visiting Boulder was in attendance and gave the band a four-star review. He called the band members "unquestionably virtuosos," a real high point for Hot Rize. But Pete told us, "Tim later mentioned that that night he said to himself, 'Ten years, that's long enough,' or something to that effect."[64] A decade is a long time in the life of a band. And Nick and Tim, the two youngest members, harbored ambitions for alternative careers of their own.

Chapter 4

THE PULL OF NASHVILLE

Tim was fully committed to Hot Rize and made immeasurable contributions to their sound, but he had found time throughout those twelve years to develop his reputation as a sort of Renaissance music man. If someone wanted a person to sing tenor harmony on their record, Tim was your man. If you wanted an instrumentalist, he could readily fill the bill on any one of several instruments. If you wanted a producer for your record, he was brimming with ideas. And, if you needed a song, Tim probably had a few that would suffice. As early as 1984 he made his own album for Flying Fish, *Hard Year Blues*, with the help of his Hot Rize friends and a few others such as Buck White and his daughters. Red Knuckles even appeared as the lead vocalist on "Honky Tonk Hardwood Floor." The album illustrated not only Tim's receptivity to a wide range of music—including two pop songs, Duke Ellington's "Cotton Tail" and Mitchell Parish's "Evening," and the gospel classic "Cabin in Gloryland"—but also revealed his deft writing skills. Two of his compositions, "Land's End" and "The High Road," presaged his interest in Irish music. "The High Road," a particularly haunting tune with an Irish ambience, became an often-covered number in the bluegrass field. It is a love story with four verses, and each one ends with a version of being carried away: from being on top a "high road lookin' down" and thinking of being let down, while hearing "the sound of the song that carried me away."

Two years later, Tim produced Laurie Lewis's first LP, *Restless Rambling Heart*, and appeared on ten of the album's eleven songs, playing mandolin, fiddle, or guitar and singing harmony on at least three cuts. Hailing from Berkeley, California, Laurie was on her way to becoming a highly regarded singer and fiddler in the bluegrass genre, taking part in the "feminization of bluegrass" that occurred in the 1980s. She told us she just had a brainstorm about inviting Tim to work with her, thinking that he would understand what she was trying to do musically and would help her see her dream to fruition without imposing his ideas on what that dream should be. In fact, she asserted, working with Tim on the album pushed her to decide that she wanted to make music full-time. Tim said that what he finds meaningful in his role as a producer entails "helping someone else achieve their vision, and then you can walk away from that project." The following year, he produced Mollie's debut solo album, *I Never Move Too Soon*, after which they did a Mother's Day concert, then decided to do an album together, with Tim choosing all the material. Mollie said that making those records with him was "kind of an eye-opener," since she, like Tim, had not grown up with traditional music and, unlike her brother, had not immersed herself in it. Sugar Hill produced *Take Me Back* in 1988, and this was the beginning of the O'Briens' work with the label, a relationship they enjoyed and that would prove crucial over the next several years.[1]

Arguably, the most portentous events for Tim involved working with fellow West Virginian Kathy Mattea. She grew up in Charleston with a childhood not dissimilar to Tim's: urban, Catholic, and scouting. Kathy had recorded hit versions of two of his songs, "Walk the Way the Wind Blows" and "Untold Stories."[2] Born Kathleen Alice Mattea on June 21, 1959, in South Charleston, West Virginia, Kathy grew up in Cross Lanes. As she recounted, "Girl Scout Camp and folk masses and guitar-playing all came along together." Kathy's father was a supervisor at the Monsanto chemical plant. Like Tim, music dominated any other career moves she might have made, and she dropped out of West Virginia University in 1978 and moved to Nashville on September 2 where she worked as a tour guide at the Country Music Hall of Fame and then as a secretary and waitress, while also performing as a demo singer. She signed with Mercury Records in 1983 and, by the following year, had become a successful recording artist. Two years later, she and Tim met at the *Mountain Stage* radio show in Charleston, but she learned about "Walk the Way the Wind Blows" from singer-songwriter and producer Paul Craft. It appeared in her breakout album, *Love at the Five and Dime*, in 1986, and the song reached Number 10 on *Billboard's* Hot Country Singles charts. Her version of Tim's "Untold Stories," released in July 1988, climbed even higher to Number 4. "Walk the Way the Wind Blows" had also garnered the Country Music Association's Single of the Year Award in 1986. Beautifully melodic, the words poignantly describe the dissolution of a relationship remembered fondly as "when you first came to me" when "all our love was sweet . . . and all our time was free." Now the protagonist is walking the way the wind blows, wiping away the tears. In 1990 Tim and Kathy recorded "Battle Hymn of Love," written by Paul Overstreet and Don Schlitz, and the song climbed to Number 9 on *Billboard's* Hot Country Singles and Tracks chart. The success of these songs whetted Tim's appetite for exploring his options in the larger and more lucrative country and western field, particularly since people like Marty Stuart, Keith Whitley, and Ricky Skaggs—all with bluegrass backgrounds— had won stardom in Nashville. As Tim recalled in an interview for *Puremusic*, "when I first got the Kathy Mattea cuts . . . it gave me an excuse to do what the heck I wanted to do. I went after a major label Country deal."[3]

Tim's fellow band members recognized his prowess and understood his ambitions beyond Hot Rize. They, therefore, could not have been completely surprised when one day in May 1989, he was called to the phone during a sound check in Boston. He returned with the news that he had been offered a contract by RCA. As Pete raised a post-gig glass to him, he conveyed the admiration and disappointment that expressed the end of an era: "Congratulations, you son of a bitch."[4]

The next day, Tim proposed that the band continue to gig another year, while he recorded his RCA album and prepared to launch his own band to tour behind the forthcoming record. Because Nick joined Hot Rize on May 1, 1978, band members agreed that April 30, 1990, would be their last gig, marking exactly the twelve years the four had played as a band. Pete explained, "We agreed to not make any announcement, tried not to draw attention to the band breaking up and having people asking about it, but just to enjoy the last year and play good music. And we managed to keep it from being known till late summer. That fall, Keith Case booked 41 early-1990 'farewell' gigs at many venues around the country where we had played, probably some 1,400 gigs altogether, in almost every state."[5]

Tim's decision seems not to have engendered hard feelings among his old friends and fellow band members, but that last year had to have been emotionally difficult, knowing that the tight and truly familial relationships they'd forged over the past twelve years would never be the same. No one at this juncture could have anticipated that Hot Rize would never *really* go away and that it would continue to reappear in various guises in the future. Ironically, the dissolution of the band occurred simultaneously with their zenith of recognition. In 1990, Hot Rize received the IBMA's Entertainer of the Year award, the first time that the award had been presented. They also recorded a highly praised album, *Take It Home*, which received a Grammy nomination, and saw one of its songs, "Colleen Malone," win an IBMA award for Best Bluegrass Song of the Year. Written by Leroy Drumm and John "Pete" Goble, the song lay squarely in the old tradition of American sentimental songs that used Ireland as the theme. This was a foretaste of the Irish/Celtic preoccupation that Tim would exhibit in the following decades. With awards flowing in like these intensifying the bittersweet recognition of the end of this leg of their journey, the band members could only have experienced this juxtaposition as "What a way to go out!"

The path to a broader world of musical achievement seemed open as Tim entered the decade of the 1990s. He was in and out of Nashville in the late 1980s and early 1990s, making contacts through his many friends in the bluegrass and acoustic worlds. He met Ken Levitan, a music business lawyer, who in turn introduced him to the influential RCA producer Mary Martin. Largely through her intervention, Tim signed a contract with RCA and appeared to be headed toward the kind of mainstream success that Ricky Skaggs and Marty Stuart had achieved crossing over from bluegrass to a larger audience.

Mary Martin was a beloved Nashville producer, known for her honesty, acerbic wit, salty language, and great skill at finding and aggressively cultivating then-young musicians such as Leonard Cohen, Van Morrison, Rodney Crowell, and Vince Gill. Born in Toronto, she relocated to New York and became active in American folk music after working as a receptionist in the office of the famed music manager Albert Grossman. Credited with signing Emmylou Harris for Warner Brothers, she also brought Bob Dylan and the Band together for their mutually productive relationship. Tim told us, "she was really hard to please, and it was amazing that she wanted to work with me. She had a sign on her desk: 'You cannot write if you cannot read.' I started trying to come up with new songs. That's when Hot Rize was in its 10th year, and I was feeling kind of restless."[6]

Tim had every right to expect a positive outcome, but that sense of security soon proved short-lived. His mother wrote about those roller-coaster days in her memoir: "When he was being groomed by RCA, they wanted him to select a psychological counselor to help him through all the trauma he was about to experience. When he told his father this in a telephone conversation from Nashville, Frank said, 'You go home and turn yourself over to Kit—she is the only therapy you need.' And he did." Tim had been working on an LP for RCA between 1989 and 1990, and the process and results had stumbled, but under record producer Garth Fundis the final product was completed. The company itself, however, was undergoing internal changes. Unfortunately, when RCA's president, Joe Galante, got transferred to New York, Martin lost her position with the corporation. Without her enthusiastic support and advocacy, Tim's audition tapes got lost in the shuffle when a new team of managers were installed and they lost interest in Tim's record. With most of his original songs shunted to the side, he finally felt he would actually do better on his own. As Jerry Douglas argued, "Tim realized he wasn't going to be in charge of his material. He recognized that he was still at a point where he could reverse that." Because he needed to make money right away, a lawyer helped wrangle him out from under the RCA contract. Tim signed an override agreement to release the songs he had done for the label. With such an agreement, if Tim sold more than one hundred thousand copies of any of the songs, he would have had to pay RCA, but he never sold nearly that many, so he never had to pay the corporation. When Tim had initially signed with RCA, Randy Travis and Ricky Skaggs had awakened audiences to the new directions Nashville's mainstream music could travel. But when Tim got ready for his record to come out, Clint Black and Garth Brooks had suggested even larger audiences for their sounds, which plumbed an altogether different vein. Although taken aback by this turn in fortune, Tim felt that "severance was definitely a mutual thing."[7]

Although Tim always tended to keep his innermost feelings hidden, RCA's actions, understandably, had first elated and then disheartened him. As Kathy Mattea put it, "It's hard to know how Tim reacted to the RCA putdown. When he is going through something, you probably would never see it on the outside," but Kit remembered that Tim was "pretty heartbroken when it happened." His son Jackson experienced the delight his parents had felt when the RCA deal was being contemplated. Their friends and family were equally thrilled for Tim. Jackson recalled that his dad moved the larger than life-size plastic figure of Nipper, the iconic Victor Talking Machine dog, from the hall by the stairs to the yard in Nashville in 1996 after the family was "well past the RCA debacle." Amy added her perspective about the effect of the RCA aftermath on her youngest son: "His ego was shattered but he spent little time licking his wounds, held his head high, tried to see the humor in it, reconciled his long-range goals with this tremendous, hurtful disappointment and started all over again. Tim and Kit's resilience has been not only amazing but touching. . . . Someday Jack and Joel will find inspiration in this meaningful story about their father."[8] We may never know exactly why the new managers of RCA rejected Tim's offerings, but Pete Wernick's judgment is probably correct. Tim "recorded a whole record that they decided not to put out because it wasn't considered country music, so they passed up on an incredible musician because he didn't sound like whatever it was they wanted."[9]

Although Tim may have been deeply wounded, he also remained highly focused and super-talented. Dusting himself off, he took his rejected project to Sugar Hill. Tim had built a solid relationship with the founder and owner, Barry Poss, from the earlier Sugar Hill albums—*Untold Stories* and *Take It Home* with Hot Rize and *Take Me Back* with Mollie. That Barry admired both Tim's musical abilities and traditional tastes was already a given.

Born in Toronto, Barry Poss had been a five-string banjo player with a love for old-time music. He was within one chapter of finishing his dissertation when he left Duke in 1975 to take a job with County Records in Virginia. In 1978 he founded Sugar Hill, named for an old southeastern fiddle tune. Tim expressed delight in being associated with Barry: "At Sugar Hill, I get to call up the president of the label and talk about Gid Tanner and stuff. You couldn't do that with most any record label guy. I mean, you can just call him up on the phone. I'm not hooked up with the country radio market. I'm back in the sort of folk market where I really belong." On the other hand, Tim fit Barry's profile of the ideal Sugar Hill performer on *Billboard*'s Hot Country Singles charts: "a consummate artist—musician, songwriter, singer—all the above in terms of artistry, plus his understanding of the roots of the music he plays. He has a deep grasp of the music, both passionate and romantic about the music he performs—both on and offstage."[10]

At Sugar Hill Tim also gained the invaluable services of the energetic and influential Bev Paul, who served independently as his manager for a brief time during these years (or at least until Brad Hunt assumed the position). As Tim told us, with Sugar Hill, he had "complete control as a producer," but Bev Paul knew how to market his music to disparate audiences. Born in Bethlehem, Pennsylvania, Bev had become an avid fan of urban folk music when she first heard the Kingston Trio back in the 1960s. After a stint as the manager of an acoustic listening room called The Gaslight in Fayetteville, North Carolina, she honed her skills in marketing, merchandising, promotion, and advertising during stints with a rock radio station and a major record retailer. She joined Sugar Hill in 1991 and discovered Tim when, during her initial interview, Barry Poss gave her a handful of cassettes. Sugar Hill had an impressive roster, and she was familiar with much of its talent—Guy Clark, Doc Watson, Townes Van Zandt—but Tim was new to her and she "fan-girled" him like crazy. "I wanted to join the label, use all my experience and figure out how to promote him."[11]

Bev also found trying "to sell Tim to retail buyers . . . so challenging." She had to learn "how to present this roots-based singer-songwriter, with his acoustic music, to the people that put music into retail stores and find ways to describe it for what it was: it's not country, not bluegrass, not folk or blues. It's hard to sell a negative image. Tim didn't fit into categories. I tried to do everything I could to position him into the folk roots genre." She felt that "Tim was a little shy about self-promotion," but he was glad to do anything that she asked of him. Having witnessed the variety of roots musical acts on the Sugar Hill roster and attending big music festivals like MerleFest in Wilkesboro, North Carolina, and South by Southwest in Austin, Texas, Bev became aware that a sizable audience and energy existed for the music. At the festivals and industry events like South by Southwest she also found a group of business colleagues who felt the same way about the music and saw the need for new ways to promote it. In fact, she said that much of Tim's rise actually occurred before the Americana label came along, and that he "was important to the creation of Americana, as was Guy Clark or Emmylou Harris. They were genre-less artists looking for a home in the marketplace." Bev continued to play multiple and significant roles in Tim's career.[12]

Along with Brad Paul from Rounder Records, entrepreneurial DJ Rob Bleetstein, Bev and other likeminded folks including publicists, magazine feature writers, and DJs wanted to promote the roots-based art form. In January 1995 they all met in Nashville to brainstorm the creation of a trade organization to help deal with the challenges genre-less artists faced. They struggled to decide what to call it: the term needed to be succinct.

"Alt-Country" got kicked around but that felt too much like a subgenre; "acoustic" was too narrow. Attendees dug down to the core of what they were looking for: contemporary music derivative of multiple forms of American roots music. In the end, they settled on Americana Music, and the Americana Music Association (AMA) was born. But Bleetstein was right on the mark when he said that it "encompassed all the elements of country music that country radio no longer played."[13]

Tim's new record for Sugar Hill, *Odd Man In* (released in 1991), contained many of the songs he had planned for RCA. Pete Wernick considered the album a much richer version of the songs "that RCA didn't like when they slicked it up." With Tim accompanied by a stellar lineup of musicians, the fourteen-song collection featured Nick Forster on guitar, Stuart Duncan on fiddle, Jerry Douglas on dobro, and Mark Schatz on bass. Tim presented his trademark variety of material, ranging from two traditional songs presumed to be of Irish origin—"Flora, the Lily of the West" and "Handsome Molly"—to a body of original numbers like "Lone Tree Standing" and "Lonely at the Bottom Too," that revealed his growing mastery of the craft of songwriting. "Lone Tree Standing" moves along in Tim's inimitable high-spirited way with lyrics that perfectly amplify the feeling when "stars are fading in the morning light," with a lover "warm beside" the singer, who therefore feels "so safe . . . so free." Among the bevy of positive reviews received by the album was one written by the dean of bluegrass reviewers, David Freeman, in his widely circulated and influential *County Sales Newsletter.* Freeman's approbation, sought and prized by all acoustic musicians, must have mightily pleased Tim when he read the opening sentences: "A wonderful 14-song collection from the highly talented O'Brien, formerly a mainstay of the great HOT RIZE band. O'Brien is one of the best song-writers in the field today, and there's so much good material here that it's overwhelming at first." Freeman cites as one of his favorites a strong and affecting affirmation of love, "Like I Used to Do," which later was covered in a popular version by the bluegrass band Seldom Scene. As one of Tim's finest, co-written with Pat Alger, it begins with images of young love, reminiscing about "the days when we'd pack our bags and run / Chasing some crazy dream into the morning sun." The song immediately moves to the perspective of a seasoned love "as the twilight falls" when satisfaction comes from "watching the fire glow" with the lover by the singer's side. The chorus contains the summation: "The only thing I still do like I used to do / Is carry this torch for you."[14]

Lyle Lovett wrote the liner notes, telling listeners that "the only thing odd about Tim O'Brien is that he is a consistently great singer, player, and songwriter," and the title reminds us "there is a world of great music that exists somewhere outside the mainstream, and he makes us ask how music this good can possibly remain on the outside." Lovett quotes the letter Tim wrote him when he sent the copy of the album, which includes Tim's honest and humorous self-assessment of his role in the music world at that moment:

> *Odd Man In* means I go by my own rules, and I've made a place for myself that I'm comfortable with. Lots of people feel like they don't fit in exactly. In fact, there are probably lots more of us out there that don't fit in than there are those that do, and it's nothing to be ashamed of.
>
> So, I'm oddly normal (and normally odd) with a wife, two sons, a Volvo, a Macintosh that I don't know how to use, and five mandolins.

Lovett closes by calling *Odd Man In* "an album of heartfelt songs and brilliant performances by a thoughtful and talented artist, Tim O'Brien. We should all be so odd." Tim dedicated the CD to "the O'Brien Clan, especially to the memories of Trip and Brigid."[15]

When Tim was working on the RCA deal, Mary Martin had encouraged him to come to Nashville to work with other songwriters. Tim met Pat Alger at that time through their common friendship with Kathy Mattea, for whom Pat had written such popular songs as "Goin' Gone" and "She Came from Fort Worth." Born in New York City and raised in LaGrange, Georgia, Pat found his path to country music through the folk revival, when he performed with the Woodstock Mountain Review. The Review included, at one time or another, Jon Sebastian, Jim Rooney, Bill Keith, and Happy and Artie Traum. By 1981 Pat was living in Nashville and pursuing a career that eventually saw him writing major hits like "Unanswered Prayers" and "The Thunder Rolls" for such luminaries as Garth Brooks. Tim could not have wished for a better songwriting partner. The two found collaboration easy. Pat told us, "A lot of what happens in co-writing is meeting the right person at the right time. The ability and respect for one another allows the collaborators to be emotionally honest with one another. . . . When I got in a room with Tim, we really enjoyed each other, and we wrote two good songs." The songs he was referring to were "Like I Used to Do" and "Time to Learn," which Tim recorded for his next Sugar Hill album. Pat talked about the way both he and Tim approach their craft:

> We aren't trying to guess what the market place wants as a hit but we write the song as closely to the idea that inspired us while keeping in mind the elements we have learned over many years that make songs accessible. I don't think I have ever known (with the one exception of "Unanswered Prayers") that a song will be a hit. I do believe that our innate sense of narrative development and our knack for memorable melodies opens the door of opportunity for a lot of our songs being popular. Sometimes that translates into a hit—other times just a really great song. I know when we finished "Like I Used to Do" we both felt we had a special song that didn't remind us of any other song. That is the hardest thing to do when you've written as many songs as we have.[16]

During his years with Sugar Hill, Tim recorded seven solo albums. While this music rested on a bluegrass foundation and included some of the greatest musicians in that genre, it ranged far beyond that original identity. After leaving Hot Rize, Tim organized a new trio, the O'Boys, with musicians who had impressive bluegrass credentials but who were comfortable in any instrumental format. In the fall of 1990 when the band formed, Tim's old friend and longtime singing partner Nick Forster played guitar with the O'Boys before he decided to give his full attention to his new *eTown* business.[17]

Scott Nygaard, a highly regarded master and student of the guitar with credentials as a rock, jazz, and bluegrass musician, replaced Nick. After a productive association with Laurie Lewis, he joined the band in the spring of 1992 and played with the O'Boys for the next five years. Bass player Mark Schatz brought both musical and visual assets to the band. Educated as a classical musician on both cello and bass at Haverford College and Berklee College of Music, he fell in love with old-time music and became fascinated with clogging after a trip to a fiddle contest at Fiddlers' Grove in North Carolina. Mark had been playing with the Tony Rice Unit and "was ready to be done" when he saw that Tim was going out on his own. Intrigued by Tim's sound, musicality, songwriting, and singing, Mark became "proactive" in going after a spot with Tim and remains to this day one of his big-

Tim and the O'Boys, from left to right: Tim, Scott Nygaard, and Mark Schatz
(photo by Anne Hamersky)

gest fans. During his years with the O'Boys, from 1990 to 1998, Schatz's
bass playing gave the band's music a solid underpinning and his solo step
dancing became a crucial ingredient of the band's popularity. At some
point during a concert Mark would step onto a small plank platform and
do his exhilarating dance to the accompaniment of a brisk fiddle tune and
sometimes slap his hands against his body in a rhythmic way—a technique
known as hamboning. Tim, Scott, and Mark formed the basic trio, but they
were often joined by various "guests," including Mollie, but most often
Jerry Douglas. As America's foremost dobro or resophonic guitar player,
Jerry came to the band after many years of service in some of the nation's
leading bluegrass and acoustic bands, including the Country Gentlemen.
By 2020 he had earned fourteen Grammy awards. Although never a permanent member of the O'Boys, he played with them when the band first
organized—when it consisted of Tim, Mark, Jerry, and Nick—and afterwards, only occasionally, but he also produced many of their albums and
continues to be a steadfast friend of Tim's.[18]

Tim had an assured network of festivals inherited from his Hot Rize
days, but he added to that an extensive array of clubs and other venues,

both in the United States and abroad. From its inception, the O'Boys played a demanding schedule of about 150 dates a year, mostly during festival season between Merlefest in the spring and Labor Day. As the Hot Rize musicians had bonded, the O'Boys enjoyed both their musical and companionable relationship. Mark told us that "the touring was always pretty much fun, and everybody liked each other, and we all got along." Scott mentioned that "the O'Boys didn't rehearse that much, since Tim tends to be 'a seat-of-the-pants kind of guy.'" Tim trusted their musicianship, and the band, according to Scott, stayed closely tied to Tim's repertoire: Scott singing harmony with Tim, playing a few instrumentals, and "performing the same list every night." Since they played so often, they had no difficulty in retaining the musical arrangements between gigs. The O'Boys usually flew to an area where they were scheduled, rented a van, and drove from festival to festival for a couple of weeks. Around Thanksgiving, the band played in Boulder, where Tim was still living in the first years of the O'Boys. When Scott joined the band, he was thinking of moving to Nashville, but he never left the Bay area. In 1994 Tim acquired an RV, and with the trio taking turns driving they were able to travel around the country during that summer. The "No Wives Aboard" rule that held sway for Hot Rize did not apply to the O'Boys, and Kit, Jack, and Joel often accompanied them on the road. But Jackson told us that, while the RV allowed the family to travel with the band, "it turned out not to be economically feasible to do that."[19]

Unlike the outgoing Mollie and Kit, Tim is both introspective and an introvert. Sometimes like Charles Sawtelle, Tim could be quirky, extremely funny, hard to pin down, "mysterious." Jerry Douglas described Tim as having many layers, "like peeling an onion." Jerry felt that the early tragedies Tim had experienced had done much to shape him. When producing Tim's recordings, Jerry "would wonder how all of those songs could come out of one guy. He's on a tier up there with some rare air." He marveled about the way Tim conveyed what he was thinking: "The way he processes things is so *different*. He has reinvented himself two or three times." Mark described Tim as "something of a closed book emotionally" and therefore a little inaccessible. Yet Mark sensed "a true warmth there, and when you're in trouble, he really understands. In his songs, there's a lot going on in there, and he finds a way to translate those emotions."[20]

The O'Boys fondly remembered the rewarding Arts America (USIA) tours during the early 1990s. Nick Forster was still with the band, but he

was reluctant to travel abroad, so bluegrass and roots musician Matt Flin-
ner played in his place. The tour to eastern Europe and the Mediterranean
in 1991 gave the O'Brien siblings their first opportunity to tour abroad
together, and Mollie was extremely grateful, even though leaving her young
children made it difficult for her and her husband, Rich. This five-week
stint on the European continent took place soon after the Berlin wall
came down and after Desert Storm. The tour began in Bulgaria "where the
audiences really hadn't heard live American music and responded enthusiastically." They traveled next to Slovakia, where Tim remembered the
people they encountered as being especially appreciative. They went on to
Malta and Cyprus "where we played both the Greek and Turkish sides of
the divided island." Mark remarked that the experience presented an interesting juxtaposition of cultures, with the Greek audience more subdued
and the Turkish audience more ecstatic. The USIA had funded the trip,
principally, so that the band could play at a reception at the American
ambassador's home in Greece honoring Jimmy Carter. By request, Mollie
sang "Georgia On My Mind," while Tim performed "This Land Is Your
Land" when someone called that song out. As this example demonstrates,
the band had to adapt to whatever limitations or prerequisites were presented by any given venue. Originally, they were to go from Greece to Tur-
key, but, "in the wake of Operation Desert Storm," the band went instead
to East Germany. According to Mollie, the electrifying energy of the era
contributed to their audiences' receptivity to the music. Tim and Mollie
included a couple of Beatles tunes, which people really wanted to hear.
Mollie found it particularly thrilling to see what American music meant to
the audiences they encountered. Mark laughed as he recalled that Tim
made up funny names for some of the countries: "'Bolemia,' where no one
could keep anything down," and "'Insomnia' where no one could get any
sleep." Mollie agreed. She said that one of the aspects of touring with Tim
that was so enjoyable had to do with her brother being "one of the funniest
people on the planet." She talked about how pleased they were to hear
local musicians wherever they traveled, both on this European tour and
the second USIA tour two years later in Central and South America—
Bolivia, Ecuador, Chile, Brazil, Guatemala—where they heard traditional
musicians in at least some of the countries where they journeyed.[21]

Tim and Mollie's commercial duet-making began back in 1988 when
they recorded *Take Me Back* for Sugar Hill, which Dave Freeman dubbed a

Tim and Mollie O'Brien publicity shot (photo by Laura Rose)

"lovely, relaxed album" graced by the siblings' flawlessly smooth singing
and Tim's and Nick Forster's minimalist acoustic accompaniment. They set
a high bar by reaching deeply into the old-time country song bag. Fans of
traditional country music could only be deeply satisfied with songs like
"Sweet Sunny South," "When the Roses Bloom in Dixie Land," "Dream of
the Miner's Child," "Down in the Valley to Pray," and "Your Long Journey."
Their interpretation of John Prine's "Unwed Fathers" constitutes the high-
light of the album, probably the best of many recorded versions of this
socially sensitive ballad. Tim appreciated the seemingly effortless harmonies he and his sister achieved and said many years later, "There's a kind of
loose, easy thing about singing with Mollie. It just falls together. She's got a
really beautiful bell tone. It's effortlessly expressive." Although Mollie's
tastes ran far beyond bluegrass and old-time music, she easily adapted her
vocal style to the songs that Tim chose.[22]

After their first tour abroad, Mollie and Tim released their second
album, *Remember Me*, in 1992 and, two years later, *Away Out on the Mountain*,
both for Sugar Hill. These recordings ranged across the stylistic map.
Enlarging their repertoire may have worked at cross-purposes, though,
since increasing their appeal to a more diverse audience may have left

tradition-minded fans wanting more. No one, however, could be dissatisfied with the harmonies they displayed. Their singing on "The Floods of South Dakota" on *Remember Me* elevated an obscure song to majestic heights. A few songs from the African American tradition, "Motherless Children" and "Stagger Lee," charged the album with energy, as did Leadbelly's "When I Was a Cowboy"—complete with a yodel that echoed that of the great Black balladeer. Tim wrote in the liner notes:

> Thirty years ago, we'd give each other a funny look when we'd venture out on a new harmonic limb. We're still giving each other that same look today. The only difference is that we're even more relaxed around each other—if that's possible—and we're still best friends. Don't get us wrong. This "biz" involves some real work and some very real heartaches, but hanging out and playing music together is a blast. We even do things together when we don't *have* to!
>
> With this, our third recording, we think we've given you an outline of the world according to Tim and Mollie. . . . What ties it all together are great musicians, great songwriters, and our own philosophy of life, "It ain't what you do, it's the way that you do it."

As a whole, this third duet collection marked a refreshing return to country roots, featuring yet another display of superb harmony. In addition to venerable songs like Jimmie Rodgers's "Away Out on the Mountain," "Tragic Romance," and "Ain't No Grave Gonna Hold My Body Down," the album included "Wichita" and "Orphan Girl," compositions by Gillian Welch, the marvelous singer-songwriter who has the knack of composing songs that sound instantaneously old. The O'Briens recorded these songs before Gillian got around to putting them out herself, and they seem to have been the first singers to record her songs. In addition to the O'Boys (Mark and Scott) playing on the album, they were joined by others, including Mollie's husband, Rich, on bass and Mike Seeger on banjo.[23]

Following the release of each album, Mollie and Tim did mostly weekend tours, but they also played at significant summer festivals: Merlefest, Telluride, Strawberry Music Festival near Yosemite National Park, and Grey Fox. In the summer of 1994, the siblings also made their first trip to Ireland together, opening for Guy Clark and his son, Travis. They played in Dublin, Kilkenny, Cork—before going to the Cambridge Folk Festival in

London, the "granddaddy of all the folk festivals in England." At every event, Tim made new friends and deepened his interest in his Irish roots, facilitating both future sojourns and musical explorations.[24]

In 1993, Tim benefited from Sugar Hill's release of his second solo album with that label, *Oh Boy, O'Boy*. Its diversity of songs contributed to his being named 1993's IBMA's Male Vocalist of the Year. Tim, of course, played his usual retinue of instruments—mandolin, fiddle, guitar, and bouzouki—but it was his singing that made the album compelling. Tim asked several friends to play on the recording, including Mollie, Pete, Edgar Meyer, Del McCoury, and Jerry Douglas, who also produced the album. Otherwise, the CD demonstrated Tim's wide-ranging choice of songs: a fiddle medley with an Irish flavor, "Johnny Don't Get Drunk/Rye Straw"; an old British ballad, "The Farmer's Cursed Wife"; a rousing tune learned from hillbilly pioneer J. E. Mainer, "Run Mountain"; a haunting song written by Jimmie Driftwood, "He Had a Long Chain On"; and several songs of his own. Two standouts from this album are, to a great extent, autobiographical: "The Church Steeple" and "Time to Learn." As Tim wrote in the liner notes about the former, with St. Michael's just up the street from his boyhood home on Lenox Avenue, the church's chimes "seemed to weave through the fabric of everyday life. . . . The details in the song are my usual combination of the 'true' and the 'could have been true.'" The lyrics deal tenderly and explicitly with the joy (Mollie's marriage to Rich) and the tragic (Trip's death in Vietnam): "Of the joys and the sorrows, the laughter and the pain / The heartbeat of the whole town is heard within that strain."[25]

He wrote "Time to Learn"—one of our favorites in Tim's repertoire—with Pat Alger. Pat told us about the simpatico he felt when he and Tim first met and the way they were able to talk honestly with each other, a quality he deemed necessary to successful collaboration. They shared their sense of sadness over deaths of loved ones—Tim's loss of his siblings, Pat's loss of his ex-wife, and other more recent deaths—and "Time to Learn" emerged. But inspiration only goes so far, as Pat said, "We both worked at it as a business." In his liner notes, Tim amplified his version of that story:

Two of my siblings died before their time. My mother tells the story of my older sister, Mollie, who would have been three years old at the time waiting on the front porch for our older sister,

Brigid, to come home from school, weeks after the funeral. My older brother's death when I was fourteen was definitely something I had a hard time understanding. I can't imagine how my parents got through all that. Pat Alger and I tried to write about the sudden and strange finality of death and how we deal with it.[26]

Tim's and Pat's personal responses relate to the universality of loss: "Your last hours we never knew / We never had a chance to say goodbye to you." And their beautifully crafted song, minimalist in its simple elegance, poignantly touches listeners everywhere.

While the early 1990s saw Tim rising to the top of his game as a singer, musician, and producer, this period also saw him blossoming as a songwriter, beginning with his working with Pat. Unlike the negativity generated by the RCA fiasco, Tim's songwriting collaboration with other writers moved the needle to the opposite pole. Before he actually moved to Nashville, in early 1995 he signed with Forerunner Publishing, owned by songwriter and publisher Allen Reynolds and musician Jim Rooney. Reynolds, Arkansas-born and Memphis-raised, directed the early careers of people like Crystal Gayle, Don Williams, and Kathy Mattea. His greatest claim to fame, though, came with his production of superstar Garth Brooks's earliest albums. Rooney, born in Boston and a longtime partner of Bill Keith (the pioneering musician who popularized the chromatic style of banjo), had also served as manager of Club 47, the Boston establishment that hosted many of the leading lights of the folk revival. His resume included working for the Newport Jazz Festival and then cofounding the New Orleans Jazz Festival. Arriving in Nashville in 1976, he soon became the chief recording engineer for the influential Jack Clement, a legendary Nashville producer. Forerunner Publishing set the scene for the upsurge in Tim's songwriting career that he was seeking.[27]

Tim's songwriting and his collaboration with other writers fully show in his Sugar Hill album of 1997, *When No One's Around*, with all thirteen songs in the collection published or co-published by Forerunner. Only two items of traditional provenance, both arranged by Tim—"Out on the Rollin' Sea" and "Love Is Pleasin'"—appear on the album. All of the others, written or co-written by Tim with such writers as Darrell Scott, Hal Ketchum, Danny O'Keefe, and Gary Nicholson, address the eternal enigma of love from a variety of perspectives. "How Come I Ain't Dead," for example, playfully deals with the dying-for-love theme when it asks, "If I can't live without her, how come I ain't dead?" "First Days of Fall," on the other hand, a beautiful country waltz, exudes no irony at all when it recalls a love that has either dissolved or been severed by death.

One of Tim's most fateful collaborations began in the lobby of the Forerunner building, probably in late 1995. Tim told Randy Barrett, in *Bluegrass Today*, "I was living in Colorado and made writing trips to Nashville. The [music] publishing company I worked for was Forerunner, run by Jim Rooney and Allen Reynolds, and they set up a co-writing date with Darrell Scott. I had never met him." Darrell's publisher was EMI. Darrell told us that one of the tenets in his philosophy of songwriting is to "tell the truth" with the other songwriter, and even though a fan of Tim's, Darrell had no expectations of this "blind date."[28]

When their respective publishers first put them together in the standard Nashville fashion, they had already achieved renown on their own as accomplished musicians and writers. While Tim was steeped in bluegrass and country, Scott straddled country and rock and roll. Darrell's song "Uncle Lloyd," Tim found "eye-opening" for the way it demonstrated Darrell's writing style, particularly his use of "plenty of biographical details." This approach helped Tim, who was moving closer to writing from that perspective. Equally responsive, Darrell explained that "two or three guys will expose themselves emotionally and vulnerably to one another," a quality he deems essential for songwriters. Or, as he put it, the "creative male" must follow the adage "Take your emotions and bring them forward in your work." Tim and Darrell hit it off immediately. As journalist, Terri Horak, later wrote:

> [Their relationship] quickly morphed from an arranged collaboration to a "Where have you been all my life?" moment for both artists. "Tim and I both felt like we met at Hank Williams," says Scott, noting that Hank's music had been a passion of his musician father[,] Wayne Scott, and those seminal records had been the younger Scott's sacred texts growing up, as they were for O'Brien, along with the bluegrass canon. "Both of us can push the country button and be there," says O'Brien of their common ground. "We just stretch toward each other till we intersect."

Forerunner proved transformative for Tim, above and beyond introducing him to Darrell. It provided him with a receptive environment in which to translate ideas into songs: a recording studio on the ground floor, writing rooms in the basement, and the publishing company offices on the second floor. As he told a journalist for *PineCone*, "I'm lucky that Forerunner likes what I do, but I don't deny that being in this town heightens your sense of what could get cut."[29]

Born on August 6, 1959, on a tobacco farm in London, Kentucky, Darrell moved with his family as his father looked for better work opportunities, first in East Gary, Indiana, and then in southern California. Although his father, Wayne Scott, worked as a carpenter as Darrell was growing up, he also played music whenever he could. Darrell soaked up the music and songwriting of his youth as well as that of the older country greats and began playing professionally before going to college. By the time Darrell enrolled at Tufts University at the age of twenty-three, he expected to "buckle down." He had already been married and divorced and been on the road as a musician. After majoring in the humanities, he had to decide whether to go into creative writing or to divert his attentions to songwriting. Choosing the latter, he moved to Nashville in 1995. A story that Darrell told about his father inspired "Daddy's on the Roof." Wayne Scott had moved his family to California because of greater prospects there and more hours of sunny daylight for the outdoor work at which he excelled. Once they moved to the Golden State, Darrell remembered, his dad "sometimes felt like getting some air and freedom up on the roof." Darrell would spend the night up there with his brother and his dad and said, "My little brother would be tied to the mattress, since he had a tendency to sleep walk." The first day they worked together, Darrell and Tim took the story and made a successful song out of it; it appeared on Tim's next Sugar Hill album, *Rock in My Shoe*, released in 1995.[30]

With Jerry Douglas producing the album and again playing the dobro, the band included the regular trio of Tim, Scott Nygaard on guitar, and Mark Schatz on bass. The album also featured the guest appearance of another musician who was destined to play a major role in Tim's career, Dirk Powell, who played the accordion, Cajun style, on a few songs. The album has an eclectic mix, including a traditional song, "Jonah and the Whale," and it prominently features Tim's songwriting and co-writing with Darrell, in "Daddy's on the Roof," and with other collaborators. One of his solo highlights is "Brother Wind." The plaintive and tenderly evocative song contains autobiographical references in its opening lines: "Made up my mind to go / Some place so far away, I headed west / Without a sad goodbye." It also confirms the emotional distance that Tim sometimes places between himself and others, with the loneliness that such distancing entails: "He knows me, my brother wind / He's lonely too and he takes me away." But the song also fits within a romanticized tradition of older wandering or hobo songs, with somewhat cliched lines like "The only home I have is open road." Tim talked with Ronni Lundy about how pieces of "Brother Wind" were with him for a long time, and the song "took a couple of years to evolve." She thought of it as one of his numbers that is "closest to the bone."[31]

The spirit of "Brother Wind" seemed to be blowing from Colorado east the following year when Kit and Tim moved their family to Nashville. They were already contemplating a possible move somewhere about the time of Joel's birth in 1990. Tim felt he had outgrown the music scene in Boulder. He told Jim Newsom:

> I was in Colorado for 22 years, with a little brief sprint up to Minneapolis for a little bit. But I got to be friendly with people in Nashville because I'd be out on the road working. It looked like, to support my family, Nashville was the place. Since I had moved there in '74, Boulder had become much more gentrified and I outgrew the music scene there. So, Nashville was the only logical place. I didn't want to go to LA or New York and raise a kid. I kind of went on my own terms. I had songs already recorded by other artists.[32]

The first two or three years on his own, Tim said that he didn't feel secure enough to move, but by 1996 he recognized that the right time had arrived. It became a default option for him: he had a performing circuit of his own; Kathy Mattea had achieved successes with his songs; and he had already benefited from collaborating with other songwriters. He hoped that by moving to Nashville he could make three revenue streams work to support his family—performing his own music, songwriting, and playing as a sideman or singing harmony on other musicians' recordings. As he expressed his self-assessment to Jim Newsom, "I don't think I was ready ten years ago. I was intimidated by the business and afraid I'd get up in the wrong priorities. I don't have any illusion that the kind of stuff I've done is going to set the woods on fire, but it's the kind of thing that can pay for my

The O'Brien family, 1994, from left to right: Joel, Kit, Tim, and Jackson (Tim O'Brien's collection)

kids' education." The O'Briens settled into their first house in Nashville in Hillsboro Village, one block away from a songwriter hangout, Brown's Diner. They lived there until the year 2000 and then moved to a house in Oak Hill where he has lived ever since. Tim's instincts turned out to be on target. Within a year after moving, he felt he had a "gold ticket," and that things were working out. The move to a larger city thrilled Jackson, who attended high school there and began playing music himself. And, as Jim Newsom confirmed, "Soon after he and Kit arrived, Garth Brooks recorded 'When There's No One Around,' Tim's collaboration with Darrell Scott that appeared on Tim's 1997 CD that bore the same name. He could not have asked for more positive reinforcement. Tim noted that his presence in Nashville meant that when somebody like the Chieftains (the immensely-popular Irish revival group) came to town, they could say 'who can we get to make this country record?' and the producer will say 'let's get this and that, and Tim O'Brien.' It's just like fishing out of the local stream there."[33]

Not only did Nashville seem to reach out and embrace Tim and Kit, they were just as up for returning the embrace. Mike Kemnitzer told us about spending time with the O'Briens after their move and about the wonderful annual party they threw for their friends in the music community:

> After Tim and Kit moved to Nashville, I went to one of their early New Year's Day parties. It was a house full of food and friends and now it was Bela [Fleck], Sam [Bush], Jerry and a who's who of the young greats, playing nonstop music. I was happy for how thoroughly Nashville had accepted Tim. Everybody loved him, and why not? Charlie Cushman said, "Tim and Kit have the GREATEST parties!" I agreed while thinking, same recipe and vibe as their parties back in the early Boulder days, how could you go wrong?
>
> I went to several of those New Year's Day parties over the years and they never waned in popularity. I can't imagine all the music greats that attended. One year, Earl Scruggs and his wife Louise were the first to arrive and it was late in the evening when I retrieved their coats from the bottom of a huge pile on a bed.[34]

Tim further noted that moving to Nashville gave one a sense of going around the track really fast: more opportunities, more stimulation, more excitement, and more pressure. He told Terri Horak for *Billboard*: "Being here has got a little fever in me. Everybody's talking about songs. I don't feel like I'm changing, just doing it more, and it's been fun." Kit thought the "move to Nashville seemed like a natural, if not overdue, progression." Always seeking perfection in his performances, Tim's presence in Nashville awakened him to demanding even more from himself. And he commented to Dylan Muhlberg:

> Things are faster and people are making more deals. Folks are more finely tuned as musicians because you have to be to compete. The competition there helps you hold your ground. You've got to keep up with people. Commercialism and the trends can also bog you down. But by following the trends you're automatically behind. That can be a trap there. Everyone is trying to get the next country radio hit. If you imitate what the hit was last week you're probably not going to make that happen.[35]

Good things kept percolating for Tim in 1996, and another Sugar Hill recording, *Red on Blonde,* became Tim's most venturesome and widely praised project yet, even though it had nothing to do with his Nashvillian emphasis on songwriting. *Red on Blonde*—an acoustic, bluegrass-driven treatment of thirteen Bob Dylan songs—became the first of Tim's concept albums. The title came from his sobriquet, Red Knuckles, and from a Dylan album called *Blonde on Blonde*, though Tim included none of its songs on that recording. Although Tim related that "Barry Poss loved *Red on Blonde*," initially he wasn't sure if it would be commercially successful. Tim had already recorded *Odd Man In* and *Rock in My Shoe* for Sugar Hill, and "record contracts generally provide for the artist to commit to follow up a release with 2 or more additional releases." So, while Barry endorsed the idea, "he said the Dylan record wouldn't be considered one of the records I was required to produce under the existing contract. He issued a separate contract just for that one." Tim's next album, *When No One's Around*, fulfilled his original contract with Poss. However, once *Red on Blonde* had been released, "it was obvious that it 'had legs' and would likely sell." By that summer Poss had already made a deal with a Brazilian record company to license two tracks—"Señor" and "Forever Young"—as dance remixes, which sold extremely well.[36]

After Hot Rize as an active band stopped performing in 1990, Charles Sawtelle, also road weary, set up his own recording studio, Rancho de Ville. But he and Tim stayed close, and Charles introduced and provided him with a batch of obscure but recorded Dylan tunes for the project.[37] In the liner notes, Tim gives Mollie big-sister credit for turning him on to Bob Dylan back in the mid-1960s and berating him for "not being aware of the greatest songwriter of the times." Tim mentioned that other bluegrass singers, such as Del McCoury and the Dillards, had covered some of Dylan's songs. And three years earlier, Mike Seeger, David Grisman, and John Hartford had worked on a similar effort, *Retrograss*, performing modern country and rock songs with vintage instruments and old-time styles. But no one in the acoustic realm had conceived an entire collection like *Red on Blonde*, which, in Tim's words, might "be a more listener-friendly batch of Bob's music."[38]

In his review of the album, George Graham noted that it lived up to O'Brien's reputation for being eclectic: "the result is a fine recording whose quality comes in the execution rather than in the concept or originality. In a way, it's a tribute from one fine songwriter to another who was a great and profound influence." Peter Blackstock noted, "given that Bob Dylan's catalog has pretty much been interpreted to death by all manner of song stylists by now, an album of all-Dylan covers would seem a rather risky proposition, but Tim O'Brien proves more than up to the task with *Red on Blonde*." Blackstock praised Tim for using his own strengths as a musician and singer to "infuse" the songs with that energy. Along with the O'Boys (Scott and Mark), Tim enlisted other musicians from his circle, including Jerry Douglas and Charlie Cushman, his sister Mollie, and his good friend Kathy Mattea to give listeners, Blackstock concludes, an "engaging, joyously listenable disc." Terri Horak convincingly tied *Red on Blonde* to Tim's larger quest to produce meaningful songs of his own, since his singing helped him discern the elements that make a good song. He told her, "'If you sing a song enough times, you realize the nuances and why you liked them. I don't claim to write like him, but singing Dylan's songs continues to teach me different things about writing. Just studying his lyrics opens up a whole new world.'"[39]

The Dylan collection contained none of Tim's original material, but it certainly reached a variety of audiences. As Scott Nygaard stated simply, "*Red on Blonde* was *big*. It was the first of Tim's albums to be nominated for a Grammy" as best bluegrass recording in 1996, and it earned Tim and the O'Boys "a lot of IBMA accolades for that, too."[40]

Tim's shifting his base from Boulder to Nashville now delivered all that he hoped it would, facilitating his ascendance to a new level in his career. He told Terri Horak, "Songwriting is an outgrowth of wanting to perform, and my main aim still is to write the kind of stuff I want to sing. I've always loved playing music, and if you write songs that touch people, you're able to reach them in a new way." Having moved only recently, he could already feel himself growing through his songwriting collaborations. Other events only reinforced this upswing. After experiencing their compatibilities as writers, Tim and Darrell found they could also make good music together. Soon after Tim moved to Nashville, he saw Darrell at Sam Bush's New Year's party, jammed with him, and asked him to be involved in his recording the following month. Darrell told us that, about the time he and Tim were writing "When There's No One Around" at Forerunner, "We wrote the song, and immediately, we played our brand-new song to someone and saw the reaction five minutes later" when Garth Brooks overheard it and decided he wanted to record it. It appeared that year on his 1997 album, *Sevens*, as well as on Tim's next record, *When No One's Around* (1997), where Scott played guitar. Darrell laughed. "Tim bought a van, and we redid the kitchen with the money made from the album that sold seven million copies." This kind of success reinforced Darrell's belief that "the atmosphere in the writing room with two people seeking the honesty and vulnerability in conversation can lead or move into a song."[41]

While maintaining their solo careers, Tim and Darrell also built a powerful duo presence. The following spring, they traveled to the United Kingdom. As Tim recalled, "We ended up on the second night, playing everything together, and it just kinda went from there. Of anybody I've ever played with, Darrell doesn't really need to know the song. There was no problem getting it together. It was just play whatever you wanted to play and he would be on it, and I was able to follow along easily with the mandolin on his stuff." Like Tim, Darrell is a multidimensional musician: a compelling singer, a master of many instruments, and a sensitive craftsman of enduring songs like "You'll Never Leave Harlan Alone" and "Long Time Gone" (made into hit recordings by Patty Loveless and the [Dixie] Chicks, respectively). Involvement with their own projects, however, meant that recording together had to take a back seat temporarily.[42]

Dropping out of Colby at the beginning of his sophomore year to devote himself to music did not mean that Tim divorced himself from intellectual pursuits. Just as he constantly challenged himself tracking and trekking down new music-making paths, he also pushed himself to explore new literary and historical realms. He remained a voracious reader. As many of our interviewees attested, Tim constantly asked friends and acquaintances for new book recommendations or told others about some article or book he had just discovered. Charles Frazier's *Cold Mountain*, published in 1997, sparked Tim's imagination. Not only does the novel depict the deprivations and tragedy of the Civil War, but the rugged setting of southern Appalachia at the narrative's center has served as a repository for many traditional southern folkways and music. As an informal, but intentional, student of the region of which his home state is so much a part, Tim, like many before him, has also romantically accepted Appalachia's music as "a living link to the past and to the Scots/Irish and English immigrants who settled the area in the late 1700s." Surely, Tim recognized that other people were there. In addition to the original Native inhabitants of the region, Germans, African Americans, and those of other European stock also populated the area. Nevertheless, the pervasive myth of the "pure" Anglo-Celtic roots of mountain music continues to override the reality of a more diverse Appalachia. Through his erudite research for his powerful novel, Frazier sprinkled references to the songs that would have been known to Civil War–era residents of western North Carolina. And Tim, in his quest to explore all that he could about the Appalachian past, found those references worth teasing out musically. In his relationship with fellow multi-instrumentalist Dirk Powell he also discovered a friend with whom to embark on this musical odyssey to the past.[43]

An extraordinarily gifted musician like Tim, Dirk Powell fell in love with American traditional music in its myriad forms. Born in Oberlin, Ohio, and classically trained in music, Dirk embraced the music and culture of his maternal grandfather, James Clarence Hay, a fiddler and banjo player from Elliot County in eastern Kentucky. Although raised in Ohio, Dirk spent as much time as possible with his maternal grandparents. He found he needed those same roots that had earlier "strangled" his parents. The music expressed to him the unconditional familial love valued by his grandfather, a love that Dirk readily reciprocated. As he expressed it, "you take from and give back to the traditional resource of that body of music." Dirk made himself an authority on traditional Appalachian music, but he also became immersed in Cajun music after he fell in love with and later married Christine Balfa, a daughter of the revered Cajun fiddler Dewey Balfa. Dirk added the Cajun accordion and fiddle to his performing repertory, made his home in Louisiana, and built his own recording studio near Breaux Bridge where many musicians have played. He and Tim shared musical interests, a common resolve to preserve and document traditional styles and songs, and a romantic perception that Celtic and Appalachian musical strains somehow intersected.[44]

Dirk told us that he was a teenager when he first met Tim, who had approached him backstage at Rocky Grass, after hearing Dirk's fiddle playing. Tim told him, "You just kicked my ass." As Dirk said, Tim "never hesitates to pay a compliment." After that brief encounter, they had overlapped at festivals where Dirk played in both the old-time and Cajun fields. He appreciates that Tim never compartmentalizes music, instead "drawing on all the sources in his world." Perhaps because Tim never forgets all those who helped him find his own path, he enjoys mentoring younger musicians like Dirk in whom he believes. In that spirit, Tim produced Dirk's first solo on Rounder, *If I Go 10,000 Miles*, in 1996, which Dirk considered an exceptionally generous "labor of love," since Tim agreed to do it in Dirk's Louisiana studio. Around the same time, Tim invited Dirk to play on *Rock in My*

Shoe, and a stronger friendship emerged. Dirk finds Tim "really gifted and fluent" in his creativity, so that he doesn't have "to prove anything." They both share the belief that "creating from your heart has a spiritual dimension, and these understandings form the basis of the friendship." The two of them also shared special moments with their mutual hero, Doc Watson, and both were mightily impressed by *Cold Mountain*.[45]

As Tim recalled, "the impetus to start the [Howdy Skies] record label was that Dirk Powell and I had talked about making a CD to be a companion to the novel *Cold Mountain*." Dirk told us, "There are lines in the text of that book that are taken from traditional music, [but] if you don't know the music, you couldn't recognize that it's a line from the music." Tim and Dirk wanted to demonstrate this intersection musically, and Tim felt strongly that "anyone who plays this music, and knows this book is going to be interested" in a collection of the historic songs and tunes referenced in the text. When they approached Charles Frazier, he agreed, because he respected both the knowledge and the intent they brought to the project. Tim and Dirk had discussed the project at a Folk Alliance convention after the book's publication, and they enlisted John Herrmann to join them on banjo. Then they reached out to Bev Paul about the best means of distribution. By this time, she had left Sugar Hill to be a freelance consultant. "We thought, originally, that we'd sell it in book stores, so we set up the idea of our own record company, Howdy Skies." The three musicians and Kit agreed with the concept, deciding that Kit—mentored by Bev—would run Howdy Skies (Tim's old nickname from his time with the Ophelia String Band) as CEO. Kit also served as art director for the project and did the illustrations for the liner notes, while Sue Meyer, who had designed most of Tim's album covers for Sugar Hill, took responsibility for the design.[46]

Although Tim and Dirk hoped that, by creating a musical product that could accompany a paperback version of the book, they could profit from the success of the critically acclaimed and commercially successful novel, those hopes were soon dashed. The Howdy Skies team faced a wall of unsolvable legalities in regards to rights, which became even more complicated after they learned that a movie version of *Cold Mountain* was forthcoming, with a soundtrack produced by T-Bone Burnett. The Howdy Skies CD, therefore, could not use the name of the book as the title. In spite of these obstacles, the Howdy Skies team did create an outstanding musical project called *Songs from the Mountain*, filled with fiddle tunes, ballads, and gospel songs that reflected the music of North Carolina during the Civil War. The album experienced good sales, with the excellent music critically praised. Jonathan Pitts, a reviewer for the *Baltimore Sun*, argued that in contrast to the movie's soundtrack, *Songs from the Mountain* is "truer in approach to the music that Dirk called 'a living link to the past and to the Scots/Irish and English immigrants who settled western North Carolina in the late 1700s.'" For example:

> O'Brien's reverence for old-time music storytelling is evident in his restraint. . . . With gentle, haunting harmonies, and such rough-hewn instruments as cigar-box fiddles and gourd banjos woven in with deftly played acoustic guitars and mandolins, the trio brings to natural life the sense of aspiration, grief and loss that drives the novel. Frazier himself calls the CD "a marvel. Dirk, Tim and John wonderfully capture the raw power and rough, sorrowful beauty of the music that sustained old America's spirit—and gave it a new life for the new century."[47]

Songs from the Mountain did not become the blockbuster that they hoped for. Distribution for a small record label proved difficult, and when the book-CD package arrived in record stores, the obvious customers for the CD had already read the book in hardcover, so they balked at purchasing the paperback. Furthermore, the Howdy Skies team found that they could sell the CD only through the year 2000, the expected release date for the movie. They had shrink-wrapped and packaged the CD and paperback together, with the unfortunate result that the bar code on the CD couldn't be scanned, resulting in CD sales that weren't being credited to Howdy Skies. Skilled radio promoter and artist manager Brad Hunt, an old friend of Barry Poss and Bev Paul, suggested they could place the barcode on the outside of the packaging to make sure that the CD/book combo actually allowed Tim to make money from those sales. This proved a fine solution until Charles Frazier, who liked the album, disapproved of marketing his book with it—and this new wrinkle added another expensive lesson when Bev, Kit, and Tim had to break up that packaging.[48]

Born in the small town of Johnson in Orange County, New York, Brad Hunt went to high school in Buffalo and on to Gettysburg College before beginning his career in radio and retail. From there, he worked first for MCA and then for Elektra, where he served as general manager for four years, before becoming senior vice-president and general manager of Zoo

Songs from the Mountain trio, from left to right: John Herrmann, Tim, and Dirk Powell (photo by Jim McGuire)

Entertainment. Brad went out on his own about the same time Tim moved to Nashville. Steve Earle, recently out of drug rehab, became his first client. In 1999 Steve toured with Del McCoury, but after two or three months into their CD release tour, the two had a falling out. Steve wanted to continue the tour with a bluegrass band, and Brad right away thought of Tim, who put a "first-rate band" together. Joining Tim were Dennis Crouch on bass, Darrell Scott on banjo, and Casey Driessen on fiddle. Casey had just graduated from high school. Tim said, "I knew him through his dad who I knew from the Colorado bluegrass scene in the '70's. He was fired up and available, so we had a band." They played festivals throughout the summer, ending with the Hardly Strictly Bluegrass Festival in October. Brad had also "negotiated an opening solo set for Tim at non-festival dates with Steve." Tim has vivid memories of heading the bluegrass backup band for the tour, giving us a clear picture of a musician's life on the road during that summer:

> We rehearsed a day in Nashville and went on the road the next week. We played Newport Folk Fest on the first few days of that summer run. After we played the Minneapolis Zoo, we headed to a country festival in North Dakota, close to the Canadian border.

We closed the show on Saturday night after Marty Stuart and then the Kentucky Headhunters, both electric bands. Then we get up on stage at about 11 PM, some of the crowd had been drinking beer all evening, and we're playing acoustically through a few mics. People were yelling for "Copperhead Road" from the get go, and Steve ignored them most of the way through the set. A few empty beer cans, a bra, and later, a half full beer can were thrown onto the stage. We ended with "Copperhead Road" each night, and then encored with "Guitar Town." It was wild and amazing how Steve just stuck to his guns, never gave an inch. He was committed to performing bluegrass the way he had learned from playing with Del, instead of us all plugging in, or even each having our own mics. We traveled by bus, I think there was one flight when we had too long of a distance between gigs. It was another experience where I didn't know much of the artist's music at the outset, and I respected his artistry much more after learning the songs and internalizing them. Steve really liked the vocal trio with Darrell and me, and he loved the freeform hippy bluegrass attitude we brought to it. Casey played every note he could think of, and Darrell just got better and better on the banjo—he'd got a real banjo for the tour and worked hard at it, and played some dobro, too.[49]

When Bev Paul decided to return to working with Sugar Hill soon after *Songs from the Mountain*, Tim and Darrell were appearing at a festival around Black Mountain and ran into Brad. As he told us, Tim asked if Brad would like to manage him, "which was a handshake deal, and that's the 'contract' under which we still operate."[50]

The 1990s began and had nearly culminated in ironically and similarly bittersweet fashion for Tim. He left Hot Rize with the expectation that the RCA contract would bring the kind of mainstream acclaim of which every musician dreams, and at the end of 1998, the hopes of achieving a major financial as well as artistic breakthrough for *Songs from the Mountain* had ultimately fizzled out. But there were many moments of glory in between. And the collaborative research and musicianship that Tim, Dirk, and John had embarked on in putting their magnificent recording together led Tim increasingly into the depths of more fulfilling projects of his own as one century closed and a new century opened.

Chapter 5

THE LURE OF IRELAND AND BACK HOME IN AMERICANA

Tim's enthusiasm for *Cold Mountain* and the consequent collaboration with Dirk Powell and John Herrmann in creating *Songs from the Mountain* likely sparked his interest in pushing his Appalachian-centered imagination back to both his real and his romantically conceived Irish roots. In the late 1990s and early 2000s the music of Ireland became Tim's principal preoccupation. Not that he considered this sensibility anything new, since he had first exhibited an interest in Irish culture at Colby. He played some Irish music in Boulder before Hot Rize was founded, visited the Emerald Isle in 1976, played Irish music during his brief sojourn in Minneapolis with Kit before they got married, and had included a few Irish tunes in his first and solo fiddle album in 1977, *Guess Who's in Town*. Still, Tim's rediscovery of his Irish great-grandfather Thomas O'Brien and his heroic walk from Cumberland, Maryland, to Wheeling in 1851 reignited Tim's interest in his presumed Celtic roots. This preoccupation then evolved into a full-scale immersion in Irish music. While Tim's Irish heritage derives from his paternal great-grandparents, there is no evidence that these or any other known Irish ancestors displayed any musical talent. This in no way diminishes the patina of his patriarchal great-grandfather's origins in Muff, a "townland" in the east of County Cavan, between Kingscourt and Bailiborough. Although Tim thinks that his great-grandmother may have hailed from Donegal, other accounts suggest that her birthplace may have been Scotland. She does not figure in his discourse like the more intimate connection he feels with his great-grandfather's story. Above all, this Irish connection and the name O'Brien gave Tim a legitimacy among Irish musicians—similar to his embracing his West Virginia origins when he moved to the Rocky Mountains—and he seldom lost an opportunity to speak of his great-grandfather's birthplace. Tim began making annual pilgrimages to Ireland in 1994, and on a trip in 1998 he actually visited the little cottage where his great-grandfather was born.[1]

This visit coincided with the end of his contract with Sugar Hill, since he had released his fifth CD that year. As Tim was considering moving in a new direction, Akira Satake—a "longtime friend" whose "musical sensibility" Tim admired—had launched Alula, a world music label. Tim approached Akira to see if they might work together, and by late 1998 they had begun to formulate plans for a major recorded exploration of Irish music.[2]

As Tim outlined in an email to us, his "initial idea was to find the intersection of Celtic and Appalachian musics." Once he got into the project, his work assumed a much more personal tone, and he began to feel that, in his performance of old southern fiddle tunes, he had actually been performing Irish music. "One day, playing an old West Virginia tune, I realized, hey, this is part of that, I am doing it after all. Maybe this is a mission I'm on, this is my Dharma or something. I feel as if everything up to now was leading to this angle. More and more I'm taking pride in being part of a tradition, even if my part is to adapt it." Tim realizes that his Irish roots do not dominate his ethnic heritage, as he told Craig Havighurst, a Nashville journalist: "Irish is just one part of my cultural background. There's the English, the German, Welsh and, I guess, a little American Indian. I'm just a mongrel, but the Irish element is somehow more fascinating because it works with all this music I've learned over the last 30 years." Nonetheless, no one can doubt his commitment to Irish music nor his ability to absorb and command its rhythms. After all, he had produced recordings of Colcannon, a Colorado-based Irish band, back in his Hot Rize years, as well as recordings of fiddler Kevin Burke's Open House band. The new project would provide Tim the opportunity to gather his "favorite players and singers on both sides of the Atlantic" who had become his friends and involve them as collaborators.[3]

In 1999 Tim's romance with the cross-fertilization of American and Irish musical styles and their presumed hybridization in the Appalachian South coalesced with the release of his most ambitious recording project, *The Crossing*. As he points out in the liner notes, "Since hearing Kevin Burke fiddle 'The Sailor's Bonnet' on an Arlo Guthrie record in 1973, I've sought Irish music wherever I could." The "common repertoire" that Tim found in the Irish antecedents shared by old-time and bluegrass musicians further piqued his interest, which was augmented as he learned about his

Irish-born great grandfather. Coupling these fascinations—music making and familial roots—he told us, "It's like I'm finished wandering around wondering what to do with my life, in fact I've been doing it all along. It reconciles the various tangents I've been on, transforming them into real tools for the task at hand."[4]

To demonstrate his musical thesis, he enlisted the talents of a wide array of American, Irish, and Scottish performers. One can debate the album's thesis—with terms like "Celtic," "Appalachian," and "Scotch-Irish" being tossed around with abandon and little precision—but, put simply, the music on the album is superb, with numerous high points. Tim played his usual assortment of instruments and also engaged Stuart Duncan, Frankie Gavin, Ciarán Tourish, and Mairéad Ní Mhaonaigh on fiddle; Edgar Meyer on arco bass; flute player Seamus Egan on bodhran—and that's just for starters. Additional musicians can be heard on a variety of other instruments, including penny whistle, low whistle, and uilleann pipes, slide guitar, and banjo. Mollie, Kathy Mattea, Jeff White, Del McCoury, and Maura O'Connell joined Tim on lead or harmony vocals. Tim opens with the hauntingly beautiful ballad "Ireland's Green Shore," inspired by an acapella version done by the Hammons Family from West Virginia, here amplified by Del McCoury's soulful harmony accompaniment. We especially like the song on which Tim and Guy Clark collaborated, "John Riley," with lyrics that tell of Irish emigrés who fought in thankless nineteenth-century wars in both the United States and Mexico. Other standouts include Tim and Kathy Mattea's duet on "Wagoner Lad," a lonesome ballad borrowed from Buell Kazee; his duet with Paul Brady on "Down in the Willow Garden"; and Tim's love song written with Craig Fuller, "A Ribbon from Your Hair," where he is joined by Maura O'Connell. His own "Mountaineers Are Always Free," a phrase that appears on the West Virginia state flag and seal, contains the refrain that repeats the motto, pairing it with "no more a wanderer, no more a refugee."

In April 1998 Tim made a pilgrimage to find his ancestral home in County Cavan, an adventure he cleverly describes in "Talkin' Cavan," an homage to Woody Guthrie's "Dust Bowl Blues." Actually, the album contains no clunkers, and the assemblage amply accomplishes Tim's mission to link the project's title to a fulfillment of his personal quest. In her review of *The Crossing* for the *Irish Times*, Victoria White's critique of the album raised issues similar to reservations we expressed about the Celtic tinge

Tim thought he found in American old-time and bluegrass music: "When you hear the magnificent Yorkshire folk singer Kate Rusby, harmonizing on Tim O'Brien's bluegrass 'Down on the Banks Below,' it makes you less certain of the specific Irish-American influence, more certain of the common ground between all folk musics, and very, very certain that we're all children of the 1960s folk revival."[5]

In 2005, Sue Kavanagh asked Tim to talk about some of his favorite musical moments, and he described the first time he presented *The Crossing* in a live performance in Dublin on January 15, 2000:

> It was an incredible thing. After sweating to get that record together and to do the subject of being Irish American justice, I finally assembled a cast that could represent it on stage. Darrell Scott and I plotted to get legends Danny Thompson and Kenny Malone to meet and play together. And Paul Brady and the members of Altan joined in. There was a tangible excitement in the room. I'd been up in Donegal a week earlier for the Frankie Kennedy week and I think the word got around the country among the traditional crowd that a cool event was going to happen in Dublin that night. The place seemed to lift off the ground.[6]

After he had exerted so much effort in conceiving, organizing, and carrying the project through successfully, the reception must have exceeded his wildest expectations and felt stunningly rewarding.

It's easy to understand why the *The Crossing* seems to have been Tim's favorite album, for he followed it in 2002 with a documentary of the same name. He joined with the Footworks Percussive Dance Ensemble to do a chronological history of the transit of Irish musical culture to the United States, featuring both traditional songs and his own compositions. The Footworks Ensemble was the creation of Eileen Carson, the wife of Tim's brilliant bass player and clog dancer, Mark Schatz. Irish step dancing or some other kind of dance sequence accompanied almost every song. As Pamela Squires noted, "both O'Brien and his superb musicians and the skilled dancers of Footworks are delighted to be in one another's production." She essentially echoed what Victoria White for the *Irish Times* had written about the album: the production "capitalized on immigrant culture's frequently idealized view of one's homeland and the fueling of this sentiment by the folk revival of the '60s."[7]

Tim continued in the Irish vein in 2001 with another CD, this one called *Two Journeys*, named for a song written by Dirk Powell and Christine Balfa, "Deux Voyages." Featuring an impressive array of both Irish and American musicians, including Dirk Powell and Darrell Scott, the album dealt with song influences that moved back and forth across the Atlantic Ocean. The CD liner notes declare that "this recording represents an ongoing celebration of the shared heritage between the USA and Ireland. Our world may continue to shrink, but it is still essential to view each other's perspectives." On the album, one hears several instrumental pieces, including an original of Tim's, "The Apple Press/The Apple Cart," written in France in 1984 while Red Knuckles and the Trailblazers were recording *The French Way* in rural Normandy. As he told us in an email, he had sat down "fiddle in hand," near an old horse-drawn apple press, and "let the music come." He and Karan Casey perform both a very traditional ballad, "Demon Lover" (also known as "The House Carpenter"), and a more recent love song, "What Does the Deep Sea Say," along with several newly composed songs, including a humorous tale built around a wild night in Ireland when Dirk fell into a bog ("Me and Dirk's Trip to Ireland") and a sweet recollection of Tim and Kit's visit to a holy spot near Union Hall, west Cork ("The Holy Well"). "Two Journeys (Deux Voyages)," beautifully sung in French by Christine Balfa's cousin Courtney Granger, and in English by Tim, makes an intriguing inclusion. Dirk and Christine wrote it to honor her father, Dewey Balfa. The song also commemorates the Acadian journeys from western France to Nova Scotia and, eventually, to Louisiana. Although not quite parallel to that of the Irish to America, this selection works nicely with the others, just as Tim's and Darrell's vocals on John Lennon and Paul McCartney's "Norwegian Wood" somehow makes a fitting final number. Tim mentioned that both Lennon and McCartney have some Irish lineage, and their compelling music, with its American antecedents, blew back across the Atlantic, recapitulating the album's thematic center. In keeping with the transatlantic mood, *The Crossing* and *Two Journeys* complement each other well.[8]

While one tends to think of Tim as being completely consumed by his own projects, he nevertheless had the strength of immense artistic energies to direct them elsewhere as well. And when his dreams of the promising solo career with RCA led to the demise of Hot Rize, the other band members followed dreams of their own. Charles played for a while with Peter

Rowan and then formed the Whippets, but his recording studio, Rancho de Ville, captured more of his interest. Pete played music with his wife, Joan, and recorded a solo album, formed Pete Wernick's Live Five band, and conducted weekend banjo camps in nearby Boulder and all around the country. Nick, after his stint with Tim in the O'Boys, returned to Boulder where he and his second wife, Helen, created a radio variety show called *eTown*, featuring a wide range of musical genres mixed with discussion about commonsense stewardship and community activism. Although Hot Rize had ceased its extensive touring as a band after 1990, Tim happily took time off from his solo ventures to participate in its celebrated reunions, playing from two to seven gigs per year. For these occasions, Hot Rize played their usual venues, including both favorite festivals and special concerts. The Strawberry Festival held special meaning for them, and some events they remembered with particular fondness. These included moments in 1992 when they played for an hour on stage at the festival after the power had gone out, and the time during a Sunday morning gospel set in the fall of 2000 when Tim, without signaling to his fellow band members, removed his clothes (except for a bathing suit), jumped off the stage, then ran and jumped into Birch Lake. The act became a ritual that he performed year after year both anticipated and accompanied by many members of the audience.[9]

Sometime during 1993 when Charles learned that he had leukemia, he still had strength enough to play gigs with the band. Even as his illness intensified, Charles and his close friend Laurie Lewis were collaborating on an album that she produced after his death as *Charles Sawtelle: Music from Rancho de Ville*, on which Tim and many other musicians played. Charles also participated in Hot Rize's extensive tour of 1996: "eleven one-nighters including both coasts," which resulted in the first Hot Rize album in over a decade, *So Long of a Journey*. Though it was not released until 2002, Nick had recorded the album surreptitiously during two concerts at the Boulder Theater in 1996. Pete said of their third live recording, "Eighteen years into the band, we'd finally have an album of us as we were on stage, just being ourselves. Way to go, Nick!" Charles had expected to mix the tapes at Rancho de Ville the following year, but he made a fateful choice in an effort to beat leukemia. His older brother, Dan, donated bone marrow for a transplant, which unfortunately only further weakened Charles, though it did somewhat subdue the disease. The tapes lingered, unmixed.[10]

The last performance of the original Hot Rize band occurred in August 1998, at the Grand Targhee Bluegrass Festival in Alta, Wyoming, as Charles's condition worsened. Pete told us, "Charles crossed the stage near the end of the set and asked me to take his breaks, and I did, and we finished the set." While Tim also played with other bands at the festival, the remaining Hot Rize members sat around, realizing this was their last time together. In the car on the way to the airport, Pete recalled, Charles rode shotgun up front, while he and Tim sat in the backseat, with Tim "massaging Charles with Woody Guthrie songs, knowing exactly what Charles needed at that moment."[11]

Two years later Charles's physical condition further deteriorated, and he went to the City of Hope in Duarte, just northeast of Los Angeles, insisting on driving to California alone. Tragically, he got pneumonia on the way. After Charles and Sumi divorced, he had had a series of relationships but never remarried. Although she remarried and was living in California, they remained friends. With Charles now dying, Sumi became the go-between with his parents so that the hospital would not be so overwhelmed by calls. He died on March 20, 1999, in Duarte, California.[12]

Nick went to Rancho de Ville after Charles's death to try to find the tapes of their Boulder concerts, but he could not locate them. About a year later his wife, Helen, found them in a closet at their home; Nick had forgotten Charles had brought them over two years before. Pete and Nick then went to Colorado Sound, where their friend Kevin Clock, who'd recorded Hot Rize and Tim, mixed the tapes for *So Long of a Journey*. Nick commented in the liner notes, that without Red Knuckles on the album, it was "just the four of us playing bluegrass the way we heard it. Charles, Tim, Pete, and I knew each other like brothers. This is what we sounded like on a good night." All three remaining Hot Rize members wrote their own essays for the liner notes. Pete commented, "Having grown up together musically, and then parting and continuing to grow in other contexts, we were now a sum of greater parts than ever. . . . What a blessing to have been a band long enough to reach that place, and what a joy to return again." Tim's testimony was the most emotional:

I miss him so much, but I hear his words come out of my mouth every hour. I mix records the way he would have. I laugh at things he showed me were funny. I know he's here inside me and I'm better for it. I'm pretty sure Nick and Pete and Frank feel the same.

I've done lots of different stuff since Hot Rize was on tour, but I'll never stop being a member of the band. The colors are too strong and they just won't wash out. I wear that uniform with pride.

The long-delayed album does exactly what only a live recording can do—it recaptures the immediacy of the moment—the next best thing to being a member of the audience on one of those two memorable nights at the Boulder Theater when Hot Rize reprised some of their stellar performances. They were happily, as Pete said, at their best.[13]

After Charles's death, Hot Rize concluded its 1999 commitments as "Charles Memorials," with various guitar players like Peter Rowan and Jeff White filling in for Charles. For over two years Hot Rize played no gigs, save for a private party in Colorado with Ronnie McCoury on guitar. In June 2002, with the release of *So Long of a Journey*, Hot Rize decided to accept some high-profile dates with a new guitar player—Bryan Sutton, the winner of numerous IBMA awards as Guitar Player of the Year. His greatest fame had been as an in-demand Nashville studio musician and a member of Ricky Skaggs's band, Kentucky Thunder. Sutton came from a country music family in Asheville, North Carolina, and has played the guitar since he was a child. He was sixteen in 1989 when he first heard Hot Rize at Doyle Lawson's festival in Denton, North Carolina. He thought they presented a "total entertainment package." Now that he would be playing with his heroes, he saw it as a "blessing in his life." With this renewed version of Hot Rize, Sutton performed his spectacular style of note-filled guitar, sang an occasional fourth part, and with Red Knuckles played a character with an ominous mien called Swayde.[14]

In 2000, when Tim and Darrell Scott finally found time to put together their first mutual recording effort with the album *Real Time*, Tim still had Charles very much on his mind. Tim's opening song, "Walk beside Me," includes lines that boldly bare his thoughts: "It's a lonesome road I have to travel. / But you will always be with me." Tim told an interviewer:

Thematically, it was putting to bed my friend Charles. . . . "Keep Your Lamp Trimmed and Burnin'" I used to sing with Charles.

Hot Rize at Rockygrass, from left to right: Pete, Tim, Nick, and Bryan Sutton
(Tim Benko photo)

And "A Memory like Mine," there's a lot of death and misery
and desperation in there. That's why I liked doing . . . "More
Love" . . . it addresses being lost in the world, but at least there's
an answer.

Every place I'd go for a year after he died was a rolling tribute
to Charles, so it was weird for a long time. I felt like he's still here
with us. We know that he's inside us now instead of standing beside
us. Then the time comes when you stop talking about him and it's
time to get on with things. . . . That's what these songs are about.
We have to get on with life, but we're not forgetting you.[15]

Darrell also shared a sense of loss on the recording. His father, Wayne,
had begun the lyrics for the second song, "With a Memory like Mine," in
1964, and Darrell completed the song and wrote the melody just before he
and Tim recorded it. Tim returns to the sense of holding onto memory in
"I'm Not Gonna Forget You," while his pleading and poignant "More Love"
provides a balm, asking that love "take us and hold us and lift us above."

Tim performing with Darrell Scott at Grand Targhee (Tim O'Brien's collection)

Perhaps the simpatico that flows between Darrell and Tim helped them adroitly balance the emotional content of the lyrics and the skilled musicianship to make this collection so satisfying. In this project, they also deliberately aimed for an informal sound, an effect similar, they hoped, to the field recordings earlier made by Alan Lomax and other folklorists. They recorded the album in Scott's home, a two-story A-frame with a corrugated tin roof, picking in the living room while microphones hung overhead. They included an a cappella version of Hank Williams's "A House of Gold" and a raucous rendition of the traditional "Little Sadie." Darrell's "Helen of Troy, Pennsylvania," tells the story of an older divorcee seducing a couple of teenage boys, while his rollicking "Long Time Gone" became a major hit for the [Dixie] Chicks two years later.[16]

Tim's solo album, *Traveler*, from 2003 offers a highly personal work, a casebook example of his role as singer-songwriter, as he mentioned at the time of its release. Ruminating about that journey is one of the overriding themes of both his lyrics and his albums. This sensibility is reflected in the liner notes: "The Australian Aboriginals speak of an individual's life as a 'songline.' You go on your walkabout, you become that line. It defines you, and that's your song." He identified his own restlessness early in his career in a song like "Brother Wind," where he personifies the wind ("Whatever pushes me / It's something only he can understand"), and he explored that impulse historically in *The Crossing* and in *Two Journeys*. Here in *Traveler*, the lyrics echo that theme even more explicitly. As Tim told an interviewer for *No Depression*: "I'm a traveler; that's what I do. . . . Being a traveling musician is something you can honor, and that's what I hope to do with this album." Tim wrote or cowrote eleven of the twelve songs on *Traveler*, all of which deal, for the most part, with life on the road. The CD is therefore more expressive of his own life as a musician than as a strictly concept album. Like any successful performer, Tim spent as much time on the way to and from Kit and his sons as he spent with them. Even though the songs might not be literally autobiographical, the yen for adventure vies with the opposite pole of yearning to be grounded—a tension without resolution. The moods swing to and fro, from the lighthearted to the more meditative. In the wistful "Travelers," he articulates the sense, "We are but travelers on a road without end / Searching for signs that the spirit may send," while in "Kelly Joe's Shoes," he muses in a more upbeat way about the places his borrowed "high-top sneakers" have seen in his travels around the world. Tim's fascination with the past can be heard in "Restless Spirit Wandering," inspired by stories told about the ghost of a Civil War soldier supposedly inhabiting the O'Briens' Nashville home. In "Family History," the lyrics reveal that "Family history will repeat, look through your history, you're sure to meet / Someone a walkin' much the same pathway as you." Ola Belle Reed's "I've Endured," though, may be the best performance on the album, with Tim's lonesome tenor singing, and Dirk Powell's opening clawhammer banjo introduction, giving this classic a distinctive "mountain" sound.[17]

One reviewer felt that on *Traveler*, "O'Brien explores both the simple and profound moments of inner and outer rambles in the eleven originals here," each song "played from the heart." Another reviewer commented that "the costs exacted by a life on the road have inspired numerous formula country tunes, but in O'Brien's hands each song deftly achieves a fresh energy." While most reviews of Tim's performances comment positively on his trio of talents—superb singing, brilliant playing, and skillful songwriting—a few have responded negatively to his singing. One reviewer, for example, commenting on "When There's No One Around," complained that while Tim's voice "belongs to a genuinely nice guy" (even though the writer didn't know him personally), he nevertheless brought "no privation and pain to the microphone." He concluded that "those of us still tripping through the darkness will take our pleasures elsewhere." While *Traveler* garnered almost universal praise, a disappointed reviewer, similar to the first, called it a "comfort album" that "does little to excite or inspire" but instead reflects the world in which Tim lives that is "comfortable, banal, and cliché and it shows up in the music."[18]

While Tim's voice typically expresses neither angst nor pain, most reviewers—including us—tend to believe that he brings a soulful warmth to his songs. And one can ask, why should Tim, who has certainly suffered loss and pain, dwell in that discomfort? Many outstanding entertainers such as Ernest Tubb, Willie Nelson, Ricky Skaggs, Roger Miller, and Doc Watson performed songs with voices that reach us in different ways from those who ask us to agonize with them—notably, George Jones, Jason Isbell, Iris Dement, or Lucinda Williams. Most critics have applauded Tim's distinctive and spot-on versatility as a singer. One may recall that back in 1977, when Tim had not yet been a lead singer, Pete Wernick thought enough of his version of "Wichita Lineman" to build a band around him.

Chris Moore became Tim's manager for the next decade, having stepped into Tim's life the same year *Traveler* was released. They first met when Chris was playing with a band called Rust Farm at festivals in the Northeast such as Grey Fox. Already aware of Chris as a songwriter, Tim joined him at his home on Peak's Island, near Portland, Maine, to produce *Snows of March*, which Rust Farm put out on their own label. Released in 2000, the album included Tim playing fiddle and bouzouki. Chris welcomed Tim's generous embrace of his talents and his support, the same traits so much appreciated by other musicians and Tim's peers in the music business. Chris told us, "I shaped what I was doing based on what I liked about Hot Rize. Musically, what's not to model yourself after? Chris Thile says that he'd like to be anything as good as Tim does when he opens his mouth to sing."[19]

After their work together in Maine, Tim encouraged Chris to move to Nashville. Chris's band, Kindling Stone (founded with Mark Wingate), played in Nashville and traveled around the Southeast when Tim and Darrell were touring. Then Tim suggested that Chris also might want to do some work for him. Chris assumed his role as a publishing liaison: coordinating with publicists, distributors, doing whatever is necessary in running a small publishing house (Howdy Skies), and then whatever Tim needed to get done at home when he was out on the road. Chris also worked with Tim's booking agent, Brad Hunt, who said that he saw his role as providing Tim with "the opportunity to work within his world." Working both at home and at Tim's, Chris truly acted as his personal assistant on many levels. As Chris said, "When you want to share your lives together, you want to be really compatible," which is an understated way of saying that Tim trusted his sound judgment.[20]

Although Tim's catholicity of taste and multifaceted endeavors have remained constant, he has always affirmed his involvement with the bluegrass community. He even served a stint as president of the IBMA, taking over the position in 2003 when Pete Wernick concluded his service of sixteen years. These two Hot Rize alumni had been the only presidents that the IBMA ever had. Tim's view of the presidency echoed that of the IBMA leadership as a whole. The position had been redesigned to be more of an ornamental or spokesman kind of leadership. At one time during his tenure he told Jonathan Pitts, "Yeah, I'm a figurehead. I don't like leaders, so I'm trying not to lead." He nevertheless had strong ideas about what bluegrass should be. Like country music as a whole, the community of bluegrass had evolved into different camps: traditional versus progressive, and fractures existed within both of those persuasions. Tim's career had taken him into many realms of musicianship, which prepared him to provide the music with the benefits of his multi-focused approach. Tim argued that the IBMA "wanted someone who hasn't just walked down the center, but who has been out on the periphery and can bring it together." In an even more direct interview with *Puremusic*, years later, he maintained that bluegrass needed to become more inclusive:

> Old time music needs to be embraced more. In some ways the kids are more into that than they are progressive bluegrass, at least a certain strata will be. I mean, the same people who love Gillian Welch will like the *Anthology of Folk Music*. So, there's that, and then the Jam Band movement, people like Leftover Salmon or The String Cheese Incident, which is a huge grossing act that started out as a Bluegrass band. And we need to be a little more involved with the commercial country market, which is kind of wondering what's happening now.

I've been places that many traditional bluegrass musicians may not have been to. John Hartford said Bluegrass is like a small town. The IBMA wants to make it a bigger town. We're not sure that's such a good thing, we like our small town. But it's a good thing to have a storehouse of information and for everyone to be aware of everybody's work in the larger field, so we can all make the most of the music.[21]

As Tim pursued his career in the early 2000s, his repertory remained wide-ranging, taking into its purview both contemporary and traditional songs. When he began preparing a new CD for 2005, he had conceived it as a project that would "show the full spectrum and diversity of folk music"—that is, "all the music that he had been playing over the years." Tim soon discovered that he had far too much material to fit on one album. He decided instead to produce two CDs simultaneously: one that would feature modern styles and instruments, both acoustic and electric, and another that would concentrate on traditional instruments. They were released in 2005 as *Fiddler's Green* and *Cornbread Nation*. The previous December, Tim had to face another loss—the imminent demise of his mother. Right after Christmas, Kit and Tim had attended Mark Schatz and Eileen Carson's wedding in Annapolis when Tim and his brother, Jim, received calls from their mother, asking that they come immediately to Wheeling. Mollie was already there. Tim recalled that Amy, courageously realistic as always, asked her children's

> permission to stop dialysis, saying it wasn't really working any-more. We didn't object, although that meant she wouldn't live very much longer. I think the next night was New Year's Eve, and she said, "I think I'll have a scotch." She talked and told us stories and . . . pretty much slept through the day and then died in the pre-dawn hours on January 2nd. She did a remarkable thing in a way: we were all there with her, and we had the funeral a few days later. She died 49 years to the day after our sister Brigid died. *Fiddler's Green* and *Cornbread Nation* were about finished then, so I dedicated those CDs to her.

The liner notes tell Tim's fans that the dedication is to his mother "whose determination, compassion, and wicked irreverence will always inspire me."[22]

Although many of the songs on both CDs come directly from the public domain, Tim's inveterate exploration of many kinds of arrangements—
from a solo with fiddle in "A Few More Years" or his vocal and fiddle and
Edgar Meyer's powerful arco bass on "Foreign Lander" on *Fiddler's Green* to
the exuberant multi-instrumental, complete with his son Joel's hambone
on "Cornbread Nation" on the companion CD of that name—show the
songwriter and arranger at his most creative. Kit illustrated the covers and
made the interior illustrations for both albums, which handsomely complement each other, reinforcing the CDs' paired relationship. Speaking of
these two albums, Tim said:

> I wanted to do the whole spectrum of folk music from one guy
> singing and playing guitar or fiddle to a full band with electric
> guitar. And that's how the pair came out, like folk music book-
> ends. *Fiddler's Green* tends toward the intimate and traditional,
> while *Cornbread Nation* is a bit funkier and tempo-driven. On both,
> however, old-time tunes sit comfortably next to originals and a few
> classic country songs by the likes of Jimmie Rodgers and Harlan
> Howard. I love stuff like "California Blues" and "Busted," which
> are like folk songs to me, and they fit with the others, and it shows
> that what is called country music is just another footstep down the
> same path. Rock and roll, a lot of that is the same too.[23]

Fiddler's Green, Tim tells us, is named for "a mythical place where old
sailors go when they die," and the title cut, as noted in the liner notes, was
written by Pete Goble, co-writer of "Colleen Malone." Several of the songs
on this lovely album, such as "Long Black Veil," "Fair Flowers in the Valley,"
"Buffalo Skinners," and "A Few More Years," deal with death in some fashion. Tim's favorite theme of travel presents itself once again in a few songs,
and he reminds listeners that "Our narrator [not unlike himself] might
just be restless . . . he wants to hop that train and leave his blues behind, or
he wishes he could afford a plane ticket home." His apt description of the
selections and their tasteful and often haunting accompaniment as "intimate" describes a quality that may help to explain why *Fiddler's Green* garnered a 2006 Grammy Award for Best Traditional Folk Album.[24] A few of
the outstanding numbers include the opening ballad, "Pretty Fair Maid in
the Garden"; Tim's original and rousing instrumental, "First Snow"; his
outstanding rendition of "Long Black Veil"; and his own rollicking "Look

Down That Lonesome Road," which won IBMA Song of the Year in 2006. This song came directly from folklorist William Ferris's book, *Mule Trader: Ray Lum's Tales of Horses, Mules, and Men*, which Ferris took from his interviews with the auctioneer. Tim said, inspired by Ray Lum's "little phrases . . . I rhymed them and told his story. I wish I had met the man." In the song, Jerry Douglas's resophonic guitar and Dan Tyminksi's harmony singing contribute to enshrining the spirit of Ray Lum.[25]

Cornbread Nation included several traditional songs, but it is decidedly modern in style. According to Tim, the album contained "more Delta and electric and southern" feeling than *Fiddler's Green*, which was "kind of mountain and Celtic and acoustic." To underscore the difference, Tim fiddled a-plenty on *Fiddler's Green* but does none of that on *Cornbread Nation*. He constructed the album around a jaunty tribute to cornbread that he wrote to accompany Ronni Lundy's collection of essays on southern cooking, *Cornbread Nation 3: Foods of the Mountain South*. Both are members of the Southern Foodways Alliance, and Tim and Ronni's friendship grew from the days she first heard him play with the Ophelia Swing Band at Telluride in 1977, their families becoming ever closer over the years. In the liner notes, he describes the album's contents as "homemade music," just like the description of cornbread in the title song. Like recipes passed along that morph from cook to cook, Tim doesn't consider traditional music a museum object: "Like good home-cooked food, it's gonna come out a little different each time you make it." *Cornbread Nation* opens with a bold and evocative version of "Hold On," graced with Mollie's bluesy harmony, Kenny Vaughan on electric guitar, Kenny Malone on conga and shaker, Dennis Crouch on bass, and Tim on guitar. His excitingly original take on traditional songs becomes an effective emotional wake-up call to the listener on numbers like "Walkin' Boss," "The Foggy, Foggy Dew," and "House of the Risin' Sun." While the lyrics of these songs convey an old-time feel, they were performed with modern instrumental backing. The electric guitar, pedal steel, and drum kits appeared on several numbers, and "The Foggy Foggy Dew"—originally performed in 1945 by Burl Ives with only a single guitar accompaniment—was embellished with tenor saxophone backing. Tim produced the album, at least in part, to show that the folk music continuum includes electric and other forms of nontraditional instruments. As he did on *Fiddler's Green*, Tim sprinkles in unexpected country classics—"Busted" and "California Blues"—and the clever original

"Runnin' Out of Memory," which he cowrote with Kit and his son Jackson. The three used the peculiar language of "computerese" to describe a failing love affair, and the inimitable voice of Del McCoury enhances the cut. Perhaps, most impressive, is the way the album showcases Tim's versatility as a singer with an always distinctive voice and style, no matter what the genre or feel. It's not surprising that in 2006 Tim also won Male Vocalist of the Year at the IBMA.[26]

Ever on a quest to create a set of challenges to scale, Tim set out to fulfill still another long-standing goal: to record a true solo album, which he accomplished in 2008 with the release of *Chameleon*. He later told Dave Stallard, "It was the one thing I hadn't done yet. It's been nagging at me. I've done many solo shows over the years, so I know there is a certain intimacy that I like about it. It's really simple—corporate downsizing." Tim wrote most of the songs, with only two collaborators—David Olney and John Hadley on "The Garden" and "Chameleon"—and he played all the instrumental accompaniment on guitar, bouzouki, mandolin, fiddle, mandola, and banjo. He told his listeners in the liner notes, "My songs mostly start with me and an instrument." Appending this statement in the interview, Tim explained, "The songs pick the instruments, mostly. But then you want more of the instruments, so you write songs for them. There's this intrigue about which instrument it should be and featuring instruments to get more textures and more sounds in there. I was just trying to give it my best shot with this solo direction and give this bunch a breadth, to make it as wide as possible and interesting to listen to."[27]

Since his early days at Forerunner in Nashville and his collaboration with songwriters for whom he had both respect and simpatico, Tim felt increasingly comfortable with more autobiographically based material. The idea for "Chameleon" came from a childhood memory of buying a chameleon at a circus the O'Brien family attended. Like so many little reptiles bought in similar situations, the chameleon got lost, then sometime later was found behind the TV where its coloration had adapted to the picture tube, which kept the lizard warm. Tim philosophically pondered its fate: "I wonder about how healthy it is to change your appearance (or actions) just to fit in, but I suspect we all do it sometimes." In the outstanding opening song, "Where's Love Come From," Tim talks about his mother's death (January 2, 2005), as she said, "Here I go," followed by "The hardest thing in life I do / Is to try to say good-bye to you." Tim had traveled a long way from his perceptions of feeling neglected during his mother's grieving for Brigid, and the resolution here expresses how much he'd come to terms with his emotions as a toddler. In "Megna's," another Wheeling-based song, he recalls Mr. Megna shouting out the produce he's ready to deliver from his pickup to those up and down the street where the O'Briens lived. But Tim also grappled with some philosophical, social, and political issues, protesting mixed with gentle humor on numbers such as "Chameleon," "World of Trouble," "Father, Forgive Me," and "When in Rome"—all delivered with his fine acoustic finger work and distinctive warm voice. The instrumentation on "The Garden," hauntingly lyrical in its evocation of unrequited love, is especially appealing. The album, then, can be appreciated on many levels, recalling Mike Seeger's ability to entertain masterfully on so many instruments, but here with the bonus of Tim's compelling singing and songwriting. As reviewer George Graham wrote, for *Chameleon*: "O'Brien bucked the tendency to add more and bigger musical backing on his CD, and instead opted for a literally pure solo album, recorded essentially live. Not a lot of artists could pull this off and have it remain interesting and engaging for close to an hour as O'Brien. . . . His performances on his various guitars, mandolins, bouzoukis and fiddles are first-rate and help to add further interest to the recording. Perhaps the tongue-in-cheek nature of the title cut sums up the chameleon's own persona: "What's on his mind we'll never know / His true colors never show," which says a great deal about the twenty-first-century society in which we live.[28]

Until the punishing summer season of 2020 caused by the COVID-19 pandemic, festivals remained a mainstay of bluegrass and Americana musicians' lives, and the Hardly Strictly Bluegrass Festival, held at Golden Gate Park in San Francisco (Speedway Meadows) became one of the favorites among the many festivals where Tim appeared. The event was the brainchild of Warren Hellman, a San Francisco native, both a well-rounded banjo-playing athlete and an extremely successful investor. He co-founded Hellman & Friedman, one of the industry's leading private equity firms, and his many civic-minded philanthropies included founding the festival. Although devoted to the music of Hazel Dickens and playing with his old-time band, the Wronglers, he also appreciated other forms of roots music, especially that of Emmylou Harris and Jimmie Dale Gilmore, who are not bluegrass musicians. Thus, the name, "Hardly Strictly." Hellman's generous funding keeps the festival free to the public, a gift that has continued since his death in 2011 at the age of seventy-seven. Tim estimated that about one hundred thousand people attended in October 2009, while he was performing "With a Memory Like Mine," accompanied by Mike Bub, Casey Driessen, Kenny Malone, Darrell Scott, and Mollie. Tim also sat in with the well-known comedian and superb banjo player Steve Martin, and played in the final set of the day with Steve Earle's Bluegrass Dukes. Since the weather turned out to be typically San Francisco chilly, he felt "glad to be wearing a Fishing Music ball cap and a polyester blend all black jersey. . . . About 40 minutes into the set, my fingers felt like stones, the only feeling the sting of the strings as they vibrated against the fingertips." He also experienced an acutely mystical moment during the festival, as he later described it:

> When it came time for my solo on Darrell's song "With a Memory Like Mine," I closed my eyes and thought of my long-lost brother Trip, who died in Vietnam back in 1968. I got lost in the music and when I finished and looked up, four Canada geese were flying right over the stage against a clear blue sky. The sight took my breath away. . . . I decided the four were Trip, my mom (both former marines), Charles Sawtelle, and Frank Edmonson, my departed Hot Rize cohorts.[29]

Tim had been a dominating presence in bluegrass and acoustic music up through the first decade of the twenty-first century, constantly leading bands or pursuing solo projects. It is ironic, then, that he closed out that decade touring as a sideman with Mark Knopfler, a major British entertainer. Mark Freuder Knopfler, born in Glasgow, Scotland, is a rock musician, a brilliant guitarist and producer who came to fame as a member of the rock band Dire Straits. An ardent partisan of country and other forms of roots music, he often played with Chet Atkins and had fronted a band called the Notting Hillbillies.

Tim often accompanied other entertainers on their occasional CDs or in concerts, but these were short-term episodes, and none was as high-profile as the association with Knopfler. Tim obtained this coveted gig because his friend and fiddler John McCusker, who had been part of Knopfler's crew, went on paternity leave and recommended Tim. Knopfler did not need much persuasion. He had earlier described Tim as "a master of

American folk music, Irish music, Scottish music—it doesn't matter; a fine songwriter and one of my favorite singers."[30]

Describing the association with Knopfler as "the holy grail of sideman gigs," Tim toured with the rock star for four weeks in April and May 2010. Tim played fiddle, mandolin, acoustic and electric guitars, bouzouki, and banjo and chimed in on vocals, giving him, as he put it, "a glimpse into another world." The gig included three weeks of paid (and very posh) rehearsal time in London and touring in a private jet. He nevertheless had some reservations about doing the stint. In a lengthy interview with Edward Morris, Tim said, "quite honestly, I wasn't going to take it. I saw the show that Knopfler did in Nashville, and I tried to imagine it through the eyes of the guy I ended up replacing. I thought, 'why does he need that guy? Everybody wants to hear Mark play guitar and sing his songs, and they want to sing along to the songs.'" Tim also wondered about adapting to a role he hadn't played since the Ophelia Swing Band days and confessed, "I didn't know if I could be a sideman. It's a much smaller cog than I'm used to being anymore. It's totally full without it. But when I got to the rehearsals, after several days, I realized he just likes the textures. He's been using folk instruments in recent years to sort of broaden the sound and keep him occupied, keep him interested. He's expanding his vision."[31]

Tim played only on the American leg of Knopfler's worldwide tour, but the experience left a deep impression. At that time, he told an interviewer for *Me and Thee Coffeehouse*, "Great gig in Boston! I learned a lot—how well you can be rehearsed for instance, also how good the production can be, and how to play less to make a bigger sound. It's serious business, he doesn't mess around. I liked playing electric guitar on a few. Killer players. Mark's a true gentleman, commands a lot of respect and gives plenty back." Although Tim had never been big on rehearsals, those with Knopfler offered him a whole new dimension to the concept. Those three intensive weeks in London came with lots of staff and state-of-the-art equipment: "It was funny staying in the same hotel room for that long." Tim said that "each person in the band had a different monitor mix, with an inner-ear monitor mold made specifically for each musician's ears. They're tweaking what you're doing. Each song had a digitally programmed mix. It's a different world being a sideman. I learned so much working with Mark, who directed the rehearsals all the way through." Recalling his participation in one of Knopfler's last gigs in the United States, at Rev. Ike's huge church in

Harlem, Tim told *M Music Mag*: "There I was playing in Manhattan for a sold-out crowd. When I was warming up, I thought—this is really, really cool. Here I am in Mark Knopfler's band—playing clawhammer banjo. I never thought I'd be here. It was cool to look out there, and it's also weird because that's what you've wanted to do. Then you do it, and think—it worked. I did it. And maybe I'll never do it again, and I can accept that too."[32]

Tim's most faithful fans probably view the Knopfler gig with some bemusement. They understand Tim's awe at being associated, if only temporarily, with a glamorous internationally revered rock star, but they also might feel that Knopfler should be the one most impressed. Measured in terms of musicianship and breadth of interest, Tim is every bit as talented and influential. And while impressed with the company he was keeping and the venues in which he was playing with Knopfler, Tim continued to push his own projects forward: he still kept busy being Tim O'Brien. "On a ten-day break between rehearsals and the tour start," he told his fans, "I went home and mixed a new record. It's now mastered and the art work is coming along. Its title is *Chicken and Egg.*"[33]

Released in 2010, *Chicken and Egg* was Tim's thirteenth album and concentrated at least obliquely on the changes taking place in his life. It carried a philosophical but whimsical message, noting the cycle of birth, aging, and death that ultimately becomes the reality for every human being. His mother had died five years earlier, and his father had passed away the year before at the age of ninety-six. His parents' passing and his two sons going out on their own brought home the realization that a generation had gone. Mortality beckoned, which Tim expressed in the title itself. On the whole, the album is a trademark display of his eclecticism, presenting a few old-time numbers like "My Girl's Waiting for Me" and Hal Cannon's adaptation of "Suzanna," and other songs written or co-written by Tim. One song carried lyrics from a poem, "The Sun Jumped Up," left behind by Woody Guthrie, which Tim put to a melody. The first song on the CD is called "You Ate the Apple?" and offers a humorous take on the confrontation between God and Adam and Eve and the sober understanding that life would forever present a stream of difficult choices. Tim dedicated the album to his father, with one of Frank O'Brien Jr's favorite sayings on the cover, "I have never had bad ham. I've had some that's better than others, but I've never had bad ham," telling the world that his long life had mostly been blessed with the good. Tim wrote two of the songs, "Not Afraid o' Dyin'" and "Letter in the Mail," directly about him. The songs recall examples of his dad's preoccupations and puzzlements, concerns shared perhaps by most elderly parents: reading a book, paying a bill, driving the widows to lunch, dozing off, forgetting what he was saying, asking about the grandchildren, expressing to Tim a concern about something called downloading and wondering how it would affect Tim's music career. Over-all, despite some of its somber themes, the reviewer Edward Morris noted that the album had "a sprightly string band effervescence that seems to pro-pel it from the speakers like champagne bubbles."[34] Into every life, however, come champagne bubbles that have already burst, and Tim's life proved no exception.

★ ★ **★** ★ ★

Chapter 6

PURSUING NEW DIRECTIONS

In the fall of 2009 Kit joined Tim for a tour in New Zealand with Gerry Paul, from Wellington, New Zealand, and Trevor Hutchison from Dublin. Tim knew Gerry from producing his traditional Irish band Grada's recording for Compass Records, and both Gerry and Tim were friendly with Trevor, a bass player with the Irish band Lunása. The three musicians, Tim noted, "actually made a record together before we were ever in the same room together." Gerry and Tim recorded some tracks in Nashville, which they sent to Trevor. They called their CD the *Two Ocean Trio* "as in Atlantic and Pacific." They were selling the CD on their tour, first on the South Island and then on the North, including the Wellington Folk Festival. Unfortunately, right before their Auckland gig, Tim learned that his father had died on October 26, from prostate cancer. Tim and Kit flew home to Nashville where they gathered the boys and drove to Wheeling.[1]

When they returned to New Zealand for the postponed tour four months later, on February 22 Christchurch suffered a magnitude 6.3 earthquake. It caused major damage in the city and in nearby Lyttelton. In all, 185 people lost their lives. Fortunately, Kit and Tim were not hurt. Unfortunately, however, the quake inadvertently contributed to a seismic shift in their marriage. Tim told us that he had skyped Jan Fabricius to tell her that he and Kit had escaped unscathed, and Kit saw the message. Tim said, "Kit asked who Jan was, and I could have lied, but I chose to let the truth be told." This happened at the start of the tour, and although Kit came to a few shows, she flew home early. Tim's brother, Jim, and his wife were vacationing and had joined Tim and Kit in New Zealand, which must have made the situation even more awkward.[2]

Although the New Zealand incident may have sparked Tim and Kit's breakup, his involvement with Jan did not solely lie at the root of the marriage's dissolution. Despite the apparent harmony of their marriage, Tim told us, his relationship with Kit had been troubled for some years. "I had painted a simple picture of my marriage to Kit for years in interviews, and I believed the overall happy part, and still do, but it was way more complicated," he told us. "I am proud of my sons and how they've grown into fine men, and I'm proud of my part in that," he added, because Tim assured us that he tried to be a good husband and father, even if he did not always succeed. In a 1999 article, he had been quoted as saying that "there's always a need to put music into perspective. With my songwriting success, I have the luxury of playing the music *I* want to play. I build in enough time to be home, and the kids know I'm there for them. I feel I'm modeling to them to follow their dreams." He stressed the need for dinner time to be family time. "The phone is turned off and that time is ours."[3]

Tim claimed that both he and Kit drank too much and that he smoked too much pot. Of course, life on the road for a touring musician carried many temptations. Tim has been honest in saying, "Part of this is being a traveling 'on stage guy,' being a child of the 60s in the 'free love' world, which I experienced, but only after I was married. But it was a slippery slope . . . not really dealing with my own marriage." Tim believed that the worst aspect of infidelity is "lying to your partner, the one person you're supposed to be able to share everything with. My own problem with honesty preceded my infidelity. I have a bad habit of stuffing problems and not confronting them, and that's been the main source of my honesty problem." He mentioned that "a couple of times when young couples were engaged to be married, they told one or the other or both of us that we were their role model for how a musician could have a solid marriage. We both would privately cringe in reaction because we knew we had trouble in our marriage." But ultimately, Kit decided their marriage was over. There is a bit of dark humor in his remark, "Someday I'll write a song: 'When you finally gave up on me's when I gave up on you.'"[4]

In 2010 Tim and Kit had acquired a second smaller home in Joelton, less than thirty minutes northeast of Nashville, initially purchased as a site for writing and painting. Tim said, "It was always more Kit's place," since it was built by an artist as a retreat. She concurred, telling us that the main part of the house is "a painting studio with great northern light." Kit was already spending most of her time there even before the marriage ended. Since their divorce in 2012, she has continued to live there and paint.[5]

Jan Fabricius grew up in western Kansas, the third generation of a German family from Russia. Her father worked five decades as a postal employee and also farmed wheat and raised some cattle; her mother was a registered nurse. An amateur mandolin player and an ardent fan of bluegrass and old-time music, Jan got into that music "partly" through her older sister Diane and her guitar-playing husband, although Jan was already listening to the Nitty Gritty Dirt Band and Pure Prairie League. At eighteen, she moved to Lindsborg, Kansas, and, two years later, traded Diane a sewing machine for a mandolin. Jan regularly began attending the famous Walnut Valley Festival in Winfield, Kansas, in 1976, missing only once, in 1980, when she was eight months pregnant. She was married for twelve years and had two sons and lived in the country in northwest McPherson County. When Jan's younger son started kindergarten, she put herself through nursing school by working as a medication aid at Bethany Home in Lindsborg. She graduated in 1989, divorced in 1991, and moved to Galva, Kansas, where she worked as an ICU cardiac nurse at a hospital in Halstead, about thirty-five minutes away. She said that her two sons grew up at the Walnut Valley Festival, spending time there year after year, and she first heard Tim there with Hot Rize in the late 1970s and saw him at other festivals as well.[6]

While living in Galva, she first met and chatted with Tim at the campgrounds during the Winfield festival where he had been "jamming with Mollie and the girls from the band Ranch Romance." They had just played "Beer Barrel Polka," and as he put his mandolin away, they struck up a conversation. Two years later at Winfield, "while walking around listening to music, I once again ran into Tim in the campgrounds and I was impressed that he had remembered my name, where I worked and everything we had talked about." She told us, "we had a brief affair," but she had no illusions about their relationship, knowing that Tim was married and committed to making it work. Despite their feelings for each other, she went on working and raising her sons. Although Tim sent Jan an occasional letter or postcard, she never responded, and a few years before the fateful Skype, they had agreed not to see each other. Jan said that the message from New Zealand came "out of the clear blue," since she had no idea that an earthquake had occurred or that Tim and Kit were there. Jan was just glad to know they were safe.[7]

She became an increasingly strong presence in Tim's life after his marriage's dissolution. After Kit moved permanently to Joelton, Tim called Jan on September 1, 2011. She said, "He told me he would like to get to know me better." By that time, Jan had moved to Wichita, and Tim went there to visit her at the end of the month. They were now free to admit, as Tim put it, that they "were and are deeply in love." In November, they went on "an eleven-day date in New York City," as part of a tour Tim was making to New York and Maine that fall (it was her first trip east). "We made time to see each other when I wasn't working or on call and had enough PTO [paid time off] built up and could get away," Jan continued. The following spring, Jan accompanied him to Ireland where he toured with Arty McGlynn. These longer times together helped them both recognize that their relationship was definitely solidifying. She wrote that, in September 2012, when visiting Tim in Nashville, he "asked me to move in with him eventually, so when he was off the road, at least I would be there."[8]

Initially, she and Tim planned to sell both their homes and find something new together. After fixing up the house for the market, Jan's home sold in April 2013. The following month, "after almost 2 years of courting and a long-distance relationship, I moved to Nashville with the help of both of my sons to be with Tim." His house, on the other hand, did not sell, so he and Jan modified their plans. Although the house required some extensive repairing and remodeling, Jan and Tim both realized that remaining there ultimately would make life easier because it already fitted his music needs. When Jan moved in, she not only thoroughly cleaned, organized, and addressed the extensive repairing of the house, she assumed both Chris Moore's job as tour manager and his wife's paid help for housekeeping and yard work. Having Jan as a partner saved the couple money, but her presence addressed many more aspects of Tim's life than the practical.[9]

Although Kit had supported Tim in many ways, she was not a musician. Playing music together created a different kind of bond. As Tim told us, "Jan and I are doing our best to be partners and make the music ours as well. We enjoyed playing fiddle tunes together. It was great playing music around the house with someone else, just for fun." He found that "the most important thing is that we do make music together. It's worth it. It's like making a commitment. Though we're not married, the musical bond has strengthened the relationship." They have worked steadily to build a life together, to support one another, and eventually, "grow old together." In December 2020, Jan and Tim announced their engagement.[10]

When Tim recorded *Pompadour* in 2015, Jan sang background vocals on several songs, an experience that emboldened her to sharpen her skills on the mandolin as well. Since that time, she has become a regular and confident part of the vocals, and Tim has moved back to the guitar, giving her more opportunity to play the mandolin in his performances. On his website in 2020, he noted that he and Jan had been singing "informally since she became my partner seven years ago, and she's always had a real natural way with the harmony, kinda pasting her sound onto mine." Tim wrote "You Were on My Mind This Morning" about Jan, and in 2014 the song appeared on the Hot Rize album *When I'm Free*. He and Jan co-wrote "The Other Woman," and she sang lead on the song when it was released on the 2019 album, *Tim O'Brien Band*. As Tim said in his bio, "The three guys in the band are really close to us, but Jan and I are the inner circle, and it feels great."[11]

Notwithstanding the immense changes in his personal life before he and Jan began performing and recording together, Tim remained ever the professional musician: writing songs, collaborating, performing, and producing CDs. His repertory during this past decade has remained far-ranging, and his method of marketing continues to be highly varied. His rate of CD production, however, has shown a steady decline—a consequence, primarily, of changes in the music industry. Earlier in his career he recognized that having a new CD on the merchandise table for each new season was indispensable, but now CDs no longer retain the primacy they once held for fans.

Tim departed from his solo efforts briefly in 2012 when he joined with a few members of his family to pay tribute to one of his and Mollie's child-hood heroes, Roger Miller. Both Kit and Tim's sons and Mollie and Rich's daughters grew up with their parents performing. Not surprisingly, the kids are likewise talented. Both generations shared, as Tim put it, "plenty of common ground on the kind of music we liked." Mollie and Tim had enjoyed playing at the Shetland Folk Festival in the Shetland Islands in the early 1990s, and they thought they could try a family band performance there in 2006. Brigid Moore, Mollie and Rich's daughter, was away at college and couldn't accompany them. But the rest of the family went to the folk festival where Jack played bass, Joel did hambone and clog dancing, and the Moore's younger daughter, Lucy, sang. Living in disparate locations, the family members had rehearsed by phone. Tim explained, "We made a plan on material but didn't ever play a note together until we got there. The kids all enjoyed themselves."[12]

Mollie and Tim had talked about doing a family tour, but Tim wanted to put out a recording first. He recalled how the album serendipitously took shape:

> One time at a dinner in Colorado at a friend's house, "Doo Wacka Doo" or something came on the stereo, and somebody said we should just make a record of all Roger Miller songs. We all chuckled and said, yeah, maybe that's it. So, we made a plan, somehow got a booking at Grey Fox festival, which paid for flights from Colorado, and then to Nashville where we played a sorta house concert in a fiddle shop. The next day we set up a studio in my house. I had my piano tuned for Lucy to play, and we hired old standby drummer and good friend John Gardner to play drums. Dave Ferguson engineered. . . .
>
> Between the start of the plan and the actual recording, Kit and I broke up, and there was certainly a question of would we follow through with the recording. I asked everyone individually if they still wanted to do it, and they all said yes. It could be viewed as either foolhardy or brave to attempt it, and it was probably a little of both. In my case I thought that, given the breakup, it might be especially good for us all to spend that time together with the potential of more time spent playing shows after the release.[13]

As Susan Viebrock wrote, "Any new Tim O'Brien album is cause for breaking out the champagne, doubly so when he is joined by his sister Mollie, because there is nothing like genetic stew for producing the tastiest (and tightest) harmonies." The more O'Briens the merrier, in fact, seemed to spark this thoroughly enjoyable collective effort. Tim had always admired Roger Miller's ability as a songwriter to encompass the whole span of human emotions in his songs, from the absurd to the sad and poignant, and to tailor his songs to the specific styles of entertainers as divergent as Ernest Tubb and Jim Reeves. Calling themselves the O'Brien Party of Seven, Tim, Jackson and Joel, along with Mollie, Rich, Lucy, and Brigid, sat down in Tim's music room in Nashville and, over the course of a few fun-filled days, recorded the album. According to Mollie, "it was comfortable, a great environment. When someone was recording their piece, someone else was cooking—we have a lot of good cooks in the family." They called the resulting album *Reincarnation: The Songs of Roger Miller.*[14]

This album, and Tim's previous recorded performances of the songs of Bob Dylan, mark the only times in his career that he failed to include songs of his own making. Tim deferred to his family in most of the songs' performances, taking the lead on only three: "In the Summertime," "Hand for the Hog," and "King of the Road." Except for these, the group ignored Miller's biggest hits, instead choosing material demonstrating both his quirkiness and his wide range of interests. Two of the songs, "Guv'ment" (performed by Jackson) and "Hand for the Hog," came from Miller's 1985 Broadway tribute to Huckleberry Finn, *Big River.* Each member of Tim's family participated actively in the making of the CD: Lucy and Brigid did a lovely duet on "You're My Kingdom"; Mollie contributed one of the best moments with "Train of Life"; and Joel sang lead on "As Long as There's a Shadow" and supplied hambone rhythms on "Hand for the Hog." Tim played seven instruments, and Rich added a different dimension with the electric and resonator guitars. The family did not promote the album widely, and the family tour portion of the plan was difficult to achieve because their kids were embarking on "their separate ways to college, to internships, to Jackson getting married and moving to Minneapolis." But the O'Briens and Moores did enjoy performing the songs on the Fred Shellman stage at Telluride on Friday, June 22, 2012. Tim referred to the entire project as a "lark," and "a means by which the family could be brought together for something other than funerals and weddings." Although he felt that "the record bombed," he remained "proud of it." The process of bringing everyone together and having a great time, even under less than ideal circumstances, undoubtedly proved more valuable than any commercial success.[15]

While Tim vigorously pursued his own independent course of avant-garde musical expression, he never abandoned his love for traditional songs and styles. His absorption with roots musical forms led to his involvement in celebrations that commemorated Woody Guthrie and the great American folk music collector Alan Lomax. Tim recorded an occasional Woody Guthrie song and, in 2012, joined an all-star cast of American musicians—including Arlo Guthrie, John Mellencamp, Ry Cooder, Rosanne Cash, Judy Collins, Ani DiFranco, Old Crow Medicine Show, and others—that celebrated the centennial birthday of the Oklahoma balladeer. During the year-long celebration Tim played with the Del McCoury Band in Tulsa on March 10 and, again with McCoury, at the Kennedy Center in Washington, DC, on October14, performing songs like "So Long, It's Been Good to Know You," "The Sun Jumped Up," and "Woody's Rag," the only all-instrumental tune that Guthrie composed.

Tim's involvement in the Alan Lomax Project came through the encouragement of Jayme Stone, an ultra-progressive banjo player from Vancouver, Canada, who had set out in 2013 to commemorate the internationally famous collector and folklorist. The project gathered samples of the material that Lomax originally collected in his excursions in the United States and around the world. Working with the Colorado Chautauqua Association, Stone wrote a successful grant proposal that involved bringing together a group of musicians at Chautauqua, an arts center in Boulder. They gathered for a week-long residency to listen to recordings in the Alan Lomax archive and then rearrange them to create a series of new performances and workshops. At the Boulder concert, Tim talked about traditional songs, presumably collected by the Lomaxes (Alan and his father, John), that he had reworked through the years. For example, he and Darrell Scott wrote "Music Tree," inspired by "Turtle Dove," which initially came from one of the Lomax field recordings.[16]

Tim returned to his collaboration with Darrell Scott in 2012 and 2013. The songs on *We're Usually a Lot Better Than This* (2012), though, had originally been recorded in 2005 and 2006 for a couple of benefit shows for the Arthur Morgan School, a progressive middle school in Burnsville, North Carolina, in which both Joel and Darrell's daughter Mahala were enrolled at the time. The album vividly captures the spontaneity and downhome improvisation of their stage show, while also showcasing the impressive diversity of both their singing and musicianship. They performed mostly standard numbers like "White Freightliner," "Mom and Dad's Waltz," "Early Morning Rain," and "House of Gold" and also presented a few original pieces, including Darrell's powerful autobiographical "Long Time Gone."

In 2013 Tim and Darrell produced an album, *Memories and Moments*, recorded for Full Skies, an amalgam of the two men's record labels. In an interview later that year, Tim and Darrell explicitly affirmed the obvious joy they found in working together: "'Our strength is playing in the moment,' says Scott, 'so if you record that way, with us across from each

other, leaking into each other's mics, there's an immediacy to it that trans-
lates to the listener. That's our hope, anyway.'" Tim concurred, "We wanted
to keep that intimate feeling. . . . It's rare that you can play with somebody
who can respond and magnify like Darrell does."[17] They included ten of
their own songs, plus four borrowed from other songwriters. "Keep Your
Dirty Lights On," co-written by Tim and Darrell, complained about the
consuming public's complicity in the coal industry's pillage of the southern
hills. Though generally lighthearted in tone, the song nevertheless was a
bold statement for a West Virginia boy to make about his state's chief industry. On still another statement about King Coal's ravages, "Paradise," they
were joined by the song's composer, John Prine, who recalled his ancestral
Kentucky homeplace obliterated by "Mr. Peabody's coal train." Speaking of
Prine, Tim said "just to have John Prine answer the phone when you call
him is an honor. He's a national treasure and to have him singing on our
album is still unbelievable for me." "Just One More," a searing honky-tonk
lament came from the pen of George Jones who had originally recorded it.
On "Alone and Forsaken," an anguished song of unrequited love from the
repertory of Hank Williams, Tim and Darrell sang the first few bars a cappella and then completed the song backed with acoustic instrumentation.
Along with "House of Gold," they had highlighted this song in their stage
shows, evidence of the binding role that Hank played in their music.[18]

A bonafide progressive in his receptivity to many forms of music, Tim
also remained faithful to traditional music and loyal to his bluegrass roots.
In 2013 he eagerly accepted an invitation to be a member of a brand-new
revival act, the Earls of Leicester, which took its name from a clever play on
words honoring the bluegrass pioneers Lester Flatt and Earl Scruggs and
the Foggy Mountain Boys. Remembering with affection the music heard
during his childhood, Jerry Douglas conceived the group as a tribute. A
session Douglas did with Charlie Cushman and Johnny Warren served as
his initial inspiration because the three together sounded like the front
line of the Foggy Mountain Boys. Warren reenacted the part of his dad,
the fiddler Paul Warren. Charlie Cushman assumed the role of Earl
Scruggs, with his dazzling three-finger banjo style. Douglas recruited Barry
Bales to play the part of bassist Jake Tullock (Cousin Jake), and Shawn
Camp took on the role of Lester Flatt. Jerry himself, of course, "became"
Josh Graves, the hero who had contributed his distinctive dobro style. Tim
was invited to sing Curly Seckler's tenor parts and play the mandolin, a

The Earls of Leicester win a Grammy in 2014, from left to right: Shawn Camp, Jerry Douglas, Charlie Cushman, Johnny Warren, and Tim (Tim O'Brien's collection)

role he happily assumed. Seckler had actually played the mandolin infrequently; Flatt and Scruggs hired him because of his searing tenor vocal style. The invitation suited Tim to a T:

> I loved Curly Seckler like crazy. That was my favorite. When Hot Rize was traveling around, Pete, he's teaching us all as we go along, giving us lectures as we drive across the country and listening to them sing. I loved Monroe stuff, and the Stanley stuff, but Curly just had this breezy light tenor. It just sounded right—always. And with Shawn, it's the right range for singing. It's not too high for me. It's a blast to do this. We all knew those parts already, but playing together with that intention was like playing an old record, except you're actually down in the grooves of it.[19]

Jerry had envisioned the Earls of Leicester as an occasional event band, but they lasted long enough to perform a few concerts, record three fine CDs, and win a Grammy award. To his regret, although Tim shared a Grammy award with his partners, he could not remain with the band throughout their short career. With Hot Rize about to release their first record since *So Long of a Journey* in 2002, Tim didn't want to miss the excitement of touring extensively with the band to promote it.

Hot Rize truly seemed like the band that would never go away. In 2014 with a new album, *When I'm Free*, and a year of touring, Pete, Nick, Bryan, and Tim found that their old magic still came alive as they played in festivals all over the country. Their old sidekicks Red Knuckles and the Trailblazers, of course, were back on the bus, ostensibly cleaning the vehicle but actually warming the hearts of fans everywhere—especially who really preferred seeing them. In an interview with WOUB, at Ohio University in Athens, Tim said: "Yes, Red Knuckles is back, too. He's come into his money in recent years. His son Verbal patented the massively successful curved shower curtain rod and rewarded his dad with a new doublewide and financial independence, but Red still likes to play music, so they're back out. It's a little threatening to hear that they got booked as a headliner at the big Rocky Grass Festival in Colorado in July. I wonder if they'll ask us to play with them there."[20]

The band recorded *When I'm Free* in 2013, sitting in a circle without headphones, close enough that they could hear each other, so "it was like you'd play music with your friends." The album contained all new material, mostly originals by all band members. Recorded in Nick's *eTown* studios in

Red Knuckles & The Trailblazers performing on the band's fortieth anniversary tour, Raleigh, North Carolina, November15, 2018. From left to right: Waldo Otto, Red Knuckles, Wendell Mercantile, and Swayde (Rob Laughter photo).

Boulder, Colorado, the album essentially reaffirmed the Rocky Mountain Myth. Released the following year, *When I'm Free* was nominated for IBMA's Album of the Year. For the next twelve months, Hot Rize performed more than ninety shows, including a trip to Europe. In 2018, the band reached its milestone fortieth anniversary, celebrated at the Boulder Theatre, where they were joined by their super musician friends Jerry Douglas, Sam Bush, and Stuart Duncan.[21]

Tim did not record another solo album until 2015, when he released *Pompadour* on his own Howdy Skies label. The album had taken root about three years earlier when Tim welcomed to Nashville a couple of musician friends, Gerry Paul from New Zealand and Trevor Hutchinson from Dublin. Jam sessions soon led to a recording session, and some of the resulting cuts ultimately appeared on *Pompadour*. On the album, Tim's most venturesome yet, he played electric guitar on some cuts, did some scat singing, and brought a trumpet and marimba into the mix. Only one song, Billy Bragg's melodic arrangement of some Woody Guthrie lyrics, "Down to the Water," was remotely traditional in style. The others included a James Brown soul classic, "Get Up Off of That Thing," featuring Tim on the five-string banjo, and a nonsensical boasting song called "Ditty Boy Twang." Tim described the CD as "a breakup record. I separated from my wife four years ago and got divorced a year after that." George Graham wrote, "Though there are songs about love affairs that are not exactly in the smooth sailing mode, the tone of the album remains fairly upbeat, and he and his musical colleagues are clearly having fun." Since Jan performed as one of the musical colleagues on *Pompadour*, we know that smoother sailing lay ahead.[22]

In these days of multidimensional activity, Tim found that many of the traditional vehicles of music exposure—LPs, tapes, CDs—were slipping away from him and other musicians. On January 6, 2015, he and Jan established a new marketing venture, Short Order Sessions, available on all digital music outlets including iTunes and Amazon. Tim told a *Mandolin Café* interviewer: "I've seen LPs, then cassettes, now CDs, come and go. The traditional album set of 10 or more songs is less viable, so is the record store that sells them. Single song releases and downloads have taken over, so Short Order Sessions is my quiet folky way of staying current." On his website, Tim cleverly described the intent of this new mode of song delivery:

Welcome to my musical kitchen. I've long viewed musical arrangements as recipes and know well that music feeds the heart and
soul. Short Order Sessions cooks up fresh sounds and delivers
them while they're still hot.

You can find Short Order Sessions tracks under my name on
all your digital outlets including iTunes and Amazon. Starting in
2016 one new track a month will be released. Ranging from rare
live performances and obscurities from various compilations to
one-off jams in my music room, Short Order Sessions will keep
you fed with new audio soul food. My pan is seasoned and the pan-
try's stocked, so come for a visit and tell your friends about Short
Order Sessions.[23]

A duet with Kathy Mattea, "Brush My Teeth with Coca-Cola," debuted
the Sessions. Inspired by a chemical spill in the Charleston area that con-
taminated the water supply of thousands of West Virginia residents, the
song served as a social comment. On his blog, Tim wrote that the tragedy
"woke many of us to the fragile nature of the environment," and that it was
"more important than ever to remain vigilant and to hold industry account-
able. We take tap water for granted, so imagine three hundred thousand
people suddenly scrambling for enough water to cook and bathe with, a
whole community stressed and afraid." Tim also mentioned that the "pro-
ceeds from 'Brush My Teeth with Coca-Cola' were to benefit West Virginia
environmental organization AWARE."[24]

His criticism of corrupt practices that sometimes occurred in his home
state did not diminish his appreciation for the place of his birth. Nor did it
deter the West Virginia Music Hall of Fame from inducting him as part of
its fifth class of luminaries at its annual ceremony on November 16, 2013.
Tim felt honored, not only because he had been instrumental in the creation of the Hall of Fame back in 2007 but also because he was part of a
group of inductees that included bluegrass pioneers Melvin and Ray Goins
and the legendary now defunct gospel group the Swan Silvertones.[25]

Tim and Mollie made their own personal homage to their native state
on February 14, 2015, when they appeared with the Wheeling Symphony
(WSO) for a Valentine's Day concert. A headline in the *Wheeling News-Register*
announced that "beer, bluegrass and the O'Briens will brighten up a winter
evening as the Wheeling Symphony Orchestra presents 'Tim and Mollie

O'Brien, a Homecoming'" at the Capitol Theater. Tim originally had been invited to do the concert alone, but Mollie joined him when it was learned she would also be in the city to play for a West Virginia Public Radio holiday. In addition to the symphony orchestra, Tim and Mollie were accompanied by Rich Moore and Ethan Ballinger. For both siblings, the event became a true homecoming because it evoked fond memories of the ways in which the symphony shaped their childhood discovery and love for music. Tim, of course, could have had only pleasant recollections as he sang from the theater stage where he had seen and heard many of country music's greatest performers. This particular collaboration was apparently successful enough to warrant a short tour of other communities around the state with the WSO in 2018 called the Celebrate America Tour, which performed in Charleston, Weirton, Davis, and Clarksburg, from July 1 to July 4. For this tour, Mollie and Tim were joined by their partners in life and music, Jan and Rich.[26]

While he ventured into other musical realms, Tim's love for traditional styles continued to shape his work. As he told Mark Hellenberg, "Yeah, my output is pretty eclectic, but if you average it over the years it boils down to a certain roots hybrid, which is where I like to live. America's melting pot in audio." His next album, *Where the River Meets the Road*, released on March 17, 2017, signaled his rediscovery and appreciation of the music of his home state. He included two profoundly autobiographical items: the title song describing his Irish great-grandfather's trek from Cumberland, Maryland, to Wheeling, and "Guardian Angel," a lovely and poignant song about the death of his older sister, Brigid, and his struggle to come to terms with it. Among the twelve songs found on the album, Tim sampled a wide range of styles featured by West Virginia singers, including "Grandma's Hands," from the soul singer Bill Withers; "Drunkard's Grave," from the repertory of the Bailes Brothers; "A Few Old Memories," from Hazel Dickens; "Windy Mountain," from the bluegrass fiddler Curly Ray Cline; and "Little Annie," a song learned from the Lilly Brothers but ultimately traceable to Stephen Foster. Tim was supported in this labor of love by an all-star cast of performers, with backup singers that included Jan, Mollie, Kathy Mattea, and the country and western superstar Chris Stapleton. As Hellenberg commented, "*Where the River Meets the Road* is an impressive and affectionate showcase for the songwriting talents of all these West Virginians (including O'Brien himself) alongside his own considerable gifts as a talented musician and interpreter of songs."[27]

As his *Chicken and Egg* album indicated, Tim had entered a phase where he became both more aware of the people who had molded his life and more determined to acknowledge his indebtedness to them. In fact, he had never completely cut his ties with any of the people, from high school on, who had added something worthwhile to his life. A few mentors, though, remained particularly memorable, and he paid special tribute to them: JD Hutchison, Dale Bruning, and Doc Watson. As a revered link to his earliest years as a musician, Tim remained close to JD Hutchison throughout his professional performing career. Tim told Mike Kemnitzer that JD was the only person he could talk to when he got down, and he was never too busy to make a phone call or visit to JD's home near Athens, Ohio. Tim told Terry Smith, "I'm always looking for an excuse to come up here and visit JD." Between April 18 and 24, 2016, Tim helped to produce an album by JD, *You and the World Outside*. They recorded the album with JD's band, Realbilly Jive, at the Peachfork Studios in Meigs County. Tim sang and played mandolin, fiddle, banjo, and bouzouki. He and local friends of JD had launched an IndieGoGo campaign to raise money for recording, mixing, mastering, packaging, shipping, and producing the CD. Tim had experience with Kickstarter campaigns, since he and Darrell Scott had used the process in 2013 for their album *Memories and Moments*, eventually raising $31,952. Tim said, "We're asking people to buy into JD. We're asking them to help documenting and supporting a living treasure. It's like funding a national park, or a library."[28]

Tim's relationship with Mike Kemnitzer remained a constant from the day they first met and discussed the mandolin Mike was creating for him. As Tim's first mandolin, it was famous throughout the Hot Rize years, especially. Other Nugget-made instruments followed as Tim expanded his musical repertoire. That he and Mike were JD's biggest fans only reinforced the friendship. Reminiscing about Tim, Mike wrote, "It's been my pleasure to have Tim as a friend and his music has greatly enriched my life. . . . Tim and Darrell . . . bring out the greatness in each other. No singer on earth sings as well with Tim than Darrell Scott, except Mollie."[29]

In February 2015 Tim fulfilled a longtime dream of repaying his debt to Dale Bruning, the master jazz guitarist who had befriended him and taught him not long after he first arrived in Boulder. He met with Dale and another of his students, highly regarded guitarist Bill Frisell, at the *eTown* studio in Boulder and recorded a body of songs that eventually became an

Nick Forster, Bill Frisell, Dale Bruning, and Tim (Zach Littlefield photo)

album called *Life Lessons,* on the Wendell World label. Frisell echoed Tim's evaluation, saying, "It is impossible for me to imagine where I'd be if I hadn't met Dale Bruning. He really did change the course of my life." Unfortunately, a concert designed to celebrate the album, scheduled for the *eTown* radio show in Boulder, April 15, 2020, was canceled because of the COVID-19 pandemic. On August 25, 2021, when the event was rescheduled, the quartet played to a sold-out crowd (with more viewers catching the concert on livestream), and *Life Lessons* was made available for purchase.[30]

No musician has mattered more to Tim than Doc Watson, who introduced the young teenaged boy to old-time music and to the role that the guitar played in its shaping and popularization. While Hot Rize had once opened for the great folk musician, Tim was thrilled to appear and play on the same stage with Doc at MerleFest. On October 13, 2012, following Doc's death earlier that year, Tim performed a fourteen-minute one-man tribute to him at the Kennedy Center in Washington, DC, interpreting his career while maintaining an uninterrupted finger-picked version of Doc's signature rendition of "Deep River Blues" on his guitar. As he played, Tim interspersed spoken comments and recollections of the great North Carolina musician: it was an amazing and poignant performance.[31]

One of Tim's most affecting stories recalled the day that he dropped by Doc's home unannounced in Deep Gap, about ten miles from Boone. Tim had checked out of his motel and decided he'd like to pay a visit to his longtime idol. He called Doc and told him his name, but Doc did not immediately recall who Tim was. Doc's daughter, Nancy, told him, "You remember him, Daddy. He's the fiddle player who plays at Merlefest." And Doc said to Tim, "'You're the fiddle player who plays at Merlefest.' One thing led to another, and I was invited up to the house." Arriving at his home during a light snow fall, Tim could hear guitar playing and Doc singing, "While Roving on a Winter's Night." Tim described the afternoon quite movingly:

> It was just a beautiful thing. I waited for him to finish, then knocked on his door. He was living by himself, a blind man, very self-sufficient. I brought my guitar in, and we played, and he told stories. . . . I got there about 1:00 and didn't leave until 4:30 . . . just a wonderful afternoon with my hero. Doc kept talking about a certain guitar he had, a Bourgeois [crafted by Louis Bourgeois in Lewiston, Maine], then went down to the basement to retrieve it. After being down there about 20 minutes, he brought a guitar case up, opened it, strummed it, and said "this isn't the right guitar, is it?" But he told me it was a good guitar anyway. It was a great afternoon, and if you care about somebody, and if you think maybe you don't want to bother him, you can call him up and see if you're bothering him. I thought I might be bothering Doc, but it turned out he was really glad to get to be Doc Watson for the day, and I was really glad to be his student one more day.[32]

While Tim remained loyal to the musicians who had been indispensable to his career, he had also become a mentor to many musicians in his own time. When asked about his influence on younger musicians, he said: "I guess it's happened, that I've become this role model. It surprises you, but if you look at who my role models were, a lot of them aren't there anymore. That means I'm getting closer to the checkout line, so I've become a role model because I'm still out there doing it. So, I guess it's an honor, but it gets to be intimidating to continue, because you think you're not coming up with your best stuff all the time, and you wonder if you can even show it."[33]

Tim's influence on younger musicians, in bluegrass and beyond, had begun as far back as the early days of Hot Rize. Songs like "Nellie Kane" and "Blue Night" had moved into the repertories of both amateur and professional musicians and could be heard in campfire jam sessions as well as on stage. One of Tim's songs, in fact, became the inspiration for the naming of a Colorado old-time string band: Hard Pressed. Cory Obert and Andrea Lecos, a husband and wife fiddle and banjo duo, organized their group in Durango, and they chose Tim's song as their performing title because it reaffirmed the power of love through adversity.[34]

Tim's positive effect on individual musicians was also profound, whether judged by the success of such mainstream bluegrass performers as Laurie Lewis, by young traditionalists like Old Man Luedecke, or by the testimonies given by ultra-progressives like Chris Stapleton and Chris Thile. Stapleton, a singer with great vocal power, who became one of the dominant performers in mainstream country music, paid tribute to Tim and Darrell Scott at the 2018 Country Radio Seminar when he sang their earlier recording of 2000, "There Ain't No Easy Way." Talking about Stapleton, Carena Liptak wrote, "It's clear from the strong storytelling and troubled lyrical themes—*Please do me a favor, won't you write on my grave / Say there ain't no easy way*" he sings in the last verse—that Stapleton's own songwriting style takes influence from the song's original performers."[35]

Thile, the fiery mandolinist who played with groups like Nickel Creek and the Punch Brothers before emceeing the nationally syndicated NPR radio program *Live From Here*, declared, "everything I need to know about acoustic music I learned from Tim O'Brien. This is what the Telluride Bluegrass Festival is all about: genre-blind, multigenerational communion with our fellow music lovers." An early piece of evidence documenting Thile's fascination with Tim's music can be found in a photograph, reprinted on Tim's Facebook page, that shows Thile as an eight-year-old prodigy checking out Tim's Nugget mandolin at the 1989 Grass Valley Mid-Summer Festival in Nevada County, California. He supposedly told Tim that his goal at the time was to stay up past midnight.[36]

Tim's influence and that of Hot Rize extended into the realm of Jamband Music, the wild, improvisatory child of bluegrass, where musicians became known for their multi-minute instrumental breaks and their unrestrained excursions into rock, jazz, and other musical genres. Some of the best known jam bands, in fact—such as Leftover Salmon, Yonder Mountain String Band, and String Cheese Incident,—"graduated" from the Colorado music scene and particularly the free-wheeling Telluride Festival. Hot Rize was the band that had really fired them up. Drew Emmitt, mandolin player and singer for Leftover Salmon, had taken lessons from Tim soon after he arrived in Colorado from Nashville. His first group, the Left Hand Band, was an immediate predecessor of Leftover Salmon and a progenitor of the Jamband movement. Hot Rize and the Telluride spirit actually had enlivened all of the Jamband groups. Ben Kaufmann and Jeff Austin of the Yonder Mountain String Band summed up the prevailing attitude of these bands when Kaufmann said, "if it wasn't for Hot Rize, we couldn't do what we do." Austin echoed his sentiments: "Hot Rize showed the world the power of infusing incredible original music with the passion of each musician onstage. They made it o.k. to play with guts *and* brains . . . to allow the audience in by showing them that they were having as much fun as those watching." In writing about Yonder Mountain's post-Christmas concerts in Boulder, a *Bluegrass Today* contributor said, "For those who don't follow them closely, the Bowling League is the members of Yonder Mountain dressed up in ridiculous outfits, à la Red Knuckles & the Trailblazers with Hot Rize."[37]

When Tim met Chris Luedecke in England sometime in 2009, he found a Canadian singer and musician with kindred interests. They became acquainted through their mutual booking agent, Andy Cooper, who suggested that Chris open for Tim in a weeklong tour of the United Kingdom. Tim confirmed, "He comes onstage wearing a snap brim hat with an open back banjo, and I just didn't expect the tragic-comic songs and his self-deprecating MC work. He grabbed the audience within the first five minutes." They further deepened their friendship as they "bonded" while spending the night at Phil Davidson's in the village of Wyck, after a snowstorm canceled a festival. Finding a common love for books and traditional country music, the two of them resolved to jointly embark on a common set of musical projects. Like so many roots musicians since the 1950s, Chris had embraced American traditional music after hearing Harry Smith's *Anthology of American Folk Music*. Playing the five-string banjo in the fashion of Uncle Dave Macon, Chris performed both traditional songs and his own compositions.[38]

In 2010 Tim traveled to Vancouver to appear on Chris's Juno award–winning recording, *My Hands Are on Fire*—Tim played or sang on all cuts. Since that time, he has appeared on all of Chris's recordings and has sometimes acted as his producer, as on *Tender Is the Night*. During a lengthy snowbound stay in 2015 at Chris's self-made cabin in Chester, Nova Scotia, Chris and Tim made a joint recording of highly personal songs extolling the joys of home life called *Domestic Eccentric*. A journalist in Toronto wrote, "Luedecke has always insisted on a solid poetic heft in the way he uses words, and highly personal stories are what have always connected him to the universal in his audience. Recording with Tim O'Brien in an intimate setting at home has yielded an album where the songs take the starring role." Later, Chris told journalist Gregory Adams that working with Chris's favorite musician in his cabin home was "a waking dream." These recording enterprises emboldened the two musicians to embark on a series of tours in Canada and the United States. Performing as "Old Man Luedecke" (a moniker given him by his wife), Chris typically played a solo set, then joined Tim and Jan in a combined musical presentation. One of the highlights of this collaboration, recalls Chris, was a series of shows given in North Carolina and Tennessee with Tim, Jan, and JD Hutchison, as the Banjo Tramps. They themselves perhaps did not realize that this group represented a succession of mentors and proteges—from Hutchison to O'Brien to Luedecke.[39]

Tim never lost his penchant for eclectic performance and collaboration with other musicians, but he also never stopped honoring his bluegrass roots. In 2019 he organized the Tim O'Brien Band, assembling a group of outstanding musicians. As Craig Shelburne commented, "In an effort to find players adept at both Irish and bluegrass music, the impeccable ensemble is rounded out by Mike Bub on bass, Shad Cobb on fiddle, and Patrick Sauber on banjo and guitar. Released one day after O'Brien's 65th birthday," the ensemble also featured Jan on mandolin and vocals. Jan had by now become a permanent and integral part of Tim's music making, with their duets constituting a vital facet of the band's vocal sound. As a reviewer for *Rogue Folk* wrote, "[Jan's] distinctly folky voice is serendipitously matched with Tim's, and consonant with his arrival at the bluegrass world from the side of a folk musician." The album marked "a return to where it all started for Tim—as a guitarist. As audiences can attest, Tim's elastic yet menacingly groovy guitar playing is as pivotal to his sound as his mandolin playing. 'Something about lead singer and guitar player makes so much sense,' says Tim. With his 1937 Martin OO-18, Tim O'Brien Band marks a return to the place that Jimmy Martin, Lester Flatt and Carter Stanley held at the helm of their bands."[40]

In selecting songs for their first CD, *Tim O'Brien Band*, Tim deliberately tried to make a *bluegrass* album, including a couple of wordless instrumentals because the older bands had always followed that pattern when they made albums. He told an interviewer, "I'd like to think I'm trying to put in some of the elements I miss in bluegrass when I hear it on the radio."[41] Tim and the band also included Big Bill Broonzy's "Diggin' My Potatoes," a blues classic done in hard-driving bluegrass fashion; a few traditional numbers like the cowboy song "Doney Gal" (learned from an old cowboy poet, Buck Ramsey) and Woody Guthrie's "Pastures of Plenty." "Pastures of Plenty" seemed particularly timely, given the continuing gap between migrant workers' dreams and the abundance of the crops in which they worked. Tim explained to interviewer Craig Shelburne that, in looking for material, he would sometimes go to his record shelves to find songs he had neglected. One of these included Norman Blake's plaintive "Last Train from Poor Valley." Speaking of the great acoustic guitar player, Tim paid Blake a mighty compliment:

> Oh, man, Norman Blake is my hero! I saw him first probably in 1972. He was on that first *Will the Circle Be Unbroken* record, and some other friends that were playing bluegrass already knew about him. They had that first Norman Blake record. . . . And when I started playing with Hot Rize, we'd play these festivals and we would meet up with him.
>
> Norman and Nancy are old friends, and I go back to see them every now and again in recent years. Their music is just so different from what I do . . . and yet all these years later, it's a lot closer. . . . I just love the sentiment of that song ["Last Train from Poor Valley"], and I knew that song from when his record came out. I like to pay tribute to somebody like that. He's not on the circuit anymore, and I don't want him to be forgotten.

Tim said that one of the great things about living in Nashville was that you kept running into people like Blake, in grocery stores and other local shops.[42]

Jan and Tim performing at Rockygrass, 2019 (Tim O'Brien's collection)

The Tim O'Brien Band began their career with an ambitious schedule in the spring of 2019 and festival gigs booked well into 2020. The future seemed secure. Tim's experience differed little from that of other musicians during these months. But as COVID-19 tightened its grip on the United States, the entertainment industry slowly ground to a halt, beginning in March 2020, with live bookings repeatedly finding cancelations or delays. Musicians scrambled to make music available in any format they could, trying to keep their heads above financially treacherous waters. While Short Order Sessions had pretty much become dormant, Tim and Jan sometimes streamed their shows online. Tim also took the opportunity to re-release what constituted perhaps his favorite album out of the many he had produced: *The Crossing*, made available again on May 1, 2020. He described the project as "near and dear to his heart," and since he and Jan were off the road for the foreseeable future, he hoped that the record would "help you get through to the other side."[43]

Being unable to meet with his many friends on an intimate basis became particularly depressing for Tim. Ever since he arrived in Nashville, he had become well known for his picking parties, replete with copious food, drink, and of course, music. From time to time, Tim participated in online concerts with other musicians, such as John McCutcheon and, more rarely, even ventured out to play a live recording session with other musicians, but usually in a contained, socially distanced setting. For example, he took part in Sturgill Simpson's venture into bluegrass, recorded in 2020, *Cuttin' Grass*, vol. 1, *The Butcher Shoppe Sessions*. Tim regarded Simpson as the best bluegrass songwriter of 2020, and he appeared with him on television's *Colbert Show* as part of an all-star bluegrass band called the Hillbilly Avengers. Tim played guitar and sang an occasional part. When asked how he was spending his time, Tim said, "for Jan and me, the pandemic has meant hanging out, planting a garden, watching birds pair up and reading too much news. We've also been playing a lot of informal music. It seems like a good time to learn some new old songs." As he saw his monthly bookings increasingly discontinued, Tim, from time to time, did some online musing or conducted intellectual discourse with friends about philosophical, literary, political, and musical questions. With the number of COVID-related fatalities rising rapidly, John Prine's death in April 2020 hit him particularly hard. He recalled seeing John at the grocery store or favorite eateries and remembered musical collaborations with him. Then again, he said that Prine's death "reminded me that he brought so many together with his songs, and there's been an amazing world-wide ovation to Prine's curtain call." Tim reflected on loss and sought songs that soothed the sense of grief, mourning, and isolation:

> Jan's brother-in-law Wayne Avery, a fine Kansas musician, passed in mid-March after a long illness, so we've been singing "You Ain't Goin Nowhere," one of his favorites. We're also singing "I Just Dropped In To See What Condition My Condition Was In," "Lean On Me" and "Hello In There." We honor Wayne along with the late great Kenny Rogers, Bill Withers and John Prine as we sing them here at the house. We plan to sing them for others soon on a streaming concert. I guess that's how we connect with the community as we go through this process.[44]

When the Telluride Festival announced in May 2020 that the summer bluegrass festival would not be held—for the first time in its history—Tim knew he had reached a pivotal moment in his career. He, of course, did not miss Telluride any more than its faithful fans missed him, like the one who spoke with a tone that surely echoed that of thousands of others.

Remembering all of the good times associated with the festival, she said, "Tim is probably my favorite artist in the park each year. His voice is reassuring and warm, and his stage patter is by turn earnest and corny. He's an astounding multi-instrumentalist and has written some of the finest songs to have spilled off the Fred Shellman Memorial Stage." She concluded her observations with the faith that "holding on to the dream of better days is all we have."[45]

Tim well understood Telluride's impact: "It's a yearly high point, a full-on summer launch, the weekend when you'd bring new songs and debut a new concept in your presentation. Everything anticipated and then followed it. In my world, it set the tone for the whole year." He went on discussing the role that Telluride and other festivals that he'd frequented for over forty years held such importance for him and others. "Every weekend through the summer there are such events, and there are whole societies that form at them over the years. People camp in the same spaces and celebrate their own traditions."[46]

On his blog in April 2020, Tim further ruminated about coping with the pandemic, "The one thing we can and should feel is we're in it together. Let's all grab that and take this time to study it, reflect on it, and since it's going to be a while, just be in it." The situation helped him appreciate his relative good fortune compared to others, writing, "I sit in a pretty secure place compared to a lot of people. I feel and worry for those who have no savings, who have little or no income. I feel such sadness for those who are sick, and for their families and friends." He told Kyle Knox, "I have to say I miss the opportunity to get together with folks in the same room. As public people, we performers guard our privacy, but we also make it our business to get people together. Music creates community, and it's still doing that, but with filters and time delays."[47]

As he continued to reflect on the pandemic's far-reaching effects on all "modern day humans . . . on hold," he also pondered, "How about making a record during this time off? Well, let's see if we can keep virus free and let's wait until we can document if our collaborators are also virus free before we start. So, I guess it's best to hunker down and write some songs." And that's exactly what he did. Ruminating turned into songwriting, possibly initiated by a completely unexpected proposal from autoharp master Bryan Bowers. Bowers told Tim that in case he did not survive the pandemic before being vaccinated (when vaccinations were not yet available), he planned to send some of his instruments to various musicians. Tim said, "It was a tearful phone call, but I accepted the loan of his old Gibson mandocello. It came in a box padded with old extra-large festival t-shirts." The gift prompted Tim to think about how to use the mandocello in a new piece, so he arranged "a mandolin quartet version of an old Irish harp tune" by the seventeenth–eighteenth-century blind Irish harpist Turlough O'Carolan, called "Dermot O'Dowd." He recorded "a version with Jan playing on some of the parts."[48]

Tim's thoughtful response to the pandemic and the strained political and social environment that surrounded it resulted in a new album, released in June 2021 and entitled *He Walked On*. It contains some of the most powerful and socially sensitive material he has ever written or sung. A few other writers contributed songs to the album, including R. B. Morris, whose sobering "That's How Every Empire Falls," with its picture of societal decay, provided a kind of portentous context for the collection as a whole. The song seemed particularly relevant in the wake of the George Floyd murder in the summer of 2020 and the revival of the Black Lives Matter movement. Tim wrote or co-wrote eight of the album's thirteen songs. His coverage ranged widely, including a relatively light-hearted foray against our enslavement to devices, "Pushing On Buttons (Staring at Screens)," and "Nervous," a clever

Jan and Tim (Tim O'Brien's collection)

critique of ills troubling folks in today's rapidly changing social contexts. But overall, Tim aimed much higher. "When You Pray, Move Your Feet" came from a quote made by the late Congressman John Lewis and became a fitting testimonial to the great civil rights icon. A moving and sobering trip to Nogales on the southern border of Arizona with Jan and migrant advocate Randy Mayer of the Green Valley Samaritans inspired one of the most affecting songs on the album, "El Comedor," co-written with Jan. "I can see la frontera from where I stand in line at El Comedor / just over that wall is the promised land in line at El Comedor." Still another eloquent song, "Can You See Me Sister?" came from Tim's avid interest in history and his passion for social justice. He had long been fascinated by the story of Sally Hemings and her children who were fathered by Thomas Jefferson. Tim built a song around an imagined encounter between two of the children. He shared his interest with the Scottish songwriter Paul McKenna, who wrote a first verse and Tim added a chorus. "In a few days we had a song that was simple and real I think and I'm proud of it. I took my work with the mandolin quartets and wrote a little string part to play under the spoken intro." These and other songs on the album mark Tim's way of dealing with the myriad problems and anxieties of Pandemic America. As he told us, "I was under a spell of trying to make sense of the pandemic and the race situation like everyone else, and the record reflects that." Stumbling on Yip Harburg and Earl Robinson's "The Same Boat Brother" reaffirmed his conviction that humankind was indeed on trial as it had been during the Great Depression and World War II.[49]

Songwriting is more than a part of Tim's musical career; it's a calling. "Those records are like my children," he said, "and I hope like some parents that they'll do well in their lives. Maybe even reach the equivalent of becoming president. I also know they are something I just do for my own satisfaction. There will be lots of artistic statements relating to the past year, and *He Walked On* is my attempt." The album speaks to both a personal and a national moment, a statement of our ability to live through a doubly trying time: simultaneously, a mourning and a rebirth of sorts. Similarly, Tim and Jan's marriage on July 31, 2021, speaks to their commitment to each other, their music making, and their faith in a post-pandemic future when they will once again play live to the audiences that love the music that fulfills them both.[50]

ACKNOWLEDGMENTS

When we called Tim O'Brien to tell him we wanted to write this biography, almost immediately we were met by silence, then a surprised chuckle to ask if we were joking. Since the two of us—one, an acknowledged expert on American Country Music and the other, his loving accomplice—had enjoyed working as coauthors of *Nashville's Songwriting Sweethearts: The Boudleaux and Felice Bryant Story*, we had discussed doing another biography of someone we both valued and wanted to explore in depth. Tim quickly rose to the top. Once he recovered from the shock of our call, he made himself available for many telephone conversations and email follow-ups, along the way providing us with invaluable contact information for the interviews we conducted among his old friends, colleagues, and family members, which all proved invaluable in helping us build a more complete portrait of this multitalented musical genius. We want to thank Tim, a very private individual, for graciously allowing us into his life as more than appreciative fans and casual acquaintances. Thanks to his wife, Jan Fabricius, for her frankness in telling us about their love story. Tim's talented sister and duet partner, Mollie O'Brien Moore, shared stories of their Wheeling childhood and adolescence in which their early musical aptitudes were nourished by their nonmusical but supportive parents. She described the joy of their joint ventures on the albums on which they sang together, the tours they made, and the loving relationships between their own families. Tim's older brother, Jim, shared the memoir that their mother, Amelia Gaines O'Brien, wrote for her children, an indispensable resource in helping us become more fully acquainted with the O'Briens' Wheeling upbringing. Kit Swaggert, Tim's first wife, and their older son, Jackson filled in details about their music-centered household.

Once Tim made friends, he tended to keep them throughout his lifetime. Those with whom we spoke helped us get a more three-dimensional view of Tim's life. Willie Neuman from the Linsly years; Jeff (Smokey) McKeen from Colby; Matt Montagne from Teton Valley Ranch Camp; John Sidle from Jackson Hole; Ritchie Mintz, who enticed Tim to move to Colorado; Ned Alterman, owner of Folk Arts Music in Boulder, who provided Tim with his first job there; Tim's first musical mentor and "blood brother," JD Hutchison; mandolin builder and dear friend, Mike (Nugget) Kemnitzer; Harry Tuft, founder of the Denver Folk Center; Dan Sadowsky, who organized the Ophelia Swing Band; guitar master and Tim's teacher, Dale Bruning, all bring us up to the Hot Rize years. Pete Wernick, the "official" historian of the band, offered, literally, hours of interviews, comments, photos, and editorial suggestions. Nick Forster gave us great material as well. Laurie Lewis, Sumi Seacat, Jerry Mills, Mary Stribling, and Charles Sawtelle's brother, Dan, all offered compelling stories about the impact of Charles on the group's unique attributes that made them such a successful band. Joan Wernick, Kit Swaggert, Robin Claire, and Sumi Seacat told us about life on the home front while they were married to those Hot Rize guys. Bryan Sutton let us know how excited he was to move from being a fan to a band member after Charles's death. Bluegrass journalist and author Ronni Lundy added lots of spice along with her keen observations and insights. Sam Bush and Jerry Douglas joined Tim's circle during those years and continue to be important to him. Working with fellow West Virginian singer Kathy Mattea inspired Tim to break out on his own and, ultimately, relocate to Nashville. Pat Alger and Darrell Scott helped us understand the process and pleasures of co-writing songs with Tim. Darrell also talked about the joys of their playing together. Scott Nygaard and Mark Schatz shared their tales of performing and touring as O'Boys. Barry Poss related memories of working with Tim at Sugar Hill, and Bev Paul, who got to know Tim there, helped us understand the germination and evolution of Americana music and her working with him in that context. Dirk Powell told us about the musical explorations upon which he and Tim embarked; Chris (Old Man) Luedecke described Tim's mentoring and support; Chris Moore shared memories of doing advance work for Tim, among many other aspects of their relationship. We also want to thank Brad Hunt for helping us understand the many ways he worked to get Tim "out there," and Hal Cannon for his perspective on the impact of Tim's work. It's only fitting to wind up back in West Virginia where *Mountain Stage* cofounder Larry Groce told us about Tim's graciousness as a performer. While some of those we interviewed shared photos from their collections, we also want to single out Tim Benko, Rick Gardner, Anne Hamersky, Rob Laughter, Zach Littlefield, Laura Rose, Cindy Schaefer Sax, and Scott Simontacchi for granting us permission to use their work.

In addition to all of the folks above who know Tim, we talked about the Wyoming country music scene with Bob Badeau and with old friends Elaine and Patrick Maney and Jeanne and Dave Zoromski, who shared their memories of the excitement of folk masses when they were undergraduates. At a crucial moment Dan Miller, editor of *Bluegrass Unlimited*, provided us with a copy of an essential article that could no longer be accessed online. Of course, working with fellow Texan and dear friend Kent Calder, editorial director of the University of Oklahoma Press, is nearly as much fun as picking and singing together. Others at the press who facilitated publication of this book include Steven Baker and Anna María Rodríguez for directing the editorial and production process. We thank Tony Roberts for the handsome cover design, Katie Baker and Amy Hernandez for marketing and promotions, and, of course, Pippa Letsky for her painstaking copyediting. The entire team is praiseworthy.

★ ★ **★** ★ ★

TIM O'BRIEN DISCOGRAPHY

With the Ophelia Swing Band

1977   Dan Sadowsky and the Ophelia String Band. *Swing Tunes of the 30s and 40s.* Biscuit City Records.

1978   Dan Sadowsky and the Ophelia String Band. *Spreadin' Rhythm Around.* Catapult.

With Mollie O'Brien

1988   *Take Me Back.* Sugar Hill

1992   *Remember Me.* Sugar Hill

1994   *Away Out on the Mountain.* Sugar Hill

With Hot Rize

1979   *Hot Rize.* Flying Fish.

1981   *Radio Boogie.* Flying Fish.

1982   *Hot Rize Presents: Red Knuckles and the Trailblazers.* Flying Fish.

1984   *Hot Rize Extra Added Attraction: Red Knuckles and the Trailblazers in Concert.* Flying Fish.

1985   *Traditional Ties.* Sugar Hill.

1987   *Untold Stories.* Sugar Hill.

1988   *Hot Rize Presents Red Knuckles and the Trailblazers Shades of the Past.* Sugar Hill,

1990   *Take It Home.* Sugar Hill.

2002   *So Long of a Journey (Live at the Boulder Theater).* Sugar Hill.

2014   *When I'm Free.* Ten in Hand Records.

2018   *Fortieth Anniversary Bash.* Ten in Hand Records.

With Dirk Powell and John Herrmann

1998   *Songs from the Mountain.* Howdy Skies.

With Darrell Scott

2000   *Real Time.* Full Skies (originally released on Howdy Skies).

2012   *Live: We're Usually A Lot Better than This.* Full Skies (originally released on Full Light).

2013   *Memories and Moments.* Full Skies.

Solo Albums

1977   *Guess Who's in Town.* Biscuit City Records.

1984   *Hard Year Blues.* Flying Fish.

1991   *Odd Man In.* Sugar Hill.

1993   *Oh Boy! O'Boy!* Sugar Hill.

1995   *Rock in My Shoe.* Sugar Hill.

1996   *Red on Blonde.* Sugar Hill.

1997   *When No One's Around.* Sugar Hill.

1999   *The Crossing.* Alula.

2001   *Two Journeys.* Howdy Skies.

2003   *Traveler.* Sugar Hill.

2005   *Cornbread Nation.* Sugar Hill.

2005   *Fiddler's Green.* Sugar Hill.

2008   *Chameleon.* Howdy Skies.

2010   *Chicken and Egg.* Howdy Skies.

2015   *Pompadour.* Howdy Skies.

2017   *Where the River Meets the Road.* Howdy Skies.

2019   *The Tim O'Brien Band.* Howdy Skies.

2021   *He Walked On.* Howdy Skies.

Appendix B

LYRICS TO SELECTED SONGS

Can You See Me Sister?

Spoken intro:

Some years after the death of his wife, Thomas Jefferson took his slave Sally Hemings as his consort. She had several children by Jefferson, and all those who survived were eventually granted their freedom. One of the younger sons, Madison, corresponded with his older, light-skinned sister Harriet, who had married and passed into white Washington society. At some point she stopped returning his letters. This song imagines a chance encounter between the two on a street somewhere.

Can you see me sister, do you remember me
Can you feel my presence, I'm still on my knees
I can see you sister, oh how your life has changed
I'm still here in the shadows, you're just out of range
> Father can you help me now
> The chains are gone but I still feel bound
> Father please look down on me
> Until the day that I feel free
Can you see me sister, in my shabby clothes
My life so different from the one you know
I do not blame you, for we share a name
If my skin was lighter I might do the same
> Father can you help me now
> The chains are gone but I still feel bound
> Father please look down on me
> Until the day that I feel free
Bought and sold like cattle

People just like us
Couldn't look you in the eye
I could be whipped or worse
> Mother can you help me now
> The chains are gone but I still feel bound
> Mother please look down on me
> Until the day that I feel free
> Father can you help me now
> The chains are gone but I still feel bound
> Father please look down on me
> Until the day that I feel free

Can you see me sister
Paul McKenna and Tim O'Brien / No Bad Ham Music

El Comedor

I can see la Frontera from where I stand *in line at el Comedor*
Just over that wall is the promised land *in line at el Comedor*
It's a long, long way from my home to here
I was driven by hope and by fear
I pray to the Madre hold back my tears *in line at el Comedor*
I hold you and feed you here in my arms *in line at el Comedor*
If I can stay strong I'll keep you from harm *in line at el Comedor*
We walk and we wait we run and we ride
In daytime we rest and we hide
Now Coyote tells me be ready tonight *in line at el Comedor*
We arrived here so hungry just three days ago *in line at el Comedor*
We stand with our brothers we met on the road *in line at el Comedor*
Sister Cecilia welcomes us in
She leads us in prayer to begin
If we don't move tonight she'll feed us again *in line at el Comedor*
La gringa vieja is small as I am *in line at el Comedor*
She draws out the trail on the palm of my hand *in line at el Comedor*
She says that the new moon will help me to see
Marks places where water will be
She tells me her friends will watch for me *in line at el Comedor*
Tim O'Brien and Jan Fabricius / No Bad Ham Music /
    ASCAP/ BMI

Footsteps So Near

There's a tale they tell down in old Wolf County
Of a murderous husband and his family of three
One day a neighbor from over the hill
He found them dead in the cabin it was so deathly still

The killer he left a note and I know how it read
I hope you don't find me I'd rather be dead
Than to live in your jailhouse for the rest of my days
Until a jury it hangs me for my wicked ways

[Chorus:]
> Sometimes at night I wake to the sound
> Of the men in the distance and the baying of hounds
> Once on a full moon in the spring of the year
> I heard breaking branches and footsteps so near

Well the posse it searched it was five days or more
He hid in a cave by the steep river shore
'Til he gave himself up he started walking downtown
Before he got to the courthouse a man shot him down

He said I'm not sorry for what I have done
But I cannot live like a man on the run
I'm glad that you killed me you can dig me my grave
It can't be much worse than that dark lonely cave

[Chorus:]
> Sometimes at night I wake to the sound
> Of the men in the distance and the baying of hounds
> Once on a full moon in the spring of the year
> I heard breaking branches and footsteps so near

Tim O'Brien and Nick Forster / Howdy Skies Music / ASCAP
/ BMI

Guardian Angel

I guess there's no time when I can't recall
That picture hanging up there on the wall
Of a little girl walking by a snake in the grass
And her guardian angel is guiding her past
I lost a big sister when the picture was new
Nineteen fifty-six just before I turned two
I took part of my memory, added stories and things
I made her my angel, she has her own wings
I made her my angel, she has her own wings
She would have held my hand, she would have called
    my name
Too young to remember I miss her the same
My guardian angel, I miss her the same
Don't know much about her, there's not much to know
Just six years of living then she had to go
My parents they grieved, somehow they moved on
And I grew up knowing my sister was gone
I found an old letter that my mom wrote that year
And each time I read it I shed a new tear
It helps me to feel some of what my parents felt then
I think of my own kids and feel it again
I think of my own kids and feel it again
I would have held her hand, I know I called her name
My guardian angel I miss her the same
She would have held my hand, she would have called
    my name
Too young to remember her, miss her the same
My guardian angel, I miss her the same
My guardian angel, I miss her the same
I guess there's no time when I can't recall
The picture a hanging up there on the wall
Tim O'Brien / No Bad Ham Music / ASCAP

The High Road
Up on the high road lookin' down
Thinking how you let me down
And deep in my heart I hear the sound
Of the song that carried me away

We would come here years ago
And the stars would shine and the wind would blow
You'd look in my eyes and I would know
That you would carry me away

Late last week in the marketplace
I heard your voice and I saw your face
You were gone without a trace
It sure did carry me away

I'll play a tune and watch the stars
Hope the wind will carry it far
And if you hear me wherever you are
Just let it carry you away

Play old fiddle and carry me away
To another life and another day
Well, here's a little tune I always play
It sure does carry me away
Tim O'Brien / Howdy Skies Music / ASCAP

I Breathe In

[Chorus:]

> I breathe in and I reach out for you
> I breathe out and call your name
> I breathe in and I know I love you
> I breathe out and you love me just the same

The only way I know to love you is with my soul and with
  my heart
I don't claim to know love's ending, I can't find out where it
  starts
When I'm walking in the morning, when I'm talking to
  my friends
There's a light that burns inside me, it's a flame that never
  ends

[Chorus:]

> I breathe in and I reach out for you
> I breathe out and call your name
> I breathe in and I know I love you
> I breathe out and you love me just the same

If you see me from a distance, I'm the same man when
  I'm near
And my heart is always calling, even though you cannot hear
In the shadows growing longer, in the darkness spreading
  'round
In my dreams and in my waking, in the early morning sounds

[Chorus:]

> I breathe in and I reach out for you
> I breathe out and call your name
> I breathe in and I know I love you
> I breathe out and you love me just the same

Now the time has come to leave you, I'm gonna hurt to say
  goodbye
I'll remember all our good times as the teardrops dim
  my eyes

It's all just a part of the story, in our dying we can live
All the love that I am taking is all the love I have to
    give

[Chorus:]

> I breathe in and I reach out for you
> I breathe out and call your name
> I breathe in and I know I love you
> I breathe out and you love me just the same
> Tim O'Brien / No Bad Ham Music / ASCAP

Lone Tree Standing

Now the stars are fading in the morning light
And you're warm beside me in the early bright
You're the one I wanted, you're the one I need
And I feel so safe here and I feel so free

I'd like to freeze this moment, I want to take this time
I want to keep it with me, I want to make it mine
But why cheat the future, why be afraid
Cause when you have what I have, you know you got it
    made

[Chorus:]
        Like a lone tree standing on a mountain top
        One that keeps on living, one that just can't stop
        That's the kind of loving that I have for you
        And when the storm is over, I'll be there and true

Many times I'm humbled by the ways of life
And how a man can stumble onto fate's sharp knife
But I'm never worried, no I'm never scared
When you're here beside me, I know that I'll be spared

Cause you don't take chances, you don't like loose talk
And your ways are constant, you're a solid rock
You're the one I wanted, you're the one I need
And you showed me a new life and you helped me
    to be

[Chorus:]
        Like a lone tree standing on a mountain top
        One that keeps on living, one that just can't stop
        That's the kind of loving that I have for you
        And when the storm is over, I'll be there and true
Tim O'Brien / Howdy Skies Music / ASCAP

You Were on My Mind This Morning

[Chorus:]

> You were on my mind this morning, you were on my mind today
>
> We had our good times together, we sure had our special way

Guess those happy days are gone now, just like water through my hand

Wonder if I'll ever see you, ever kiss your lips again

If you hear me and I'm singin' some old lonesome song like this

You'll know I'm not over you and I am longing for your kiss

Wish that I could linger longer, sit down in some evenin' shade

But you know I have to ramble, guess that's just the way I'm made

[Chorus:]

> You were on my mind this morning, you were on my mind today
>
> We had our good times together, we sure had our special way

I was doin' good and I was flush and I was fancy fine

Threw it all away on women, whiskey, cards, dice, and wine

I will roll and I will tumble, I will rise and fall again

Ridin' on this roller coaster doesn't ever seem to end

I would leave this town this morning, I would leave this town today

If I thought you'd have me back, I would soon be on my way

The lame would get up start to walkin' and the blind would somehow see

If ever I forgot about you, all the things you meant to me

[Chorus:]
You were on my mind this morning, you were on my
mind today
We had our good times together, we sure had our special
way
Tim O'Brien / No Bad Ham Music / ASCAP

NOTES

INTRODUCTION

1. Kathy S-B, "Quick Q and A with Tim O'Brien," Me & Thee Coffeehouse, September 18, 2010, https://meandthee.org/OldSite/blog/txp/quick-q-and-a-with -tim-o-brien-2010.
2. Hal Cannon, interview, June 2, 2020. (All interviews were conducted with authors by telephone, and the notes are in the possession of the authors.)

Chapter 1. **A WHEELING BOYHOOD**

1. Derek Halsey, "Tim O'Brien: Digging Deep in to His West Virginia Roots," *Bluegrass Unlimited*, April, 2017, 24–27. In an interview with the authors on April 20, 2020, Tim told us that he learned that his grandfather's cottage in Ireland was west of Kingscourt in County Cavan. Robert McNamara, "The National Road: America's First Major Highway," *ThoughtCo.*, https://www.thoughtco.com/the -national-road-1774053, accessed March 16, 2019; David Sibray, editor, "B&O Railroad Completed to Wheeling on Jan. 1, 1853," *West Virginia Explorer*, https://wvexplorer.com/2018/01/01/bo-railroad-completed-wheeling-jan-1-1853.
2. Tim O'Brien, interview, December 16, 2019. See also "Our History," City of Wheeling, WV, https://www.wheelingwv.gov/our-history, accessed December 2, 2020; "Historic Population, 1840–2014, Wheeling, West Virginia," *Population.US*, https://population.us/wv/wheeling, accessed December 2, 2020; Rebekah Karelis, "That Wheeling Feeling," *Goldenseal* (Fall 2019): 13.
3. Tim O'Brien, interview, March 27, 2020.
4. Amelia Gaines O'Brien, "This Will Be All She Wrote," unpublished memoir, typescript, n.d., Jim O'Brien personal collection (hereafter cited as Amelia O'Brien, memoir); "Amelia O'Brien, October 14, 1919–January 2, 2005," *Altmeyer Funeral Homes*, http://obituaryarchive.altmeyer.com/obituary/amelia -obrien, accessed October 6, 202;1 Clara Varney in *Family Search*, https:// ancestors.familysearch.org/en/KWBB-DGT/clara-varney-1885-1972, accessed October 6, 2021; "Elbert H. Gaines," in *Compendium of History, Reminiscence, and Biography of Nebraska*, http://www.usgennet.org/usa/ne/topic/resources /OLLibrary/Comp_NE/cmp0843.htm, accessed October 6, 2021; "Elbert H.

Gaines," in "Genealogy Trails History Group," Custer County, Nebraska, http:// genealogytrails.com/neb/custer/biographies_g.html, accessed December 4, 2020; Tim O'Brien, interview, December 16, 2019; Tim O'Brien, email to authors, September 8, 2020.

5. Tim O'Brien, email, September 8, 2020.

6. Amelia O'Brien, memoir.

7. Tim O'Brien, email, September 20, 2020. As Mollie O'Brien put it: "Our dad's mother was 100 percent German, so we're only a quarter Irish." Mollie O'Brien, interview with authors, December 1, 2019.

8. Tim O'Brien, email, September 8, 2020; Amelia O'Brien, memoir.

9. Amelia O'Brien, memoir.

10. Amelia O'Brien, memoir.

11. Mollie O'Brien, interview, December 6, 2019; Tim O'Brien, email, September 8, 2020.

12. Tim O'Brien, email, September 8, 2020. See also Amelia O'Brien, memoir; Jason Scott, "B Sides and Badlands: Tim O'Brien Taps into the Spirit of WV Roots and Life Sorrows," *Hashtag WV*, September 6, 2018, https://hashtagwv .com/2018/09/b-sides-badlands-tim-obrien-taps-into-the-spirit-of-wv-roots -lifes-sorrows-jason-scott. Brigid's death put a great strain on his parents' marriage, and they "pulled it together in some ways by playing tennis together," both playing singles and on a doubles team with other couples. Tim O'Brien, email, September 8, 2020.

13. Tim O'Brien, interview, March 27, 2020.

14. Amelia O'Brien, memoir; Mollie O'Brien, "Wheeling Music and Me," *Goldenseal* (Fall 2019); Sue Kavanagh, "Tim O'Brien Interview," *Rogue Folk* (2005), http://www.roguefolk.bc.ca/gallery/articles/tim-o-brien-interview.

15. Amelia O'Brien, memoir; Halsey, "Digging Deep."

16. Mollie O'Brien, "Wheeling Music and Me," *Goldenseal* (Fall 2019); Amelia O'Brien, memoir; Tim quoted from Halsey, "Digging Deep."

17. David A. Maurer, "In-Demand Tim O'Brien Takes a Breather for Sold-Out Charlottesville Show at the Southern," *Daily Progress*, February 27, 2015, https:// dailyprogress.com/entertainment/in-demand-tim-obrien-takes-a-breather-for -sold-out-charlottesville-show-at-the-southern/article_b9114002-bd13-11e4 -b60b-e783d8c0245e.html; Amelia O'Brien, memoir; Tim O'Brien, interview, December 16, 2019. See also Joni Deutsch, "'There's a Mystery to West Virginia': Tim O'Brien Unlocks the Magic of #WVmusic," *West Virginia Public Broadcasting*, June 30, 2017, https://www.wvpublic.org/news/2017-06-30/theres-a-mystery-to -west-virginia-tim-obrien-unlocks-the-magic-of-wvmusic#stream/0.

18. Kerry Dexter, *Dirty Linen* 133 (December 2007/January 2008): 37.

19. Nick Stock, "Tim O'Brien: It's Time Again," *New Scene*, February 15, 2019, https://Scenenoco.com/2019/02/15/tim-obrien-its-time-again (no longer available; last accessed November 20, 2020).

Lisa Snedeker, "Seven Questions with Tim O'Brien," *Huffpost*, December 29, 2014, https://www.huffpost.com/entry/seven-questions-with-tim_b_6392890.

20. Amelia O'Brien, memoir; also Halsey, "Digging Deep"; Maurer, "In Demand."

21. Amelia O'Brien, memoir; also Mollie O'Brien, interview, December 1, 2019; Tim O'Brien, interview, December 16, 2019.

22. Amelia O'Brien, memoir; Steven Stone, "Tim O'Brien: Trailblazing Triple Threat, *Vintage Guitar Magazine*, https://www.vintageguitar.com/2932/tim-obrien -2, accessed December 16, 2020. See also Tim O'Brien, interview, March 16, 2020; Kavanagh, "Tim O'Brien Interview."

23. Richard Cuccaro, "Tim O'Brien, Ambassador from Cornbread Nation," *Acoustic Live* (February 2009), https://acousticlive.com/February_2009.html.

24. "Playlist: '60s Catholic Folk Mass," *Napster*, https://us.napster.com/blog/post /60s-catholic-folk-mass, accessed October 14, 2020. Our good friends Patrick Maney and Dave Zoromski talked about their own experiences with folk masses in the late 1960s when they were college students at the University of Wisconsin–Stevens Point. Patrick Maney, interview with authors, November 30, 2019; conversation with Dave Zoromski, December 2, 2019.

25. Cuccaro, "Ambassador from Cornbread Nation."

26. Merlin David, "Tim O'Brien Web-Exclusive Interview with *M Music and Musicians*" (2017), http://mmusicmag.com/m/2017/11/videoexclusive-interview -tim-obrien.

27. Cuccaro, "Ambassador from Cornbread Nation"; Mollie O'Brien, interview, December 1, 2019.

28. Tim O'Brien, interview, March 27, 2020.

29. John Lawless, "Martin Tim O'Brien 00-18," https://bluegrasstoday.com/martin -tim-obrien-00-18, *Bluegrass Today*, July 8, 2008. See also Bill C. Malone, *Country Music USA* (Austin: University of Texas Press, 2018), 328–29.

30. Cuccaro, "Ambassador from Cornbread Nation"; Tim O'Brien, interview, March 27, 2020.

31. Amelia O'Brien, memoir; Lawless, "Martin Tim O'Brien." See also Jim Newsome, "The Tim O'Brien Jamboree," *Veer Magazine* (October 15, 2012), http:// www.jimnewsome.com/VEE2021?1012-TimOBrien.html; Stone, "Trailblazing Triple Threat"; Tim O'Brien, interview, December 16, 2019.

32. Tim O'Brien interview, December 16, 2019; "Wheeling Feeling," *Banjo Hangout*, https://www.banjohangout.org/archive/189073, posted October 15, 2010.

33. Tim O'Brien, interview, March 27, 2020; Bill C. Malone, *Country Music USA*, 393. See also Craig Harris, "Tim O'Brien Bio," http://albumlinernotes.com /Tim_O_Brien.html, accessed October 7, 2021; Eddie Collins, "Tim O'Brien: A Life in Balance," *Bluegrass Now* 9, no. 2 (February 1999): 5.

34. Ivan Tribe, *Mountaineer Jamboree: Country Music in West Virginia* (Lexington: University Press of Kentucky, 1983). A good history of WWVA appeared in a 1976 fiftieth-anniversary booklet published by WWVA, online as "History of

WWVA, Wheeling," https://jeff560.tripod.com/wwva.html, December 22, 2020.

35. Halsey, "Digging Deep."

36. Amelia O'Brien, memoir. In our interview with Jim O'Brien, November 29, 2019, he told us, he had planned to become a lawyer after his service in the Navy, but after his deployments as a helicopter pilot in Vietnam, he was told by the dean of the law school at the University of West Virginia that "baby killers" were not wanted. In response to that conversation, Jim made the Navy his career for the next twenty-six years.

37. Amelia O'Brien, memoir. See also Oglebay Park History, *Oglebay*, https://oglebay.com/experience-oglebay, accessed December 22, 2020.

38. Amelia O'Brien, memoir.

39. Amelia O'Brien, memoir; Halsey, "Digging Deep."

40. Tim O'Brien, email, September 8, 2020. See also Stone, "Trailblazing Triple Threat."

41. Tim O'Brien, interview, December 16, 2019. When asked for a nontechnical description of a bouzouki, luthier Mike Kemnitzer replied, "There are different types of bouzoukis and technical explanations for them but in this country, and perhaps also in Ireland, it usually refers to an eight-string instrument with four courses of strings and the lower courses are paired with octave strings. With that definition, you could say that I built Tim O'Brien a guitar shaped octave-mandolin and he turned it into a bouzouki by restringing it with octave strings on the low D and G courses. It gave the instrument a unique sound, especially in the hands of Tim." Mike Kemnitzer, email, June 26, 2021.

42. Willie Neumann, interview with authors, March 29, 2020; Mollie O'Brien, "Wheeling Music and Me."

43. Tim O'Brien, interview, December 16, 2019; Willie Neumann, interview, March 29, 2020.

44. Kavanagh, "Tim O'Brien Interview"; Willie Neumann, interview, March 29, 202.

45. Mollie O'Brien, interview, December 1, 2019; Mollie O'Brien, email, October 11, 2020.

46. Tim O'Brien, interview, December 16, 2019; Mollie O'Brien, interview, December 1, 2019; Kavanagh, "Tim O'Brien Interview"; Amelia O'Brien's memoir.

47. Mollie O'Brien, interview, December 1, 2019; Tim O'Brien, interview, March 27, 2020.

48. "About Philmont," *Philmont Scout Ranch*, https://www.philmontscoutranch.org/about, accessed December 26, 2020.

49. Tim O'Brien, email, October 9, 2020; also Matt Montagne, interview with authors, February 27, 2020.

50. Halsey, "Digging Deep"; also Tim O'Brien, email, August 14, 2020.

Chapter 2. **THE CALL OF THE WEST**

1. Tim O'Brien, email, February 19, 2021. See also Joseph Terrell, "The Unbroken Circle: An Interview with Tim O'Brien," *Bluegrass Situation*, https://
   thebluegrasssituation.com/read/the-unbroken-circle-an-interview-with-tim
   -obrien, accessed December 29, 2020.

2. "About Colby, https://www.colby.edu/about, accessed December 29, 2020;
   Tim O'Brien, interview, December 16, 2019.

3. Stephen Collins, "A Half Century of Jan Plan," *Colby Magazine* (Winter 2012),
   https://www.colby.edu/magazine/a-half-century-of-jan-plan-4; Tim O'Brien,
   interview, December 16, 2019. See also Tim O'Brien, email, October 21, 2020.

4. Jeff "Smokey" McKeen, interview with authors, March 27, 2020; also Tim
   O'Brien, email, April 7, 2021.

5. Jeff "Smokey" McKeen, interview with authors, March 27, 2020.

6. Jeff "Smokey" McKeen, interview with authors, March 27, 2020; "Shirley Swipes
   Again," *Colby Magazine* (Summer 2000): 30, https://digitalcommons.colby.edu
   /cgi/viewcontent.cgi?article=1831&context=colbymagazine.

7. "About the Artist," *Colby Magazine* (Summer 2000): 30, https://digitalcommons
   .colby.edu/cgi/viewcontent.cgi?article=1831&context=colbymagazine;   Tim
   O'Brien, interview, January 10, 2020.

8. Tim O'Brien, email, October 9, 2020; Matt Montagne, interview, February 27,
   2020.

9. John Lawless, "Grammy Winner Tim O'Brien Pays Tribute to Doc Watson,
   Jim Morton," *Watauga Democrat Mountain Times*, April 6, 2017, https://www
   .wataugademocrat.com/mountaintimes/grammy-winner-tim-obrien-pays
   -tribute-to-doc-watson-jim-morton/article_751e9d40-f5e8-56dc-a529
   -7e683b5ab4bf.html; "About the Artist," *Colby Magazine* (Summer 2000): 30,
   https://digitalcommons.colby.edu/cgi/viewcontent.cgi?article=1831&context
   =colbymagazine. See also Joni Deutsch, "There's a Mystery to West Virginia:
   Tim O'Brien Unlocks the Magic of WVmusic," West Virginia Public Broadcasting, June 30, 2017, https://www.wvpublic.org/post/there-s-mystery-west-virginia
   -tim-obrien-unlocks-magic-wvmusic#stream/0.

10. Halsey, "Digging Deep"; Amelia O'Brien, memoir; Mollie O'Brien interview,
    December 1, 2019; Tim O'Brien, interview, December 16, 2019. See also Jim
    O'Brien interview, November 29, 2019.

11. Halsey, "Digging Deep"; Tim O'Brien, email, October 20, 2020.

12. Kavanagh, "Tim O'Brien Interview"; Amelia O'Brien, memoir.

13. John Sidle, interview with authors, February 6, 2020; Tim O'Brien, interview,
    January 10, 2020. See also Tim O'Brien, emails, April 7, 8, 2021.

14. Halsey, "Digging Deep"; Tim O'Brien, email, February 19, 2021.

15. Tim O'Brien, emails, February 19, April 8, 2021. See also John Spina, "Calico
    Marks 50 Years of Feeding Jackson," September 28, 2016, https://www

.jhnewsandguide.com/news/features/calico-marks-50-years-of-feeding
-jackson/article_15988fac-bc8e-52a9-a36e-d9f158cd284b.html.

16. Ritchie Mintz, interview with authors, February 18, 2020; Tim O'Brien, email,
    October 16, 2020.

17. Tim O'Brien, email, October 23, 2020; Ritchie Mintz, interview, February 18,
    2020.

18. Ritchie Mintz, interview, February 18, 2020.

19. Ned Alterman, interview, February 28, 2020; Ritchie Mintz, interview, Febru-
    ary 18, 2020; Ned Alterman, interview, February 28, 2020.

20. "History," *Colorado Bluegrass Music* Society, https://www.coloradobluegrass.org
    /history, accessed January 2, 2021.

21. "About," *Rapidgrass*, http://rapidgrass.com, accessed January 4, 2021; Brian Turk,
    "Tim O'Brien Helps Gold Hill Celebrate 50 Year Anniversary," *Marquee Magazine*,
    June 1, 2012, http://marqueemag.com/2012/06/tim-o%e2%80%99brien; also
    Adam Stetson, "Expressing Identity in Colorado Bluegrass Music Sub-Culture:
    Negotiating Modernity in the American West through Music, Humor, and
    Shared Experience," honor's thesis (Honors Department, University of Colo-
    rado, May 9, 2006).

22. Stewart Oksenhorn, "Cornbread Nation," *Aspen Times*, March 16, 2006,
    https://www.aspentimes.com/news/cornbread-nation; "When I'm Free—A
    Hot Rize Interview with Tim O'Brien," *Mandolin Café*, September 9, 2014,
    https://www.mandolincafe.com/news/publish/mandolins_001658.shtml.

23. Tim O'Brien, emails, October 16 and 23, 2020; "Tim O'Brien," *Lone Star Music*,
    http://www.lonestarmusic.com/TimOBrien, accessed January 5, 2021.

24. Tim O'Brien, interview, March 27, 2020.

25. Tim O'Brien, email, January 7, 2021.

26. JD Hutchison, interview with authors, November 30, 2019. See also Tim
    O'Brien, email, January 7, 2021; Terry Smith, "40 Years Later, Old Bluegrass
    Allies Come Full Circle on Legacy Project," *Athens News*, July 17, 2016, https://
    www.athensnews.com/culture/arts_and_entertainment/40-years-later-old
    -bluegrass-allies-come-full-circle-in-legacy-project/article_ec508b00-4c49
    -11e6-bac8-a717a0f87e9b.html.

27. JD Hutchison, interview, November 30, 2019; Tim quoted from Smith, "40 Years
    Later."

28. JD Hutchison, interview, November 30, 2019; Mike Kemnitzer, interview with
    authors, January 20, 2020; Ritchie Mintz interview, February 18, 2020.

29. Mike Kemnitzer, email, February 18, 2020.

30. Mike Kemnitzer, interview, January 20, 2020; Mike Kemnitzer, email, Feb-
    ruary 18, 2020. See also Tim O'Brien, interviews, December 16, 2019, and
    March 27, 2020. For more information on Mike Kemnitzer, see Patty
    Lanque Stearns, "Nugget," *Traverse* (March, 2002): 45–49, http://www
    .pattywrites.com/wp-content/uploads/2019/11/0302_Mandolin_web.pdf.
    For a detailed description of the Nugget company and its varying models,

see "Nugget Mandolins," *Mandolin Café*, reprinted with permission from Michael Kemnitzer, Nugget Mandolins, Central Lake, Michigan. See also Steven Stone, "Tim O'Brien: Trailblazing Triple-Threat," *Vintage Guitar Magazine*, https://www.vintageguitar.com/2835/tim-obrien, accessed December 13, 2020.

31. Turk, "Tim O'Brien Helps Gold Hill."
32. Margalit Fox, "Izzy Young, Who Presided Over the Folk Revival, Is Dead at 90," *New York Times*, February 5, 2019, https://www.nytimes.com/2019/02/05/obituaries/izzy-young-dead.html; also "Harry Tuft," *Colorado Encyclopedia:* https://coloradoencyclopedia.org/article/harry-tuft, accessed January 8, 2021; Harry Tuft, interview with authors, December 17, 2019.
33. Harry Tuft interview, December 17, 2019.
34. Tim O'Brien, interview, March 27, 2020.
35. Tribute to David Kelly (DK) McNish on Tim's FaceBook page, August 7, 2016, https://m.facebook.com/timobrienmusic/photos/a.128099660562192/1128575653847916/?type=3&locale2=ko_KR; Duck Baker, *Plymouth Rock*, http://duckbaker.com/discography/duck-baker-solo/plymouth-rock, accessed January 8, 2021.
36. Tim O'Brien, email, February 19, 2021.
37. Dan Sadowsky, interview, December 12, 2019; Tim O'Brien, "Ophelia Swing Band and Wheeling, West Virginia," Tim O'Brien blog, September 23, 2009, https://timobrien.net/articles?page=2.
38. Dan Sadowsky interview, December 12, 2019; Stewart Oksenhorn, "Back in the Swing," *Aspen Times*, November 12, 2003, https://www.aspentimes.com/news/back-in-the-swing,; Tim O'Brien, "Ophelia Swing Band and Wheeling, West Virginia," Tim O'Brien blog, September 23, 2009, https://timobrien.net/articles?page=2, accessed October 9, 2021.
39. Mike Kemnitzer, email, February 18, 2020.
40. Tim quoted in Dick Kimmel, "Hot Rize: Pete Wernick's Secret Ingredient,"in *The Bluegrass Reader*, ed. by Thomas Goldsmith (Urbana: University of Illinois Press, 2004), 241; Ophelia Swing Band Facebook page, https://www.facebook.com/Ophelia-Swing-Band-161198710646057 (no longer available; last accessed, December 22, 2019); Susan D. Brock, "Interview with Dan Sadowsky," *Telluride Inside and Out*, https://soundcloud.com/telluride-inside/dan-sadowsky-aka-pastor-mustard-host-of-bluegrass-with-mustard, accessed December 22, 2019; "Telluride Bluegrass Festival's Longtime MC Reflects on Colorado's Most Storied Music Fest," *Westword* (June 11, 2014), https://www.westword.com/music/telluride-bluegrass-festivals-longtime-mc-reflects-on-colorados-most-storied-music-fest-5675552.
41. Pete Wernick, interview, December 12, 2019.
42. Liner notes for *Guess Who's Coming to Town*, Biscuit City, 1977. According to Mike Kemnitzer JD had once referred to Tim as that "little red-haired boy." Mike Kemnitzer interview, January 20, 2020.

43. Dale Bruning, interview with authors, November 28, 2020; Tim O'Brien, interview, March 27, 2020. See also "Dale Bruning Biography," *Jazz Link Enterprises*, https://jazzlinkenterprises.com/dale-bruning-biography, accessed January 11, 2021.
44. Dan Sadowsky, interview, December 12, 2019. See also Sam Bock, "How 'Beer and Steer' Parties Put Colorado at the Center of the Craft Beer World," *CPR News*, October 1, 2014, https://www.cpr.org/2014/10/01/how-beer-and-steer -parties-put-colorado-at-the-center-of-the-craft-beer-world; Kit Swaggert, interview with authors, April 22, 2020.
45. Kit Swaggert, interview, April 22, 2020.
46. Tim O'Brien, email, December 16, 2021.
47. Tim O'Brien, interview, March 27, 2020.
48. Amelia O'Brien, memoir. See also Tim O'Brien, email, February 21, 2021.
49. Kit Swaggert, email, October 30, 2020.
50. Kit Swaggert, email, October 30, 2020.

Chapter 3. **THE REMARKABLE RISE OF HOT RIZE**

1. Pete Wernick, interview, December 12, 2019. Hometown Food Company owns Martha White Food and all of its marks and have granted us permission to use the lyrics.
2. Pete Wernick, interview, December 12, 2019.
3. Michael R. Shea, "Stepping Out with 'Dr. Banjo,' Pete Wernick '66," *Columbia College Today* (Winter 2013–2014), https://www.college.columbia.edu/cct /archive/winter13/alumni_profiles.
4. Shea, "Stepping Out with 'Dr. Banjo.'"
5. Pete Wernick, interview with Dick Kimmel, "Hot Rize—So Long of a Journey," *Hot Bands* (March 2004), http://hotbands.com/reviews/20040301review .php, November 4, 2020. No longer available. Last accessed December 3, 2020; "Hot Rize: Pete Wernick's Secret Ingredient," *Bluegrass Unlimited*, March, 1979, 16.
6. Pete Wernick, interview, December 12, 2019; Pete Wernick, email, August 9, 2020; Nick Forster, interview with authors, January 9, 2020. See also Kristin Brown, "Q & A: Bluegrass Quartet Hot Rize," *Cowboys & Indians Magazine* (October 22, 1918), https://www.cowboysindians.com/2018/10/qa-bluegrass-quartet-hot-rize.
7. Nick Forster, interview, January 9, 2020; Pete Wernick, email, May 13, 2021.
8. Sumi Seacat, interview with authors, April 20, 2020.
9. Mary Stribling, interview with authors, April 24, 2020; also Sumi Seacat, interview, April 20, 2020.
10. Jerry Mills, "The XX String Bluegrass Band," *Bluegrass Unlimited* 5, no. 9 (March 1971).
11. Nick Forster, interview, November 27, 2019; Sumi Seacat, interview, April 20, 2020; Jerry Mills, interview with authors, May 9, 2020; Laurie Lewis, interview with authors, March 25, 2020.

12. Nick Forster, interview, November 27, 2019.

13. Nick Forster, interview, January 9, 2020. See also Nick Forster, interview with Tyller Gummersall, "Tales from the Trail Podcast S1: #P7," *Cowboys & Indians Magazine* (August 28, 2019), https://www.youtube.com/watch?v=Br-FLMkYy-A.

14. John Lehndorff, "On the Rize-Landmark Bluegrass Band Still Hot After All These Years," *Bluegrass Unlimited* (2010), http://bluegrassmusic.co/content/2010/feature/on-the-rize-landmark-bluegrass-band-still hot. See also Kathy Foster-Patton, "Hot Rize: From Old Grass to New Grass," *JamBase*, July 28, 2009, https://www.jambase.com/article/hot-rize-from-old-grass-to-new-grass; Karen McLaughlin, "Hot Rize Celebrates 40 Years Together," *DC Music Review*, November 16, 2018, https://dcmusicreview.com/hot-rize-celebrates-40-years-together.

15. Foster-Patton, "Old Grass to New Grass."

16. Kimmel, "So Long of a Journey," 15.

17. Pete Wernick, email, May 13, 2021. Pete told us that initially Harley Stumbaugh joined the band members in 1979 as the group's first roadie, who sometimes drove the bus they acquired the following year. When he quit, Hot Rize hired Frank Edmondson.

18. Pete paid tribute to Frank in "What Sound Technicians Can Do to Help and Hurt Bluegrass," in his February 2004 column, *DrBanjo.com*, originally written for *Bluegrass Unlimited.*

19. Foster-Patton, "Old Grass to New Grass."

20. Nick Forster quoted from Foster-Patton, "Old Grass to New Grass"; Tim O'Brien, email, April 7, 2021; Pete Wernick, interview, December 12, 2019.

21. Nick Forster, interview, November 27, 2019.

22. Charlie Brennan, "Pearl Street Mall, Boulder's Pulsing Heart, Turns 40," *Fort Morgan Times*, August 3, 2017, https://www.fortmorgantimes.com/2017/08/03/pearl-street-mall-boulders-pulsing-heart-turns-40; Nick Forster, interview, January 9, 2020.

23. Pete Wernick, interview, December 12, 2019; Nick Forster, interview, November 19, 2019; Pete Wernick, email, August 13, 2020.

24. Pete Wernick, email, February 13, 2020.

25. John Sidle, interview, February 6, 2020.

26. This performance can be heard on "Anonymous Collection Cassette #263," *Internet Archive*, made available by the Steam Powered Preservation Society, uploaded on April 25, 2017, described by Mitchell Wittenberg as "the earliest circulating tape of a Hot Rize performance," https://archive.org/details/spps-anon001-C263.

27. A sampling of early Hot Rize performances can be found online: "Ashes of Love," recorded at the first Minnesota Bluegrass Festival, May 19–21, 1978, https://archive.org/details/spps-anon001-C263/spps-anon001-C263-HotRize-SideAt05.flac; "Ninety Nine Years (and One Dark Day)," recorded at

the Telluride Bluegrass Festival, June 24, 1979, https://www.youtube.com/watch
?v=Sp6Tfc5EWak; "I'm Gonna Sleep with One Eye Open," recorded at the
Birchmere Restaurant, Alexandria, Virginia (1980), https://www.youtube.com
/watch?v=eSchFAbXJs0.

28. Ronni Lundy, interview with authors, May 21, 2020.

29. "Thoughts about Charles," *Sandy Munro Music.com*, http://www.sandymunromu-
sic.com/Thoughts_about_Charles.html, accessed April 8, 2021.

30. Tim O'Brien, liner notes for *So Long of a Journey*, Sugar Hill, 2002.

31. Pete Wernick from Jeff Tamarkin, "Hot Rize: So Long of a Journey," *Relix*,
November 27, 2018, https://relix.com/articles/detail/hot-rize-so-long-of-a
-journey; Kavanagh, "Tim O'Brien."

32. Tim O'Brien, email, April 7, 2021.

33. "Tim O'Brien Talks Songwriting with Randy Barrett," *Bluegrass Today*, https://
bluegrasstoday.com/tim-obrien-talks-songwriting-with-randy-barrett,
accessed October 11, 2021. Tim said that "Nellie Kane" and "Train on the
Island" "are almost the same melody as "Look Down that Lonesome Road"
(written later). This interview was conducted in February 2018 but was not
posted until April 21, 2020.

34. Pete Wernick, interview, December 12, 2019; Nick Stock, "Tim O'Brien: It's
Time Again," *New Scene*, February 15, 2019, https://sceneoco.com/2019/02/15
/tim-obrien-its-time-again (no longer available; last accessed, November 1,
2020). The frequency of performances of "Nellie Kane" made by Phish in the
1990s and early 2000s is outlined on the band's website, and it appeared as an
instrumental on the band's album *The White Tape*, https://phish.net/song
/nellie-kane/history, accessed November 2, 2020.

35. Recordings of the Hot Rize performance at the first annual Minnesota Bluegrass Festival.

36. Pete Wernick, interview, December 19, 2020; "40th Anniversary Memories—
Hot Rize," *Live From Here*, September 23, 2014, https://www.youtube.com
/watch?v=ib9ZwJ6AUM8. See also Rachel Tashjan, "The Battle for the Heart
of the American Nudie Suit," *GQ*, April 19, 2019, https://www.gq.com/story
/nudie-suit-legacy. Pete told us, "I shelled out the $100 for 7 outfits (and I gave
one to each Hot Rize member, one to Tony Trishka . . . one to Sam Bush, one
to Peter Rowan). The Troubadours were definitely NOT wearing those outfits
that night (that could have been a bit gross, as musicians sweat!)." Pete Wernick, email, May 13, 2020.

37. Pete Wernick, interview, December 13, 2019.

38. Pete Wernick, interview, December 13, 2019.

39. Tim O'Brien, email, April 7, 2021.

40. Tim O'Brien, email, April 7, 2021.

41. Ronni Lundy, interview, May 8, 2020.

42. Geoffrey Himes, "Jerry Jeff Walker," *Washington Post*, May 16, 1983; Karen
Boren Swedin, "Red Knuckles and Trailblazers Knock 'Em Out," *Deseret News*,

May 18, 1989. The Trailblazers' popularity was international. They were in fact recorded in Fremontel, Normandy, in France in June 1984, for *The French Way*, an album of thirteen honky-tonk songs.

43. The standard history of bluegrass is Neil V. Rosenberg, *Bluegrass: A History* (Urbana: University of Illinois Press, 1985).

44. Alan Lomax, "Bluegrass Background: Folk Music with Overdrive," *Esquire*, October 1, 1959, https://classic.esquire.com/article/1959/10/1/bluegrass-background.

45. Tim and John both quoted from Jared Keller, "An Oral History of the Telluride Bluegrass Festival," June 17, 2013, https://www.outsideonline.com/adventure-travel/destinations/north-america/oral-history-telluride-bluegrass-festival. YouTube has many years of festival tapes available for interested listeners.

46. Dick Kimmel, "Hot Rize: Pete Wernick's Secret Ingredient," *Bluegrass Unlimited* 13, March 1979.

47. Pete Wernick, email, February 13, 2020.

48. Nick Forster, interview, March 9, 2020; Pete Wernick, interview with Anne Dyni, Maria Rogers Oral History Project, Boulder Public Library December 20, 2007, https://www.youtube.com/watch?v=4SMZHWgQimU.

49. Nick Forster, interview, March 16, 2020.

50. Nick Forster, interview, March 16, 2020; Mike Kemnitzer, interview, February 18, 2020; Tim O'Brien, email, April 7, 2021.

51. Pete Wernick, email, December 20, 2019; Tim quoted from Foster-Patton, "Old Grass to New Grass."

52. Pete Wernick, email, November 5, 2020. In fact, Pete was so sure of the importance of having these rules of engagement that he wrote *How to Make a Band Work*, published by Mel Bay in 2001.

53. Robin Clare, interview, November 25, 2020; Joan Wernick, interview, November 23, 2020.

54. Robin Clare, interview, November 25, 2020; Tim O'Brien, emails, January 21, April 7, 2021.

55. Tim O'Brien, email, April 7, 2021; Joan Wernick, interview, November 23, 2020; also Kit Swaggert, interviews, April 22, November 11, 2020.

56. Pete Wernick, interview, December 19, 2019. See the Hot Rize performance at Winterhawk Festival, July 1989, https://vimeo.com/381476600, accessed October 11, 2021.

57. Pete Wernick, email, February 13, 2020. See also Pete Wernick, interview, January 9, 2020.

58. Tim O'Brien, email, October 23, 2020.

59. Nick Forster, "Remembering Dr. Ralph Stanley," *eTown News*, January 24, 2016, https://www.etown.org/remembering-ralph-stanley; Tim O'Brien, email, January 21, 2021.

60. *Nashville Tennessean*, September 11, 1981, 38.

61. Larry Groce, interview with authors, May 8, 2020.

62. "History of Austin City Limits," *Austin City Limits*, https://acltv.com/history -of-acl, accessed November 11, 2020. Tracey E. W. Laird's *Austin City Limits* (Oxford University Press, 2014) is the ultimate resource on the history of this program; see also *tv.com*, http://www.tv.com/shows/austin-city-limits/riders -in-the-sky-followed-by-hot-rize-1137907, accessed November 11, 2020.

63. Angus Phillips, "Bluegrass: The Friendliest Festival of All," *Washington Post*, June 2, 1978; Tim O'Brien, email, September 27, 2020.

64. Wernick, email, May 13, 2021. We are grateful to Pete, as Hot Rize's self-appointed historian, for adding anecdotes and correcting errors.

Chapter 4. **THE PULL OF NASHVILLE**

1. Laurie Lewis, interview, March 25, 2020; Tim O'Brien, interview, March 27, 2020; Mollie O'Brien, interview, December 1, 2019. See also Kit Swaggert, interview, April 28, 2020.

2. "Untold Stories" was inspired by a bitter difference and its resolution between his cousin Tony Ames and Tim's father. Tony totally opposed the Vietnam War, while Tim's daddy merely found it "troubling." Trip's death in combat only accentuated an estrangement that lasted for years.

3. Kathy Mattea, interview with authors, March 24, 2020; "A Conversation with Tim O'Brien," *Puremusic*, http://www.puremusic.com/obrien3.html, accessed February 15, 2021.

4. Pete Wernick, interview, December 13, 2019.

5. Pete Wernick, email, May 13, 2021.

6. Tim O'Brien, interview, March 27, 2020. Mary Martin was also honored at the third annual Louise Scruggs Memorial Forum, on November 17, 2009. Michael McCall, "Mary Martin," and video interview with Jay Orr at the Country Music Hall of Fame, https://countrymusichalloffame.org/plan-your-visit/exhibits -activities/public-programs/the-louise-scruggs-memorial-forum/mary -martin, accessed January 26, 2021;

7. Amelia O'Brien, memoir; Jerry Douglas, interview with authors, March 11, 2020; Tim O'Brien, interview March 27, 2020; also Tim O'Brien, email, January 27, 2021.

8. Kathy Mattea, interview, March 24, 2020; Kit Swaggert, interview, April 20, 2020; Jackson O'Brien, interview with authors, January 17, 2020; Amelia O'Brien, memoir. See also Tim O'Brien, email, April 17, 2021.

9. Pete Wernick, interview with Patrick Ferris, "So Long of a Journey," in *Hotbands: The Music Resource* (March 2004); reprinted on Pete's website, Dr.Banjo .com, https://drbanjo.com/hot-bands.

10. Barry Poss, interview with authors, April 23, 2020; Pam Parrish, "Bluegrass and Beyond," *Tucson Weekly*, February 2–8, 1995, https://www.tucsonweekly .com/tw/02-02-95/music.htm. See also "Profile: Sugar Hill Records Founder Barry Poss," *Blue Ridge Outdoors*, August 1, 2008, https://www.blueridgeoutdoors

.com/music/front-porch/profile-sugar-hill-records-founder-barry-poss; Steve
Horowitz, "Sugar Hill Records: 25 Years and Going Strong," October 1, 2006,
https://www.popmatters.com/various-artists-sugar-hill-records-a-retrospective
-2495696995.html.

11. Tim O'Brien, interview, January 10, 2020. Bev Paul, interview, May 21, 2020.
See also "Thirteenth Memorial Louise Scruggs Memorial Forum Honoring
Bev Paul," press release, January 22, 2020, https://countrymusichalloffame
.org/press-release/thirteenth-annual-louise-scruggs-memorial-forum-to
-honor-bev-paul; Bev Paul, email, February 8, 2021.

12. Bev Paul, interview, May 21, 2020; Bev Paul, email, February 8, 2021.

13. Bill Frater, "Grateful Jam with SiriusXM's Rod Bleetstein," *No Depression*,
June 29, 2018, https://www.nodepression.com/grateful-jam-with-siriusxms
-rob-bleetstein. Special thanks go to Bev Paul for helping us navigate the
shoals of Americana in her email, February 8, 2021.

14. Pete Wernick, interview, December 13, 2019; Dave Freeman, "Tim O'Brien:
'Odd Man In," County Sales, https://www.countysales.com/products/25914
?variant=12292091183207, accessed January 29, 2021.

15. Lyle Lovett, liner notes, *Odd Man In*, Sugar Hill, 1991.

16. Pat Alger, interview with authors, February 28, 2020; Pat Alger, email, March 4,
2020.

17. Nick established *eTown* in 1991 and has hosted it ever since as "a nonprofit,
nationally syndicated radio broadcast/podcast, multimedia and events production company . . . that produces live-audience musical, social, and environmental programming to uplift and inspire listeners around the world." *eTown*,
https://www.etown.org/about, accessed January 30, 2021.

18. Mark Schatz, interview, March 5, 2020.

19. Mark Schatz, interview, March 5, 2020; Scott Nygaard, interview, March 18,
2020; Jackson O'Brien, interview, January 17, 2020.

20. Jerry Douglas, interview, March 11, 2020; Mark Schatz, interview, March 5,
2020.

21. Tim O'Brien, email attachment, April 17, 2021; Tim O'Brien, interview,
May 27, 2020; Mollie O'Brien, interview, December 6, 2019; Mark Schatz,
interview.

22. Dave Freeman, "Tim and Mollie O'Brien, *Take Me Back*," *County Sales*, https://
www.countysales.com/products/23801?variant=12292190994535, accessed February 12, 2021; Jeremy Jones, "Tim O'Brien Says Singing, Performing with
Sister Just Falls Together," https://www.goupstate.com/news/20130913/tim
-obrien-says-singing-performing-with-sister-just-falls-together, accessed February 12, 2021.

23. Tim O'Brien, liner notes for *Away Out on the Mountain*, Sugar Hill, 1994.

24. Tim O'Brien, interview, April 30, 2020. See also Mollie O'Brien, interview,
December 6, 2019.

25. Tim O'Brien, liner notes for *Oh Boy! O'Boy!*, Sugar Hill, 1993.

26. Pat Alger, interview, February 28, 2020; Tim O'Brien, liner notes for *Oh Boy! O'Boy!*, Sugar Hill, 1993.

27. Between 1986 and 2000, Jim Rooney and Allen Reynolds built a "successful and innovative, artist-first music publishing house" with writers who produced hits for Kathy Mattea, Garth Brooks, Patty Loveless, Vince Gill, and others. "Famed Recording Producer Jim Rooney to Keynote May 16–20 SERFA [Southeast Regional Folk Alliance] Conference in Montreat," press release (2018), https://www.serfa.org/rooney-press-release. See also Jack Hurst, "Nashville's Star Tracker," *Chicago Tribune*, June 21, 1992, https://www.chicagotribune.com /news/ct-xpm-1992-06-21-9202240947-story.html; Jim Rooney, *In It for the Long Run: A Musical Odyssey* (Champaign-Urbana: University of Illinois Press, 2014).

28. "Tim O'Brien Talks Songwriting with Randy Barrett," *Bluegrass Today* (February 2018), posted April 21, 2020, https://bluegrasstoday.com/tim-obrien-talks -songwriting-with-randy-barrett; Darrell Scott, interview, March 14, 2020.

29. Tim O'Brien, interview, November 16, 2020; Darrell Scott, interview, March 14, 2020; Terri Horak, "O'Brien Honors Songwriting via Dylan Set, Nashville Move," *Billboard*, October 19, 1996, https://books.google.com/books?id=yQkE AAAAMBAJ&pg=PA52&dq=horak+and+tim+o%27brien+Billboard+1996&hl =en&sa=X&ved=2ahUKEwi4gbnI7eDuAhXULc0KHTiyAX4Q6AEwAHoECA EQAg#v=onepage&q=horak%20and%20tim%20o'brien%20Billboard%20 1996&f=false; "Tim O'Brien & Darrell Scott," *PineCone*, https://pinecone.org /artists/tim-obrien-darrell-scott, accessed February 15, 2021.

30. Wayne Bledsoe, "Darrell Scott Lets the Song Make the Rules," *Knoxville News Sentinel*, April 21, 2016, http://archive.knoxnews.com/entertainment/music /darrell-scott-lets-the-song-make-the-rules-30dcae05-1fde-2a04-e053 -0100007f8eb2-376567871.html; Darrell Scott, interview, March 14, 2020. See also Tim O'Brien, interviews, January 10 and March 27, 2020.

31. Ronni Lundy, interview, May 21, 2020.

32. Jim Newsom, "The Tim O'Brien Jamboree," *Veer Magazine*, October 15, 2012, http://www.jimnewsom.com/VEER2012/1012-TimOBrien.html.

33. Newsom, "The Tim O'Brien Jamboree"; Tim O'Brien, interview, March 27, 2020; Newsom, "Tim O'Brien Jamboree"; also Jackson O'Brien, interview, January 17, 2020.

34. Mike Kemnitzer, "A Few Words about Tim O'Brien," email, May 18, 2020.

35. Horak, "O'Brien Honors Songwriting"; Dylan Muhlberg, "Grateful Web Interview with Tim O'Brien," July 24, 2013, https://www.gratefulweb.com/articles /grateful-web-interview-tim-obrien.

36. Tim O'Brien, email, February 10, 2021.

37. Pete Wernick told us that, during Hot Rize's heyday, Tim could be moody, which irritated Nick and Pete, but Charles always supported and sided with Tim in any argument: "Tim was touchier than anyone else in the band, so it was easier to stay on his right side, even though he was very reasonable. Charles

was always very deferential to Tim, so that made the two of them a 'bloc.'" Pete Wernick, interview, December 13, 2019.

38. Tim O'Brien, liner notes for *Red on Blonde*, Sugar Hill, 1996, in which Tim also thanks Charles for help with the repertoire. See also Sumi Seacat, interview, April 20, 2020.

39. George Graham, "Tim O'Brien: *Red on Blonde*," *Graham Weekly Album Review* #1037 (1996), http://georgegraham.com/obrienr.html; Peter Blackstock, "Tim O'Brien: Red on Blonde," posted September 1, 1996, https://www.nodepression .com/album-reviews/tim-obrien-red-on-blonde-tony-rice-sings-gordon -lightfoot; Horak, "O'Brien Honors Songwriting."

40. Scott Nygaard, interview, March 18, 2020.

41. Horak, "O'Brien Honors Songwriting"; Darrell Scott, interview, March 14, 2020.

42. Tim O'Brien, interview, November 16, 2020. See also Jay Orr, "Real Music in Real Time: Tim O'Brien and Darrell Scott Take a 'Field Recording' Approach to New Project," *CMT*, June 23, 2003, http://www.cmt.com/news/1473124 /real-music-in-real-time-tim-obrien-and-darrell-scott-take-a-field-recording -approach-to-new-project; Darrell Scott, interview.

43. Tim O'Brien, liner notes to *Songs from the Mountain* (Dirk Powell, Tim O'Brien, John Herrmann), Howdy Skies Records, 1998.

44. Dirk Powell, interview with authors, April 5, 2020. Silas House wrote, "Powell believes that lineage plays a huge role in music. 'I don't believe lineage is absolutely necessary to being a good musician, but it sure helps. It's a mix of nature and nurture, but things do really reside in our blood.'" Silas House, "Dirk Powell—Family Traditions," *No Depression*, May 1, 2004, https://www .nodepression.com/dirk-powell-family-traditions.

45. Dirk Powell, interview with authors, April 5, 2020.

46. Frank Goodman, "Puremusic Interview with Tim O'Brien" (2002), http:// www.puremusic.com/obrien1.html; Dirk Powell, interview, April 5, 2020; Michael Kenney, "Music Moves the Mountain," *Boston Globe*, March 1, 2000, https://greensboro.com/music-moves-the-mountain/article_81ffacd2-09ad -55ef-b682-11cdc4217821.html; Kit Swaggert, interview, April 22, 2020.

47. Jonathan Pitts, "'Mountain' Soundtrack Cold, Too, to Music Trio," *Baltimore Sun*, January 3, 2004, http://www.baltimoresun.com/news/bs-xpm-2004-01-03 -0401030002-story.html. See also Goodman, "Puremusic Interview"; Brad Hunt, interview with authors, March 5, 2021; Tim O'Brien, interview, April 30, 2020.

48. Brad Hunt, interview, March 5, 2021; Tim O'Brien, interview, April 30, 2020.

49. Tim O'Brien, email, March 23, 2021.

50. Brad Hunt, interview, March 5, 2021.

Chapter 5. **THE LURE OF IRELAND AND BACK HOME IN AMERICANA**

1. Tim O'Brien, interview, April 30, 2020; Catherine Gillespie O'Brien, *Find a Grave*, https://www.findagrave.com/memorial/27188067/catherine-o'brien, accessed March 15, 2021; "Tim O'Brien Interview with Rodger Hara," *Celtic*

Connection, April 1, 2018, https://celticconnection.com/2018/04/01/tim-obrien
-interview-with-rodger-hara; "A Conversation with Tim O'Brien," *Puremusic*,
https://www.puremusic.com/obrien3.html, accessed February 24, 2021.

2. Tim O'Brien, "The Crossing," *Tim O'Brien.net*, https://timobrien.net/music-cd
/crossing, accessed April 27, 2020.

3. Tim O'Brien, email, November 29, 1998; Craig Havighurst, "Bluegrasser Tim
O'Brien Embraces 'Journeys,'" *The Tennessean*, November 3, 2001.

4. Tim O'Brien, liner notes of *The Crossing*, Alula, 1999; Tim O'Brien, email,
November 29, 1998.

5. Victoria White, "The Crossing," *Irish Times*, November 7, 2000, https://www
.irishtimes.com/culture/the-crossing-1.1114244.

6. Sue Kavanagh, "Tim O'Brien Interview," *Rogue Folk* (2005), http://www
.roguefolk.bc.ca/gallery/articles/tim-o-brien-interview.

7. Pamela Squires, "The Crossing: A Breath of Fresh Eire," *Washington Post*,
November 4, 2002, https://www.washingtonpost.com/archive/lifestyle/2002
/11/04/the-crossing-a-breath-of-fresh-eire/3ca78d77-22f4-405b-aa6b
-59325c642665; Victoria White, "The Crossing,"

8. Tim O'Brien, liner notes, *Two Journeys*, Howdy Skies, 2001; Tim O'Brien, email,
April 17, 2021.

9. Patrick Ferris, "So Long of a Journey: Interview with Pete Wernick," *Dr.Banjo
.com*, https://drbanjo.com/hot-bands, accessed October 17, 2021; *eTown*, https://
www.etown.org/about/about-etown, accessed February 25, 2021; Sumi Seacat,
interview, April 20, 2020; Pete Wernick, interview, December 19, 2019.

10. All quotes from the liner notes, *Hot Rize: So Long of a Journey*, Sugar Hill, 2002.
See also Laurie Lewis and Charles Sawtelle, *Charles Sawtelle: Music from Rancho
de Ville*, Acoustic Disc, 2001, on which Laurie and Pete Wernick each wrote a
loving tribute to Charles in the liner notes.

11. Pete Wernick, interview, December 19, 2019; Wernick, email, February 25,
2021.

12. Sumi Seacat, interview, April 20, 2020; Dan Sawtelle, interview with authors,
April 16, 2020.

13. Liner notes, *Hot Rize: So Long of a Journey*.

14. Bryan Sutton, interview with authors, March 23, 2020.

15. "Tim O'Brien—Time after Time," *No Depression*, July 1, 2000, https://www
.nodepression.com/tim-obrien-time-after-time/#:~:text=%E2%80%9CEvery%
20place%20I'd%20go,to%20get%200n%20with%20things.

16. "Tim O'Brien—Time after Time."

17. Liner notes, *Traveler*, Sugar Hill, 2003; "Tim O'Brien—Traveler," *No Depression*,
September 1, 2003, https://www.nodepression.com/album-reviews/tim-obrien
-traveler.

18. "Tim O'Brien—Traveler," *No Depression*; Dean Barnett, "Tim O'Brien: Traveler,"
Glide Magazine, April 1, 2004, https://glidemagazine.com/983/tim-obrien;

Grant Alden, "Tim O'Brien—When There's No One Around," *No Depression*, September 1, 1997, https://www.nodepression.com/album-reviews/tim-obrien -when-no-ones-around; "Tim O'Brien: Traveler," *PopMatters*, December 18, 2003, https://popmatters.com/obrientim-traveler-2496021761.html.

19. Chris Moore, interview with authors, December 12, 2019.

20. Brad Hunt, interview, March 5, 2021; Chris Moore, interview, December 12, 2019. See also "Chris Moore—317 Main," *317 Main*, https://www.317main.org /dt_team/chris-moore, accessed February 28, 2021.

21. Jonathan Pitts, "Picking and Choosing with Tim O'Brien," *Baltimore Sun*, September 12, 2003, https://www.baltimoresun.com/news/bs-xpm-2003-09-12 -0309120097-story.html; "A Conversation with Tim O'Brien," *puremusic.com*, http://www.puremusic.com/obrien5.html, March 21, 2021.

22. Tim O'Brien, interview, April 30, 2020; Tim O'Brien, email, March 23, 2021; Tim O'Brien, liner notes, *Fiddler's Green* and *Cornbread Nation*, Howdy Skies, 2005.

23. Tim O'Brien, interview, April 30, 2020; Tim O'Brien bio, March 13, 2008, https://web.archive.org/web/20080313073415; http://www.timobrien.net/bio .cfm. See also Tim O'Brien, liner notes, *Fiddler's Green* and *Cornbread Nation*, Howdy Skies, 2005; "Cornbread Nation: The Bluegrass/Americana World of Tim O'Brien" *Centrum*, March 20, 2008, https://centrum.org/2008/03/cornbread .nat; Stewart Oksenhorn, "Cornbread Nation, *Aspen Times*, March 16, 2006, https://www.aspentimes.com/news/cornbread-nation.

24. Tim O'Brien, email, April 17, 2021; Tim O'Brien, liner notes, *Fiddler's Green*. Tim mentioned he later learned that Pete Goble bought the lyrics for "Fiddler's Green" from Leroy Drumm (who had co-written "Colleen Malone" with him). "Pete told me to look through a whole bunch of lyrics and, if anything appealed to me, he'd send a recording. I liked 'Fiddler's Green' enough to imagine my own music. I sent that back to Pete, and he said he liked it better than his music. I wonder if he really had any music when he sent the lyrics. It seems I co-wrote that song with Leroy Drumm." Tim O'Brien, email, April 17, 2021.

25. "Tim O'Brien Talks Songwriting with Randy Barrett," *Bluegrass Today*, April 21, 2020, https://bluegrasstoday.com/tim-obrien-talks-songwriting-with-randy -barrett.

26. Steve Oksenhorn, "Cornbread Nation"; liner notes for *Cornbread Nation*, Sugar Hill, 200s. See also Ronni Lundy, *Cornbread Nation 3: Foods of the Mountain South* (University of Mississippi Press, 2005), https://uncpress.org/book /9780807856567/cornbread-nation-3, April 12, 2021. Liane Hanson, interview with Tim O'Brien, *What's in a Song*, National Public Radio, January 29, 2006, https://www.npr.org/templates/story/story.php?storyId=5176877; Ronni Lundy, email, May 8, 2020; Ronni Lundy, interview, May 21, 2020.

27. Dave Stallard, "Profile of Tim O'Brien," *Blue Ridge Outdoors*, https://www .blueridgeoutdoors.com/music/front-porch/profile-tim-o-brien/?amp,

March 13, 2021; Tim O'Brien, *Chameleon* liner notes, Howdy Skies, 2008; Stallard, "Profile."

28. George Graham, "Tim O'Brien: Chameleon," *The George Graham Weekly Album Review* #1520 (2008), http://georgegraham.com/reviews/obrien08.html. See also Chris Boros, "Tim O'Brien: A 'Chameleon' Unto Himself," *Favorite Sessions, NPR Music*, February 17, 2009, https://www.npr.org/templates/story/story.php?storyId=100683728.

29. O'Brien's blog, https://timobrien.net/articles?page=2, accessed March 13, 2021. See also Warren Hellman, conversation with authors, summer 2008; "Warren Hellman: One of the Good Guys," *Hellman & Friedman*, https://hf.com/warren-hellman, accessed March 13, 2021.

30. *Caravan Music Club*, Facebook, November 22, 2016, https://www.facebook.com/caravanmusicclub/photos/mark-knopfler-thinks-tim-obrien-is-a-master-of-american-folk-music-irish-music-s/1138149912887078.

31. Edward Morris, "Tim O'Brien Talks about Latest Album, Touring with Mark Knopfler," *CMT*, September 28, 2010, http://www.cmt.com/news/1648901/tim-obrien-talks-about-latest-album-touring-with-mark-knopfler.

32. Kathy S-B, "Quick Q and A with Tim O'Brien, *Me and Thee*, https://meandthee.org/OldSite/blog/txp/quick-q-and-a-with-tim-o-brien-2010, accessed March 13, 2021; "Mark Knopfler North American Tour Begins," Tim O'Brien blog, https://timobrien.net/articles?page=1, accessed October 17, 2020; "Video Exclusive Interview with Tim O'Brien," *M Music and Musicians Magazine*, https://mmusicmag.com/m/2017/11/videoexclusive-interview-tim-obrien, accessed November 21, 2020. Other basic information on the Mark Knopfler interlude comes from Tim O'Brien, interview, June 11, 2020.

33. Tim O'Brien's blog, https://timobrien.net/articles?page=1, accessed March 13, 2021.

34. Album cover, *Chicken and Egg*, Howdy Skies, 2010; Edward Morris, "Tim O'Brien Talks about Latest Album," *CMT News*, September 28, 2010, http://www.cmt.com/news/1648901/tim-obrien-talk-about-latest-album.

Chapter 6. **PURSUING NEW DIRECTIONS**

1. Tim O'Brien, email, March 23, 2021.

2. Tim O'Brien, interview, November 16, 2020. "Christchurch Earthquake Kills 185," *New Zealand History*, February 22, 2011, https://nzhistory.govt.nz/page/christchurch-earthquake-kills-185; Jan Fabricius, interview with authors, December 17, 2019.

3. Tim O'Brien, email, April 18, 2021; Eddie Collins, "Tim O'Brien: A Life in Balance," *Bluegrass Now* 9, no. 2 (1999).

4. Tim O'Brien, emails, March 23 and April 17, 2021.

5. Tim O'Brien, interview, March 27, 2020; Kit Swaggert, interview, April 28, 2020.

6. Jan Fabricius, interview, December 17, 2019; Jan Fabricius, email forwarded to authors, April 17, 2021.

7. Jan Fabricius, interview, December 17, 2019.

8. Jan Fabricius, interviews, December 17, 2019, June 15, 2020; Jan Fabricius, email, April 18, 2021; Tim O'Brien, email, March 23, 2021.

9. Jan Fabricius, email forwarded to authors, April 17, 2021; Tim O'Brien, email, April 17 and 18, 2021.

10. Tim O'Brien, interview, June 11, 2020.

11. Tim O'Brien, interview, June 11, 2020; "Bio/Tim O'Brien Band (long version)," https://timobrien.net/bio, accessed March 17, 2021.

12. Tim O'Brien, email, March 23, 2021.

13. Tim O'Brien, email, March 23, 2021.

14. Susan Viebrock, "O'Brien Party of Seven at Telluride Bluegrass #39," https://www.tellurideinside.com/2012/06/obrien-party-of-seven-at-telluride-bluegrass-39.html, accessed March 19, 2021; Mollie O'Brien Moore, interview, July 23, 2021.

15. Susan Viebrock, "O'Brien Party of Seven at Telluride Bluegrass #39," https://www.tellurideinside.com/2012/06/obrien-party-of-seven-at-telluride-bluegrass-39.html, accessed March 19, 2021; Tim O'Brien, email, March 23, 2021.

16. On the recording by Jayme Stone and Friends, "Jayme Stone's Lomax Project," *Discogs* (Borealis 235), 2015, nineteen tracks pay tribute to Lomax who would have been one hundred years old in 2012, https://www.discogs.com/Jayme-Stone-Jayme-Stones-Lomax-Project/release/9902296, accessed April 1, 2021. See also Ricardo Baca, "Folk Music, Reinvented via Chautauqua's Lomax Project, *Denver Post*, May 8, 2013, https://theknow.denverpost.com/2013/05/09/folk-music-reinvented-via-lomax-at-chautauqua/68438. You can listen to Tim playing "Jayme Stone Lomax Project featuring Tim O'Brien in Bristol, VA" on Youtube, https://www.youtube.com/playlist?list=PLWK4Hxvj6hEfoDY-4qRB-NBpKlsERStAt, accessed October 19, 2021.

17. "A Little Back History on Tim & Darrell," *Kate Wolf Music Festival*, December 29, 2013, http://katewolfmusicfestival.com/tim-o-brien-darrell-scott.

18. Rob Adams, "Tim O'Brien—Making the Celtic Connection," *Rob Adams Journalist*, http://www.robadamsjournalist.com/timobrien.asp, accessed March 19, 2021.

19. Nick Stock, "Tim O'Brien: It's Time Again," *New Scene*, February 15, 2019, https://scenenoco.com/2019/02/15/tim-obrien-its-time-again (no longer available; last accessed April 20, 2021). For a full account of the Earls of Leicester, see Larry Nager, "Great Pretenders: All-Star Earls Are Perfectly Foggy," *Bluegrass Unlimited* 49, no. 4 (October 2014): 26–33.

20. Mark Hellenberg, "A Talk with Americana/Roots Legend Tim O'Brien," *WOUB Public Media*, February 9, 2015, https://woub.org/2015/02/09/talk-americanaroots-legend-tim-obrien.

21. "When I'm Free—a Hot Rize Interview with Tim O'Brien," *Mandolin Café*, September 9, 2014, https://www.mandolincafe.com/news/publish/mandolins_001658.shtml. See also Derek Halsey, "Go West, Young Man: How the Innovative Group Hot Rize Became Legends," *Bluegrass Unlimited* 50, no. 5 (November 2015), 18–21.

22. "Tim O'Brien, Pompadour," *Bluegrass Unlimited*, April 1, 2016, https://www.bluegrassunlimited.com/article/tim-obrien-pompadour; George Graham, "Tim O'Brien: *Pompadour*," *George Graham Review #1841*, http://georgegraham.com/reviews/obrien-pomp.html, accessed March 20, 2021.

23. "Tim O'Brien Launches Short Order Sessions," *Mandolincafe*, January 5, 2015, https://www.mandolincafe.com/news/publish/mandolins_001688.shtml; Tim O'Brien, "Short Order Sessions," https://timobrien.net/short-order-sessions, accessed March 21, 2021.

24. Tim O'Brien, "Press Release: Short Order Sessions 2015," https://timobrien.net/articles.

25. "Video: The West Virginia Music Hall of Fame 5th Induction Ceremony Vignettes," *WV Public Broadcasting*, https://www.wvpublic.org/news/2013-11-15/video-the-west-virginia-music-hall-of-fame-5th-induction-ceremony-vignettes, accessed March 21, 2021.

26. "O'Brien Siblings at Valentine's Symphony Concert," *Intelligencer. Wheeling News-Register*, February 1, 2015, https://www.theintelligencer.net/life/features/2015/02/o-brien-siblings-at-valentine-s-symphony-concert. See also "Wheeling Symphony Orchestra Celebrates America: Annual 4th of July Tour Set," *Intelligencer. Wheeling News-Register*, June 29, 2018, https://www.theintelligencer.net/life/out-about/2018/06/wheeling-symphony-orchestra-celebrates-america.

27. Maria Wallace, "Tim O'Brien: Where the River Meets the Road," *Folk Radio*, May 4, 2017, https://www.folkradio.co.uk/2017/05/tim-obrien-where-the-river-meets-the-road; Mark Hellenberg, "A Talk with Americana/Roots Legend Tim O'Brien."

28. Mike Kemnitzer, interview with authors, January 20, 2020; Terry Smith, "40 Years Later, Old Bluegrass Allies Come Full Circle in Legacy Project," *Athens News*, https://www.athensnews.com/culture/arts_and_entertainment/40-years-later-old-bluegrass-allies-come-full-circle-in-legacy-project/article_ec508b00-4c49-11e6-bac8-a717a0f87e9b.html, accessed October 19, 2021.

29. Mike Kemnitzer, email, May 18, 2020.

30. "Bill Frisell: Testimonial about Dale Bruning," Jazz Link Enterprises, https://jazzlinkenterprises.com, accessed March 22, 2021. See also "*Cancelled* Live eTown Radio Show Taping with Bill Frisell, Tim O'Brien & Dale Bruning," April 15, 2020, *eTown Tapings*, https://www.etown.org/events/live-etown-radio-show-taping-bill-frisell-tim-obrien-dale-bruning (no longer available; last accessed March 22, 2021); "Sold Out: Album Release: Tim O'Brien, Bill Frisell, Dale Bruning, w/Nick Forster," *etown*, https://www.etown.org/events/album_release_wtih-tim-obrien-bill-frisell-dale-bruning, accessed October 19, 2021;

"Sold Out @ eTown—"Life Lessons" Release—Now Also a Livestream!" etown blog, https://www.etown.org/sold-etown-life-lessons-release-now-also -livestream, accessed October 19, 2021.

31. "Tim O'Brien Remembers the Late Doc Watson, Kennedy Center, Washing-ton, D.C., October 13, 2012," *YouTube*, https://www.youtube.com/watch?v =igdUPEHm5wk.

32. "Tim O'Brien Remembers the Late Doc Watson."

33. "Tim O'Brien Remembers the Late Doc Watson."

34. Mckenzie Moore, "Hard Pressed Isn't Pressed for Inspiration and Connection Through Music," *Delta County Independent*, July 20, 2020, https://www.deltacounty independent.com/news/hard-pressed-isn-t-pressed-for-inspiration-and -connection-through-music/article_75dc2b42-c77d-11ea-ba34-0ffe1c732d19 .html.

35. Carena Liptak, "Chris Stapleton Performs Bluegrass Homage to O'Brien, Scott," *The Boot*, February 7, 2018, https://theboot.com/chris-stapleton-aint-no -easy-way.

36. "Chris Thile & Tim O'Brien, Telluride 2018," *Mandolin Café*, https://www .mandolincafe.com/forum/threads/140199-Chris-Thile-amp-Tim-O-Brien -Telluride-2018, accessed October 19, 2021; Tim's Facebook page, posted August 7, 2014, https://www.facebook.com/timobrienmusic. It might also be noted that the first release made by Thile and his super-progressive band, Nickel Creek, was "When You Come Back Down," written by Tim and Danny O'Keefe.

37. Ben Kaufmann and Jeff Austin quoted on HotRize.com, https://www.hotrize .com/quotes, accessed March 30, 2021."Yonder Mountain String Band in Boulder," *Bluegrass Today*, December 31, 2013, https://bluegrasstoday.com /yonder-mountain-string-band-in-boulder. See also Susan Viebrock, "Tellu-ride Bluegrass: Leftover Salmon, Smelling Great after 30 Years in the Sun," *Telluride Inside . . . and Out*, June 11, 2018, https://www.tellurideinside.com /2018/06/telluride-bluegrass-leftover-salmon-still-smelling-great-after-30 -years.html.

38. Tim quoted from "Tim O'Brien and Old Man Luedecke," *Southern Café and Music Hall*, Charlottesville, Virginia, October 29, 2015, http://www.thesoutherncville .com/events/detail/tim-obrien. See also Chris Luedecke, interview with authors, March 23, 2020.

39. "Tim O'Brien and Old Man Luedecke," *Hugh's Room Live*, April 14, 2016, https:// hughsroomlive.com/event/tim-obrien-and-old-man-luedecke; Gregory Adams, "Old Man Luedecke Unveils 'Domestic Eccentric,'" May 27, 2015, *Exclaim*, https:// exclaim.ca/music/article/old_man_luedecke_unveils_domestic_eccentric_lp; "Tim O'Brien and the Banjo Tramps, featuring Jan Fabricius, J D Hutchison, & Old Man Luedecke," *Pinecone*, January 27, 2018, https://pinecone.org/events/tim -obrien-and-banjo-tramps-featuring-jan-fabricius-jd-hutchison-old-man -luedecke.

40. Craig Shelburne, "The Tim O'Brien Band Reaches Beyond," *Bluegrass Situation*, March 20, 2019, https://thebluegrasssituation.com/read/the-tim-obrien-band-reaches-beyond; "Tim O'Brien Band," *Rogue Folk*, November 22, 2019, https://www.facebook.com/events/1092273910965898 (no longer available; last accessed, April 8, 2020; now found as "Tim O'Brien Bio," IVPR, https://ivpr.com/tim-obrien, accessed October 31, 2021). See also Jon Freeman, "Tim O'Brien Returns with New Album," *Rolling Stone*, January 16, 2019, https://www.rollingstone.com/music/music-country/tim-obrien-band-new-album-dan-auerbach-780163.

41. Neal Loevinger, "Tim O'Brien—An Interview," *Hudson Valley Bluegrass Association*, April 6, 2019, https://hvbluegrass.org/tim-obrien-an-exclusive-interview.

42. Craig Shelburne, "Tim O'Brien Band Reaches Beyond."

43. Tim O'Brien, "Re-release of The Crossing," May 1, 2020, Tim O'Brien.net, https://timobrien.net/articles.

44. Tim O'Brien, "The Day the Music Died, Part 2," Noteworthymusic.org, July 3, 2020, https://www.noteworthymusic.org/the-day-the-music-died.

45. Suzanne Cheavens, "Hold to a Dream," *The Watch*, June 17, 2020, https://www.telluridenews.com/the_watch/watch_listen_show/article_410da894-b0eb-11ea-8c99-771b91b31354.html.

46. Tim O'Brien, "Spring without John Prine," April 8, 2020, Tim O'Brien.net, https://timobrien.net/articles

47. Tim O'Brien, "Spring without John Prine"; Kyle Knox, "Keeping Music Alive—A Musician's Life during COVID-19," *Weelunk*, June 9, 2020, https://weelunk.com/keeping-music-live-musicians-life-during-covid-19.

48. Tim O'Brien, "Spring without John Prine"; Tim O'Brien, "re: He Walked On," email, March 23, 2021.

49. Tim O'Brien, "Re: He Walked On," email, March 23, 2021.

50. Tim O'Brien, "Re: He Walked On," email, March 23, 2021.

INDEX OF SONGS AND ALBUMS

GENERAL INDEX

References to illustrations appear in italic type.